about glass

Contemporary Sculpture
and Installations

EVA-MARIA FAHRNER-TUTSEK PETRA GILOY-HIRTZ

about glass

Contemporary Sculpture and Installations

ALEXANDER
TUTSEK——
—STIFTUNG

HIRMER

Contents

Andrea Lissoni

Preface

How might we start to think about the relationship between glass and contemporary art? And from what angle—that of its function or its use?

In actual fact, this is a question that presents itself to me every time I reflect on the relationship between a new material, a technological medium, a discipline, or a field and contemporary art. Whether it's plastic, for example, or glass, dance, or AI, the angle shifts constantly: the introduction of plastic materials radically and permanently transformed painting and provided sculpture with hitherto unimaginable possibilities; video expanded the film tradition, adding an unseen degree of flexibility and manipulability; dance broadened to embrace choreographic models unknown throughout its age-old history, while artificial intelligence is dramatically rewriting the roles of authorship and representation. They have all opened up extraordinary paths for art, ushering in new forms of knowledge, energetically refueling critique, and most of all, driving theory ever further.

I am persuaded that the answer must always be sought in a moment of rupture with the past, in a radical—or rather a transformative—gesture. In other words, I cannot but go back, time after time, to *Élevage de Poussière* (1920).

This photograph by Man Ray, which captures the dust lying on the surface of Marcel Duchamp's *Grand Verre* (1915–1923), is that transformative moment. It is triggered by the dialogue between two extraordinary artists, and at the same time, it is itself a revolutionary artistic dialogue between two highly sensitive media—photography and glass—representing the introduction of an unprecedented dimension, one inviting us to reflect on the complex relationship between chance and intentionality, between matter and form, and between temporality and spatiality in contemporary art. Glass, deemed a transparent and fragile material, becomes the support for an artwork that challenges all the conventions of representation and creation, and which highlights the tension between the control of the artist and the unforeseeable nature of chance. The dust gathered on the surface of the glass, as captured by Man Ray, becomes something else: a path, a language, a landscape. At the same time, it is the foundational statement of a temporality and materiality of the artwork, which challenges our perception of the form, of the structure, and of linguistic-narrative conventions.

This key moment of modernity in the relationship between glass and contemporary art inevitably leads me to consider the physical and chemical properties of the material, of which transparence, refraction, resistance, and an inherent transformation of state are all clear characteristics.

The emphasis on the material and processual aspects of artwork from the 1950s onwards found in glass a potentially ideal material to accompany a range of artistic manifestations as much as a range of theoretical reflections. Yet surprisingly, in Asia, especially with Gutai initially and then with Mono-Ha, in the Americas amidst Neo-Concretism, Fluxus, and processual art, and in Europe, especially in the field of Arte Povera, this took place to no more than a minimal degree. It was in the kinetic field and that of programmed art that it found a more relevant role, particularly in the practices of Jesus Rafael Soto and Yaacov Agam, where glass took on an active role, almost that of a medium in its own right, neither exclusively metaphorical nor decorative.

In the career of Liliane Lijn (b. 1939), glass has long played a key role: in her sculptures and installations, which incorporate technology, innovative materials, and light, Lijn has made use of glass in the form of cones or prisms, not only to create effects of refraction or projection, but also to generate forms and structures that explore the relationship between the material and light itself.

With Ljin, glass broadens its field of action, becoming the medium that hosts the dialogue between light, matter, and perception, but it also becomes part of the representation of a cyber body, of the head in particular: an element often approached by the artist also as an individual sculpture, and always in glass. Now, while in more recent art history, glass has taken on an ever more prominent position—and the collection of the Alexander Tutsek-Stiftung offers a very fine testimony to this fact—what has Liliane Lijn's pioneering practice taught us about glass?

Without doubt, the versatility of its use, i.e. the chance to deploy it among completely different types of works, coupled with a vast range of other material, preempting the most commonplace and conscientious approach in more recent artistic practices. But also, and above all, its function as a medium, its scope for representing life and liveness, fundamentally its ontological statute as living matter.

Continuing along this line—and in the awareness of overlooking a fundamental postcolonial perspective as well as an in-depth knowledge of indigenous cultures, which would lead one to reflect differently on the dynamics of power and knowledge that have shaped our understanding of glass in art—it's the specificity of the material that offers the most stimulating reflections as well as those with the greatest potential: the intrinsic nature of glass, amid sand and silica, coupling primordial and highly advanced technology, exalts its function as an interface, as an "in-between" material.

Liliane Lijn demonstrates impeccably how to give rise to new and complex interdependent worlds, experimental, hybrid and indeterminate worlds, based on the exchange of properties and capable of shifting between the human and the nonhuman.

Following in the footsteps of research by the scholar Laura Tripaldi, especially in *Parallel Minds: Discovering the Intelligence of Materials* (2022), glass appears to be a typically intelligent material, capable both of responding and adapting to external stimuli, as well as displaying unique behavior, but most of all, of interacting with the surrounding environment, of influencing and being influenced by external conditions.

The characteristics of a unique material like glass challenge the mechanical view of technologies and hint at considering nonhuman forms of sensitivity and intelligence. But just what are the technological, theoretical, artistic, cultural, and political consequences of imagining materials and forms in dialogue and interchange with each other and in constant transformation?

These are the questions discreetly asked by contemporary artists who use glass to create or who couple it with other materials; questions posed openly to those who reflect on art, on the history of art, and on the many stories bound up with it.

The artists with whom I have had the chance to share the path and dialogue at length, such as Liliane Lijn, Joan Jonas, and Philippe Parreno, have worked with glass, viewing it as a sensitive material, a living interface, a genuinely transformative medium, whether it's in the simplest of camera lenses, a monitor screen, an aquarium, a vitrine, a lamp, a light conductor, or a face, be it a humanoid or an alien one.

Glass is a medium based on relations, in every sense, amid material and technological components, but also amid prime materials, communities, in both human and animal environments. And it is the dialogue between Man Ray and Marcel Duchamp, on two unprecedented works by two visionary artists and the challenges to history and the thought they have made, to which I cannot help but return once more, to celebrate the potential of glass in art both as a support and as a material.

But most of all, to celebrate it as a sensitive interface and a transformative living medium.

Andrea Lissoni, PhD
Artistic Director
Haus der Kunst, Munich

Eva-Maria Fahrner-Tutsek

Glass and Art, Art and Glass

In early civilizations, glass was a material of high cultural and economic importance: melted and hand-shaped into simple glass beads some 5,000 years ago, or artfully blown into vessels for rituals and cults around the time of Christ. Whether as jewelry, a status symbol, a sign of one's identity or political allegiance, or a means of trade, glass has always been an important material in both sacred and secular life. Its qualities of transparency and purity, as well as its special relationship to light, have also made it a unique material in architecture, giving atmosphere and ambience to interior spaces. Glass has so many possibilities for use, so many different modes of appearance: clear or opaque or colored, polished or unpolished, smooth and cool to the touch, or rough or velvety. And how enormous is the multiplicity of its forms, dimensions, and textures!

Strangely enough, it is precisely the inherent beauty and brilliance of glass that has impeded its acceptance as a material for "art." Artists may have perceived glass as having too great a natural visual appeal.[1] That glass can be used not only to create beautiful everyday design and craft pieces, but also artworks, is in part thanks to the studio glass movement in Europe during the late 1960s and particularly the 1970s, inspired by the American glass scene, as Tina Oldknow explains in her essay for this book. Glass artists began to perceive themselves in a new way: they were not creating design pieces, but rather unique, stand-alone aesthetic objects with artistic qualities—works of free expression that use the material in experimental ways, beyond function and practicality and instead focused on concept and content. Without compromise, they have challenged the traditional catalogue of forms and have embraced the plastic qualities of the material during melting and solidifying, in the transition from liquid to solid. Through this almost revolutionary practice, it was, in Germany in particular, Erwin Eisch and Ann Wolff who turned glass into a sculptural medium. However, debates remain, and so-called "studio glass" still struggles to achieve recognition as "art." At the same time, glass artists have had an impact on those who were not fully aware of the material, or had not appreciated it, inspiring them to expand their spectrum of materials to include glass: they have shown the potential this substance holds.

With this as the discourse around glass art, the Alexander Tutsek-Stiftung was founded in 2000. One of the primary aims of the foundation has been to focus on this unique material and provide a space for amplifying the neglected and undervalued: bringing together outstanding works in the field of glass, exhibiting, funding, and providing support for research, while also developing an important collection. This is a rare endeavor in our time, "in a cultural landscape that neglects and marginalizes essential and established art forms," as Florian Hufnagl, then director of Die Neue Sammlung, the state museum for applied art in Munich, wrote in the foundation's first exhibition catalogue in 2004.[2] In that exhibition, recent works of the recent studio glass movement were presented by artists from western and eastern Europe, America, Australia, and Japan. These included works by Erwin Eisch, the blown glass of Dale Chihuly, pieces by Antoine Leperlier, who writes words in enamel in glass made malleable by heat, and by Naomi Shioya, in sensual shapes of kiln-molded and then sandblasted glass, as well as by Janusz Walentynowicz, who paints his figurative sculptures in molded glass and often engages with current political topics.

A tension—even a competition—between "glass" and "art," and a need to defend or legitimize artists who work with glass, is evidently less common in other countries. In Australia and the former Czechoslovakia, glass has long been a regular part of the curriculum in art schools. In countries such as China and Japan, with their traditions of ceramic sculpture, artists and university professors have been eager to learn from glass work inspired by the studio glass movement and to apply new ideas to their art. Contemporary glass artists in those countries remained, however, virtually unknown in Europe. Discovering their work in multiple trips abroad, especially to China, and acquiring pieces through a network of relationships with artists and galleries, before exhibiting those works in the foundation's "Villa" under the title *Glass: China* (2008–9), was not only an adventure, but also a meaningful contribution to the appreciation of "glass" as "art." In *Glass: China*, we were able to show how "glass has become a direction in art with global character."[3] The sculptures in *Glass: China*, primarily by younger artists, many of them being exhibited in the West for the first time, made this pioneering show a thrilling artistic experience, the likes of which had never been seen outside of China.[4] Largely unnoticed by the international art and glass scene, a first generation of artists had grown up there, who, after initial efforts imitative of Western models, began to develop their own language combining the innovations of the West with their country's traditions and craftsmanship. Content, expression, and symbolism were increasingly foregrounded, and social themes were addressed in subtle ways. So it was that the Asian focus of the Alexander Tutsek-Stiftung was formed and continued to be developed in the years since, and which has come to include photography.

"The glass world has become larger," as Dan Mølgaard, director of the Glasmuseet Ebeltoft in Denmark, writes.[5] In a globalized world, it is easier for artists to find inspiration everywhere. Meanwhile, there is a sizable network of international exchange, encompassing grants, artist residencies, and collaborations with workshops and museums and collections dedicated to glass.[6] However, this international exchange has in no way led to homogenization. One need only compare the aesthetic and technical qualities of the works of Chinese, Japanese, and European artists. As in art generally, there are specific movements and tendencies in the handling of the material, as Dan Klein observes: he describes the 1980s as "the decade of glass casting" and the 1990s as characterized by "blown glass," with "kiln-formed glass" being typical in the first decade of the new millennium.[7] The current situation is perhaps best characterized by the disappearance of trends and limitations, with new developments moving in all directions, from classical glassblowing to the latest digital approaches that take sustainability into account: from small objects placed on a pedestal in the classical manner, to arrangements hanging from the ceiling or appearing to peel off the wall or lying on the floor, whether placed inside or under the heavens, all the way to large-scale installations. Any size seems possible, and the prior limitations of the medium have largely been overcome through improvements in the production process.

These developments also show that the hierarchical categories of "contemporary art" and "studio glass" are no longer tenable. What would the criteria be? That in one case glass is handled and shaped by the artist, and in the other the artist has an idea and orders its production? Artists have vehemently, and sometimes unsuccessfully, objected to being categorized as "glass artists," including Ann Wolff, whose multidimensional heads are expressive symbols of an interior emotional state.[8] Is the Korean artist Ki-Ra Kim a "glass artist" because glass is her only, or preferred, material, even when her crane feathers represent an "understanding of and reconciliation with death, freedom from restraints and a door to the closed, invisible world," as she has put it?[9] What about Silvia Levenson, who uses glass to convey "feelings, pathos, intuitions" in order to hold on to memories of people and things? Being an expert from the classical studio glass movement, as she has been described by Tina Oldknow, does not lead to any "classification." Nevertheless, many works are left in the "reserves" of design museums, or are put in arts and crafts museums. "The ambition of liberating the glass completely as a material on all levels," as the pioneers of "modern glass art" have hoped for, remains unfulfilled.[10]

The present volume is being published on the occasion of the twenty-fifth anniversary of the Alexander Tutsek-Stiftung and its exhibition *Future Horizons*, which includes many of the works assembled here: an extraordinary selection of works from the foundation. About fifty artists of diverse geographic and cultural backgrounds—both internationally renowned and newly discovered—are presented here in alphabetical order. The publication is intended as a contribution to the discourse on glass as a material in contemporary art, guiding the reader through the diverse artistic practices of glasswork, from spectacular small objects to grand installations—an invitation both to see and to think.

[1] Helmut Ricke, "Studioglas – eine Revolution mit Hintergrund," in *Glas der Gegenwart. Katalog eins*, ed. Eva-Maria Fahrner-Tutsek, with essays by Florian Hufnagl and Helmut Ricke (Munich: Alexander Tutsek-Stiftung, 2004), 17.

[2] Florian Hufnagl, "Ein Forum für Studioglas," in Fahrner-Tutsek, *Glas der Gegenwart* (see note 1).

[3] Eva-Maria Fahrner-Tutsek, "Das Gesicht – verloren und wiedergefunden," in *Das verlorene Gesicht wiedergefunden. Katalog zwei*, ed. Eva-Maria Fahrner-Tutsek, with an essay by Dan Klein (Munich: Alexander Tutsek-Stiftung, 2006), 8.

[4] Cf. Eva-Maria Fahrner-Tutsek, ed., *Glass. China*, with essays by Eva-Maria Fahrner-Tutsek, Susanne K. Frantz, Xue Lu, and Katharina Sykora (Munich: Alexander Tutsek-Stiftung, 2009).

[5] Dan Mølgaard, "When the Present Becomes the Past – and Landmarks Emerge," in *Young Glass 2017*, ed. Sandra Blach, exh. cat. Glasmuseet Ebeltoft (2017), 11.

[6] See Susan Warner, Artistic Director, Museum of Glass, Tacoma, Washington, USA, "Intersections of Narrative and Craftmanship in Contemporary Glass," in Blach, *Young Glass 2017*, 16ff. (see note 5).

[7] Dan Klein, quoted in Mølgaard, "When the Present Becomes the Past," 13 (see note 5).

[8] Mark Gisbourne, "Die Verkörperung der Persona (Embodied Personae)," in *Ann Wolff. Persona*, Alexander Tutsek-Stiftung (Stuttgart: Arnoldsche Art Publishers, 2014), 17.

[9] Ki-Ra Kim, "Artist Statement," https://kirakimglass.com/about/.

[10] Mølgaard, "When the Present Becomes the Past," 15 (see note 5).

Petra Giloy-Hirtz

Expansion of the Mind: Glass in Contemporary Art

Recent years have seen a dramatic reassessment of glass as a medium in contemporary art. Many artists have rediscovered the unique qualities of this material. They value its immediacy and feel, its physical and emotional effect on the viewer, and its historical, philosophical, and spiritual associations and meanings. Glass has likewise become a leading material for those coming from painting or from sculpture, be it bronze, marble, or wood, as well as for those who work in video and photography. It may be the way glass interacts with light, its reflectiveness, fragility, and lucidity, its technical sophistication, its range of shapes and colors, its history and tradition, or the narrative power inherent in the medium. One of its outstanding characteristics has proven to be its capacity to transcend boundaries and lead to new configurations. Artists are increasingly using glass in combination with photography, video and performance, poetry and sound, light, electronics, and artificial intelligence. Glass has become a major element in artworks that explore the tension between science and spirituality, nature and technology.

This was not always the case. For centuries, and even longer, glass has been valued as a material for its qualities: *glas*, that which gleams, shimmers, is clear and transparent, functional and stable, created in numerous complex manufacturing processes, forms, and colors. But in the context of contemporary art, it has been forced to assert itself: glass is not a classical material such as bronze, marble, or wood. Items such as cups, windows, stained glass, and containers are made of glass; it is part of everyday life, in both profane and sacred spaces, as well as in architecture. In the field of "decorative arts" and in debates over the difference between ornament and art, between the "applied" and the "fine" arts, works in glass have traditionally been viewed as inferior. Artists have often experienced this, despite famous predecessors having elevated the status of glass in the arts, in particular Marcel Duchamp, in his legendary work *The Large Glass* (1915–23), and Josef Albers, who became director of the Bauhaus glass workshop and who created his first glass reliefs from discarded pieces of glass. Joseph Kosuth continued Duchamp's conceptual approach in *Clear, Square, Glass, Leaning* (1965), and Gerhard Richter, in his *4 Panes of Glass* (1967), rebelled against Duchamp having proclaimed the end of "retinal" art.[1]

As narrative approaches to art were rediscovered, and interest in the material's aesthetic and symbolic aspects grew, glass steadily became more appealing to artists. It's the contextual aspect of the material that makes these works so exciting and that has established the reputation of glass as an artistic medium. The discourse in contemporary art is primarily one that looks beyond how the artist works with the material, focusing instead on the artist's message. As fascinating as a work of art made of glass may be, it is not primarily about the beautiful object or about showing what can be done with glass. "It's all about meaning," as the American artist Kiki Smith says. And in this, glass has increasingly become a viable material in contemporary art. A piece such as *Hard Entry* (2004) by the artist Jana Sterbak, for example, or *Turbulence (black)* (2014) by Mona Hatoum, or *Bonded* (2017) by Monica Bonvicini: each of these sculptures belongs in the individual context of the artist's oeuvre and is embedded in the cosmos of the political and social issues to which they are seeking answers—and not in an illustrative fashion, but critically, and even sometimes subversively, in a way that challenges society.[2]

Along with the return of narrative, the younger generation has also shown a revived interest in materiality. Anni Albers, who taught at Black Mountain College after emigrating from Germany, complained that "Civilization seems in general to estrange men from materials, that is, from materials in their original form. ... But if we want to get from materials the sense of directness, the adventure of being close to the stuff the world is made of, we have to go back to the material itself, to its original state, and from there on partake in its stages of change. We use materials to satisfy our practical needs and our spiritual ones as well."[3] In the choice of material, there is a kind of magic, as Kiki Smith, who approaches everything with curiosity, has described: "Often when you make work that is representational, people [are] trying to fix the representational narrative and do not pay attention to the fact that it is materials you deal with—materials, history of materials and property of materials ... That gets lost often. ... So you get to choose which materials are appropriate and contain the meaning you want. Or you can make something in five different materials to have different emotional effects."[4]

Glass is an excellent medium for both form and content. An interest in its aesthetic and technical possibilities has led to productive collaborations between artists and workshops in recent years. Glass manufacturers and artists have shown a mutual desire to collaborate, resulting in exciting and powerful works. For instance, the Berengo Studio in Murano, Venice, has worked with such artists as Lawrence Carroll, Olafur Eliasson, Maria Roosen, Sylke von Gaza, and many others; Ross Art Studio in Hyde Park, Massachusetts, has worked with Eric Fischl, Maya Lin, and Arlene Shechet; Pilchuck Glass School in Stanwood, north of Seattle, Washington, invites artists to residencies; the National Glass Centre Sunderland in the northeast of England, "a world-leading centre for artistic practice in glass, regularly working with artists of international standing," has collaborated with Pascale Marthine Tayou and Katie Paterson, among others. The art glass center CIRVA Marseille, a nonprofit organization founded in 1986—which has collaborated with such artists as James Lee Byars, Richard Deacon, Anish Kapoor, Pierre Soulages, Jean-Michel Othoniel, Robert Morris, and Anne & Patrick Poirier—began its work at a time "when contemporary artists had little interest in craftsmanship," says Stanislas Colodiet, director of CIRVA. "The situation was very different from what we've seen in the last decade, as many artists are now working with glass or ceramics. I see the CIRVA as a pioneering institution. It doesn't address glass artists. On the contrary, it welcomes artists and designers who know nothing about its techniques. The magic springs from these unexpected encounters between international artists and highly qualified craftsmen."[5]

When artists get involved with glass, they change the material, but in most cases not their artistic "signature." Jenny Holzer (b. 1950 in Gallipolis, Ohio; lives in Hoosick, New York), known for the provocative writing she places on LED signs, has etched a message onto mirrored glass. The words are by the architect Philip Johnson, creator of the Glass House in Connecticut: "With a glass house from one side of the house you see the moon rise while from the other side you see the sun both at the same time."[6] Lynda Benglis (b. 1941, Lake Charles, Louisiana; lives in New York City and Santa Fe), famous for her amorphous abstract sculptures made from latex, foam, and cast pigmented polyurethane, has also left her signature on glass. Her series of hand-blown glass masks, created in 2010 during a residency at the Museum of Glass in Tacoma, Washington, resemble elongated, amphora-like forms—a homage to the masks of a secret African brotherhood.

Above all, glass is a preferred material in contemporary art when the work concerns themes of history, collective memory, and cultural identity. For example, María Magdalena Campos-Pons (b. 1959 in Matanzas, Cuba; lives in Boston), who has been connected with the medium for many years, created a series of glass stools that commemorate those unaccounted for and disappeared in Afro-Cuban history. This work, an installation at the Sharjah Biennial 15, *Thinking Historically in the Present* (2022), conceived by Okwui Enwezor, was cast from an heirloom handed down through generations, becoming a metaphor for absence and remembrance.

A series of glass sculptures by the Canadian-Trinidadian artist Curtis Twalst Santiago (b. 1979, Edmonton, Alberta; lives in Munich) are likewise focused on history's blind spots: the models of his own nose, cast in colored glass, are intended to draw awareness to the politically motivated vandalism that has systematically destroyed the noses of traditional sculptures in order to undermine the power of the portrait and rob the figures of their identity.

Pascale Marthine Tayou (b. 1966 in Nkongsamba, Cameroon; lives in Ghent, Belgium, and in Yaoundé, Cameroon), who participated in documenta 11 (2002) and the Venice Biennale (2005 and 2009), creates objects from transparent glass, ranging in size from small to monumental: they resemble masks, amulets, or totems, decorated with all sorts of simple recycled materials, such as chains, ribbon, straw, fabric, plastic, and feathers. Through these seemingly playful glass figures, he engages with themes of postcolonial power structures and African social conditions.

Beads of glass, thousands of them, drawn into thin cloud-like webs hanging from the ceiling on spiraling wires and woven into installations that fill entire rooms (such as *Kicking Dust* at the Kunsthalle Zürich, 2022): in the work of Igshaan Adams (b. 1982 in Cape Town, South Africa; lives in Cape Town), glass retains the originality of earlier times, partly because he, working with women, has used traditional techniques to weave the beads together with other materials. Kathleen Ryan (b. 1984 in Santa Monica, California; lives and works in New Jersey) has also turned to traditional craftsmanship in covering the surfaces of her sculptures with glass and acrylic beads. "Overturning the distinctions between 'high' art and 'low,' Ryan's practice highlights the importance of the handmade, of the intimate relation between the artist, the materials chosen for each work, and the layers of meaning they carry."[7]

In addition to more traditional approaches to glass and older methods of manufacturing, there have been some exciting technical innovations in handling the material—with results that are at times downright spectacular. The bizarre glass figures of Andra Ursuța (b. 1979 in Salonta, Romania; lives in New York), which caused a sensation at the Venice Biennale in 2019 and 2022, were created by integrating traditional sculptural skills with state-of-the-art technology: the artist combines 3-D scans of her own body with costumes and props, "void fill" packaging materials, plastic tubes, bottles, and other materials, and casts these complex assemblages into luminous, semi-transparent glass. Under high heat, the colored glass is slowly melted, resulting in a dynamically swirling marbled effect, with detailed surface textures and seams: the glass sculptures appear both as representations of the human body and as physical and metaphorical vessels.[8] Brigitte Kowanz (1957–2022; lived and worked in Vienna), one of the leading artistic pioneers of her generation, created objects, installations, and spatial interventions in which she combined glass as a material—mirrors and neon tubes—with light, speech, and sound, as in *Mindfulness* (2020) from her series of cube sculptures.

Beyond technically complex production processes, other artists take glass simply as "raw industrial material," as a "readymade," in order to give it new meaning in a different context. One groundbreaking work consists of stacked and shattered glass panes titled *On Center Shatter-or-Shatterscatter* (from the *Layered Pattern Acts series*; 1968–71) by Barry Le Va (b. 1941 in Long Beach, California; died 2021 in New York City). Isa Melsheimer (b. 1968 in Neuss, Germany; lives in Berlin) glues simple shards of glass (panes) together vertically to create entire floor landscapes in her work titled *Lichthof* (2008). Flaka Haliti (b. 1982 in Pristina, Kosovo; lives in Berlin) uses bulletproof glass: as an artist whose artistic investigations are characterized by experiences of war, she "treats" the glass by shooting it, laying the shattered and destroyed glass over her drawings of horses and dogs, representing the exploited victims of wars throughout history (*Empty but Present, Absent but Full*, 2024).

Using industrially produced glass panes, Carlos Garaicoa (b. 1967 in Havana, Cuba; lives in Madrid and Havana), participant in documenta 11 (2002) and the Venice Biennale (2005 and 2009), constructed a glass model of the monumental, neoclassical architecture of the Haus der Kunst in Munich (*Wer im Glashaus sitzt…*, 2013) to address the guilt and the innocence of architectural forms.

Some artists are inspired by everyday objects that are typically made of glass. Thea Djordjadze (b. 1971 in Tbilisi, Georgia; lives in Berlin) has clearly taken the "lampshades" of "floor lamps" as her inspiration (*Untitled (Blue Glass)*, 2020, and *Untitled (Yellow Glass)*, 2020) and used them in the same "non-functional" way as her minimalistic cubes made of glass panes (*Untitled*, 2016, or *Untitled*, 2019). Ai Weiwei (b. 1957 in Beijing; lives in Portugal) created an enormous black "chandelier," nine meters tall and weighing 2,700 kilograms, constructed out of 2,000 hand-blown glass objects that he shaped according to the iconic motifs of his work, including skulls, skeletons, organs and bones, crabs, bats, and surveillance cameras (*The Human Comedy*, 2022).

Most artists bring their own motifs and preoccupations to this material. Sean Scully (b. 1945 in Dublin, Ireland; lives in New York and Bavaria, Germany), translates the "walls of light" of his paintings into colored glass bricks, piled up into a sculpture nearly three meters tall (*Glass Stack*, 2020). Thomas Schütte (b. 1954 in Oldenburg, Germany; lives and works in Düsseldorf), who is well-known for his enormous *Große Geister* (Large Spirits) sculptures made from cast steel as well as aluminum, bronze, and steel (1995–2000), has made "small spirits" out of Murano glass, such as *Guter Geist* (Good Spirit, 2017) and *Kleiner Geisterkopf* (Small Spirit Head, 2021). Figures familiar to us from the paintings and ceramics of Leiko Ikemura (b. 1951 in Tsu, Japan; lives in Berlin), such as floating girls and cosmic landscapes with magical hybrid beings, also appear in her glass sculptures: recumbent heads in soft colors made from cast glass, as in *asleep in blue* (2022) and such figures as *Lying luz* (2020–23).

The vocabulary of forms is abundant. With glass, everything seems possible, from the expressively figurative to the minimally abstract. In her *Glass Drops* (2015–23) and *Glass Pieces* (2013–23), Karin Sander (b. 1957 in Bensberg, Germany; lives in Berlin) creates glass sculptures that flow down from pedestals and walls: liquid glass, poured in several layers on top of each other, spreads out and swells slowly over the edges before solidifying.

Ann Veronica Janssens (b. 1956 in Folkestone, England; lives in Brussels, Belgium) explores how light, color, and space are transformed into glass. Her art mainly uses a material that is immaterial, namely light (spectacularly filling a room with light and dense fog as Belgium's representative at the 48th Venice Biennale in 1999). In glass, she discovered a natural artistic medium; she has even collaborated with scientists to research the characteristics and physical phenomena of glass. Her installation at La Chapelle Saint-Vincent au Cimetière, Grignan, in Provence (2012–13) offers a wonderful example: its colorful glass monoliths placed before the windows transform the space into a backdrop of continually changing colors. Her object-like floor works, including *16 Pink Blocks* (2016) and *16 Aquatic Blocks* (2017), are minimalist in form and emotionally charged by the color and consistency of the glass.

Large objects of cast glass, which she has created since the late 1990s, figure prominently in the oeuvre of Roni Horn (b. 1955 in New York; lives in New York), whether they are in deep blue (*Untitled (Flannery)*, 1997) or strong red (*Untitled (Aretha)*, 2002–4) or even pink (*Pink Tons*, 2009). Colored molten glass is poured into a mold, where it is left to harden over a period of several months; the resulting sculptures, which are extremely heavy, have rough sides that retain traces of the mold, while the fire-polished top is smooth and crystalline, its visual aspect shifting according to the light, shadow, and space.

Such diverse artistic intentions correspond to the mission of the Alexander Tutsek-Stiftung. The foundation was established not out of some eccentric philanthropic gesture or personal passion for collecting art; rather, its purpose is in socially relevant projects with the goal of a successful, humane, shared existence. The foundation's civic engagement is rooted in its belief in humanity and trust in the potential of art to spur the imagination, to think the impossible, to sharpen our powers of perception, to bring new ideas into everyday life, to fuel inspiration, and to help shape living conditions. This is reflected in the themes of the foundation's exhibitions, with glass works by international artists from various geographical and cultural backgrounds, including such world-renowned figures as Kiki Smith, Mona Hatoum, Shirazeh Houshiary, Laure Prouvost, and Monica Bonvicini as well as artists who are young, relatively unknown, and only recently discovered—at least at the time their works were acquired—such as Kristi Cavataro, Jes Fan, and Hui Tao.

The foundation's exhibitions are always a feast for the eyes—and are intellectually stimulating as well: from the encounter with the human face (*The Face – Lost and Found Again*, 2006) to focusing on themes of seeking and desire—with sculptures by international artists, among them Christiane Budig, Jens Gussek, Ursula Huth, and Sibylle Peretti (*The Heart Forever Yearns Away*, 2007–8). Human fears and internal and external conflicts are topics present in works by Philip Baldwin & Monica Guggisberg and Janusz Walentynowicz (*Life Is Not a Beach*, 2016). It is the philosophical and psychological considerations, the existential questions, that the selected works present. They may address perception, the correlation between seeing and recognition, or the faculty of understanding (*Viewing the Other*, 2018). Exhibitions allow new light to fall upon the neglected, turning the focus to everyday functional things—such as a knot, circle, ball, spiral, bowl, or marble—and how these reflect cultural traditions (*Primary Gestures*, 2019). The surface is inverted into depth, simplicity into complexity, the banal into ambiguity, radiance into unease, familiarity into strangeness, the domestic into the unhoused: glass sculptures reveal layers of humanity, serenity, territories of community, hospitality and empathy, and new models of coexistence (*Wide Open*, 2021–22). The question of what art can accomplish in the face of violence, repression, and war—and whether its visual language and artistic practice possess the ability and competence to enlighten people or affect anything—this, too, has been posed through the medium of glass (*So Much Love and Compassion*, 2023). Contemporary art's interest in industrialization, technology, and science is evident in sculptural glass objects, be it as a swan song for an industrial age or as a prophetic look into our collective future, scenery for both utopian and dystopian visions (*Industrial Rhapsody*, 2023). As concerns the revolution in communications and media, the history of the smartphone, with its glass surface, is perceived through contemporary glass art (*The World Is in My Hand*, 2024). And the experiences and emotions of social communities, and questions around topics such as complex gender identities, diverse cultural backgrounds, and racist clichés—these have also been addressed through the medium of glass (*Love, Maybe*, 2025).

What joins all of these works together is their recognition of the ambivalence of glass. As Roni Horn has said: "In the glass pieces, what fascinates me has a lot to do with the essence of something that has one appearance but is really something completely different. For example, glass is a (super-cooled) liquid, not a solid. It's a pretty amazing thing that a material as ubiquitous as glass can masquerade like that. It's like having a mask but the mask is identical to the real thing."[9]

1 *Fragile! Alles aus Glas – Grenzbereiche des Skulpturalen*, exh. cat. Kunsthalle Vogelmann Heilbronn, 2021, 5.

2 See "Koyo Kouoh on Addressing Social/Political Concerns through Artistic Practice," May 5, 2017, https://www.youtube.com/watch?v=snHYKeQaBZM.

3 Anni Albers, "Work with Material," *Black Mountain College Bulletin* 5 (1938). Reprinted in *College Art Journal* III, no. 2 (January 1944): 51–54; in *Anni Albers: On Designing* (New Haven: Pellango Press, 1959, and Middletown: Wesleyan University Press, 1971); and in Brenda Danilowitz, ed., *Selected Writings on Design* (Middletown, CT: Wesleyan University Press / Hanover, NH: University Press of New England, 2000), 6–7.

4 Kiki Smith, in "Kiki Smith, Chuck Close, Interview," *Bomb* (Fall 1994): 38–45.

5 Y-Jean Mun-Delsalle in conversation with Stanislas Colodiet, "CIRVA Marseille: An Atypical Glass Art Centre," *TLmag* 32, Extended: Contemporary Applied (October 21, 2020), https://tlmagazine.com/cirva-marseille-an-atypical-glass-art-centre/.

6 Jenny Holzer, *In a Glass House*, 2018, etched glass mirror, 36 × 24 in., edition of 15, 5 artist proofs, signed and numbered.

7 Daria de Beauvais, "Kathleen Ryan: Sculpting Time," *Gagosian Quarterly* (Winter 2024): 65.

8 See *Andra Ursuța: Void Fill*, David Zwirner, Paris, 2021, press release.

9 Roni Horn, quoted in *Roni Horn: Everything Was Sleeping as If the Universe Were a Mistake*, exh. cat. Fundació Joan Miró (Barcelona: Fundació Joan Miró, 2014), 128.

Tina Oldknow

American Studio Glass in Context: A Snapshot

"Born" in 1962, the American studio glass movement was contemporary not so long ago. Now, well into the twenty-first century, the movement is understood as historical. It is no longer a "movement." As with other craft-associated materials such as ceramics or textiles, glass has assimilated into a wider spectrum of contemporary art and design. What follows are some notes on the early years of this phenomenon and the importance of the European influence.

The radical beginnings of American studio glass are best understood in the context of American and European mid-twentieth-century design, the environment in which it originated. A constellation of events and influences led to the instigation of the now famous 1962–63 experimental glassblowing workshops led by the American artists Harvey Littleton and Dominick Labino at the Toledo Museum of Art in Ohio **(fig. 1)**. These workshops are legendary to American artists, representing the origin of the art of contemporary hot glassworking unrelated to industry. This significant shift in approach to the material was revolutionary. Why? Because it was believed that separating glassmaking from the factory environment could not be done and, more importantly, because artists made the decision to approach the material in completely new ways. Often disregarding traditional craft techniques in order to explore their ideas, American artists pioneered new ways of working almost immediately, and their creations tended more toward the sculptural than toward the functional **(figs. 2, 3)**.

The American studio glass movement, at first, was primarily concerned with hot-working processes. Working with molten glass by blowing, molding, and sculpting it is very different than working with glass cold, as in stained glass, or working with it in kilns, as in glass fusing and casting. In the 1950s and 1960s, American designer-craftsmen—as they called themselves—were already fusing artistic glass in small kilns. Some American artists who wanted to work sculpturally with hot glass, such as the Texan artist Robert Willson, went to Venice and Murano to work with the masters there. Beginning around 1950, in Venice, the American art collector and gallerist Peggy Guggenheim invited Pablo Picasso, Max Ernst, Marc Chagall, and other well-known European artists to work with Egidio Costantini's Fucina degli Angeli. Only one American industry seemed interested in the idea of bringing artists to glass, and that was Steuben Glass in Corning, New York. Steuben sponsored a series of designs in 1939–40 by 27 international contemporary artists, including Henri Matisse, Georgia O'Keeffe, Fernand Léger, and Salvador Dalí **(fig. 4)**. For the most part, however, there was no connection between artists and industry in the United States. This was the opposite of the stronger connection between artists and industry in Europe at this time.

Studio glass in Europe had a much different history from that in the United States. After World War II, many European craft traditions were integrated into industry, while American craft generally was not. Italian and Scandinavian artists, for example, were designers in factories, and they sometimes produced unique studio pieces in addition to their limited-edition and mass-produced designs. The extraordinary and often unique objects produced by Czech artists, such as

Stanislav Libenský and Jaroslava Brychtová and Vladimir Kopecký, pioneered abstract painting and sculpture in glass. As artists representing a country behind the Iron Curtain, their groundbreaking works could only be seen in relatively few venues, such as international exhibitions and world's fairs **(fig. 5)**.

In the United States, the craft of glassblowing was almost extinct by 1960, having been gradually supplanted by automation, which was one of the reasons Harvey Littleton—who was raised in a glassmaking family in Corning, New York—was so intent on reviving it. However, thinking studio glass was not possible without industrial facilities, Littleton, as a student, turned to studio ceramics, which in the 1950s was going through its own revolution. Although he became a professor of ceramics at the University of Wisconsin in Madison, he did not forget about glass.

In 1957, Littleton took a leave from teaching to do research in Europe, which included his interest in blowing glass in the studio. In Paris, he visited the artist Jean Sala, who batched his own glass and made objects with a bellows-operated furnace. He traveled to Venice, where he visited nearly 60 small glassworks on Murano, even attempting to blow glass at Fratelli Toso.

Littleton's interest in studio glassblowing was further fueled by his disappointment in American glass design, which was apparent in the major museum exhibition *Glass 1959: A Special Exhibition of International Contemporary Glass* organized by the Corning Museum of Glass in New York. While the submissions from European designers and American designer-craftsmen were innovative and exciting **(see fig. 5)**, the examples of American industrial design seemed dull in comparison. The solution for American glass design, Littleton thought, lay in the creation of a new hybrid, like the designer-craftsman, which would be the artist-glassblower. One of the tenets of the new American studio glass movement was that the designer and maker be the same person, as opposed to the typical factory environment, where an object was created by a designer in an office and executed in the blowing room by a factory worker.

The aim of the Toledo workshops was to introduce American artists to the use of hot glass as a material for contemporary art. Littleton's strongest supporter in this endeavor was Otto Wittmann, the director of the Toledo Museum of Art. It was Wittmann who encouraged Littleton to hold his experimental workshops in Toledo, the home of the American industrial glass giant, Libbey Glass. However, Wittmann insisted that Littleton involve the glass research scientist Dominick Labino, whose knowledge and expertise proved critical for the project. Littleton and Labino's secret for successful studio glassblowing was the small furnace that Labino developed, suitable for use in an artist's studio, and the low-temperature-melting-point glass that Labino supplied. With Littleton's organization and marshalling of funds, equipment, and artists, the success of the workshops was insured.

Littleton's next move was to take the new studio glass furnace, and budding artist-glassblowers, to an international locale, which was the 1964 First World Congress of Craftsmen at Columbia University in New York City. One of the artists Littleton invited to demonstrate there was the German artist Erwin Eisch, who had a profound influence on the development of American studio glass **(fig. 6)**. Littleton first met Eisch in 1962, shortly after the initial Toledo workshop. Visiting Eisch's studio in Frauenau, Germany, Littleton realized that studio glassblowing was truly possible and that it had huge potential.

It is hard to imagine now how unlikely studio glassmaking seemed at this time. As the American curator William Warmus remembers, no one was sure this studio glass idea was going to work, not to mention prosper and grow. A critical element of Littleton's goal to introduce glass to artists in their studios was the introduction of glassblowing into American art-school and university curricula. This would insure that glass would gain acceptance as a medium for art, rather than as a material only for industry. The interest that Littleton and his ambitious students, such as Marvin Lipofsky and Dale Chihuly, generated in glass was immediate. With Littleton's encouragement and promotion, glass programs sprang up at universities, art schools, and summer programs across the United States during the late 1960s and early 1970s **(fig. 7)**.

From the 1970s through the 1980s, what had begun as a small group of American artists who shared an unusual interest quickly grew into an international phenomenon. It was during the late 1970s and 1980s that the increasing influence of European, and especially Venetian, artists was reflected in American studio glassmaking. However, the arrival of Europeans teaching in American glass programs did not represent the onset of this influence. Beginning in 1968, Ludovico Diaz de Santillana, the director of Venini Glass—the most open and outward-looking of all the Muranese glassworks—allowed young American studio glassblowers like Dale Chihuly, James Carpenter, Richard Marquis, and Benjamin Moore to come and work at their furnaces on Murano **(fig. 8)**.

What European artists such as Lino Tagliapietra, Stanislav Libenský and Jaroslava Brychtová, Bertil Vallien, and Klaus Moje, among others, brought to the United States was new and much-needed technical knowledge about blowing, casting, and fusing processes. In turn, American artists offered the European artists new ways to think about how glass might be expressed in art, influencing how studio glass would develop there. The Europeans liked the way that Americans were so free and untraditional with glass, and how they were drawn to an activity that, at the time, had little commercial value.

By 1995, the American studio glass movement, as a "movement," had ended. American studio glass artists were working in ever-larger scale, making sculpture and installations that explored an expanding universe of ideas **(fig. 9)**. There were also the painters, sculptors, and designers who came to glass from outside the studio glass world, assimilating the medium into the larger worlds of contemporary art and design **(fig. 10)**. This assimilation has been largely the result of increased access to glass in the form of studio glassblowers and glass casters for hire, and open-access studios, none of which existed prior to the early 1990s. Wider access to glass meant that any artist who had ideas for glass could use a glass studio like a bronze foundry. They could rent facilities and engage artists to work with them to produce blown, cast, hot-sculpted, and flameworked artworks in glass.

The end of the American studio glass movement does not imply that studio glass is no longer of interest in the United States and abroad. On the contrary, glass is more popular than ever. Works made in glass by artists from inside and outside the glass community are what comprise the landscape of American art in glass today. Young American studio glass artists continue to push material and process in new directions, reexamining and reclaiming the radical beginnings of American studio glass in their development of new works of art that may reference European glass traditions, but that are uniquely American.

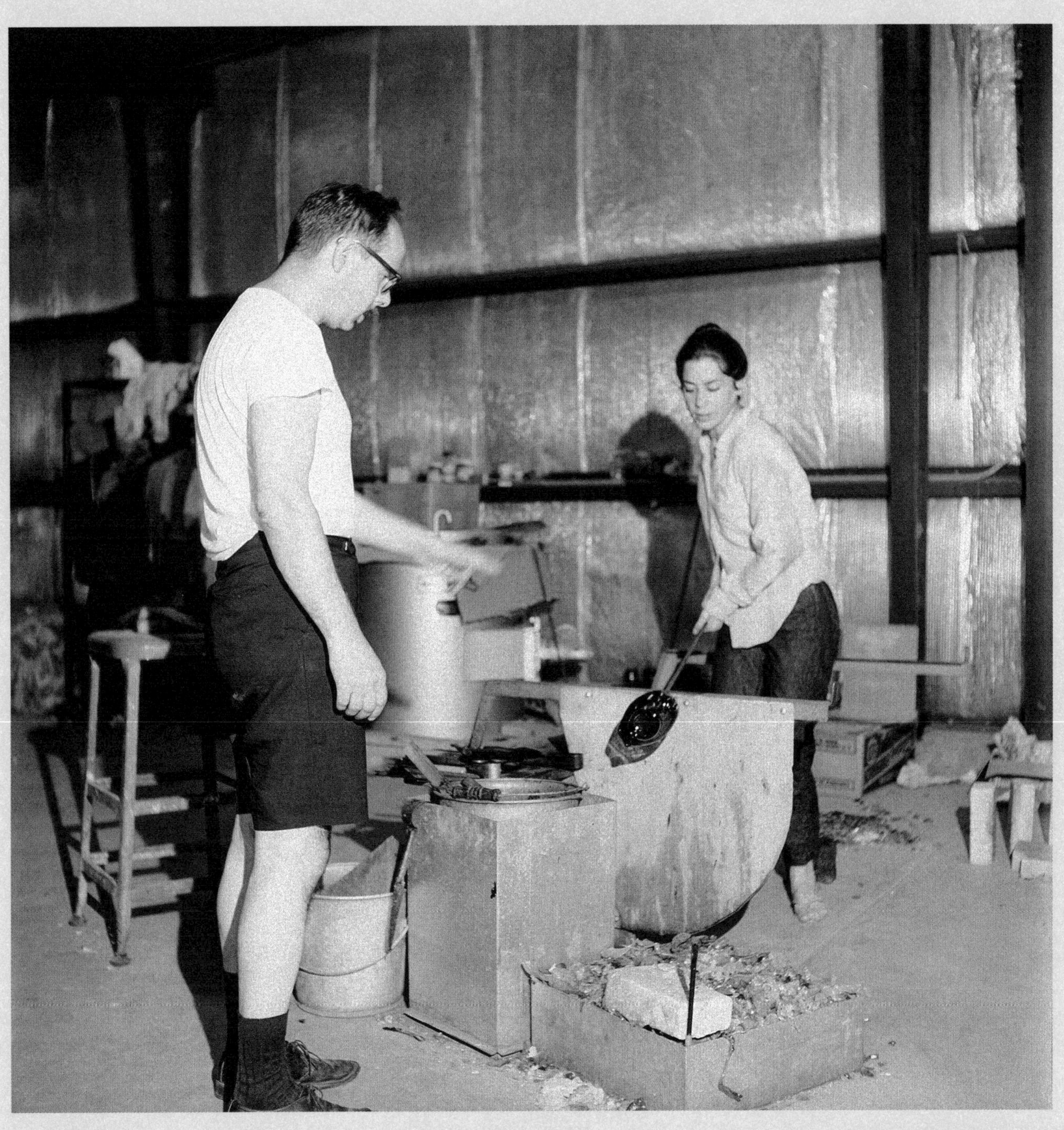

Fig. 1. Harvey Littleton and Rosemary Gulassa blowing glass at the Toledo Workshop, 1962.
Photo: Robert Florian, Robert Florian Collection, Rakow Research Library, The Corning Museum of Glass.

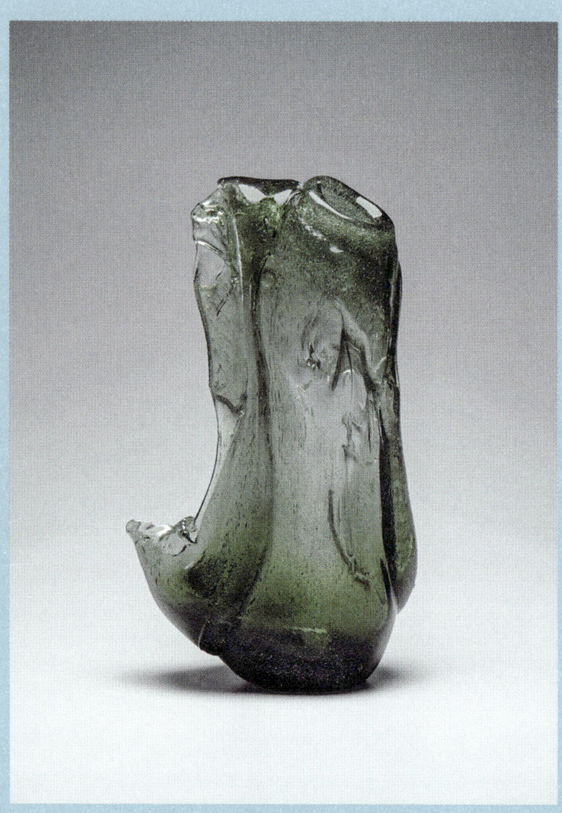

Fig. 2. Harvey K. Littleton (American, 1922–2013). *Exploded Green Vase*, 1965. This is typical of the free-form, tradition-breaking objects characteristic of the early years of American studio glass. Yale University Art Gallery, New Haven, Connecticut (2009.22.1, Janet and Simeon Braguin Fund). Photo: Yale University Art Gallery.

Fig. 3. Fritz Dreisbach (American, b. 1941). *Opaline Bottle*, 1970. The white-opal glass was researched and batched by Dreisbach, as such specialty glasses were not yet commercially available in the United States. The Corning Museum of Glass, Corning, New York (2005.4.174). Photo: The Corning Museum of Glass.

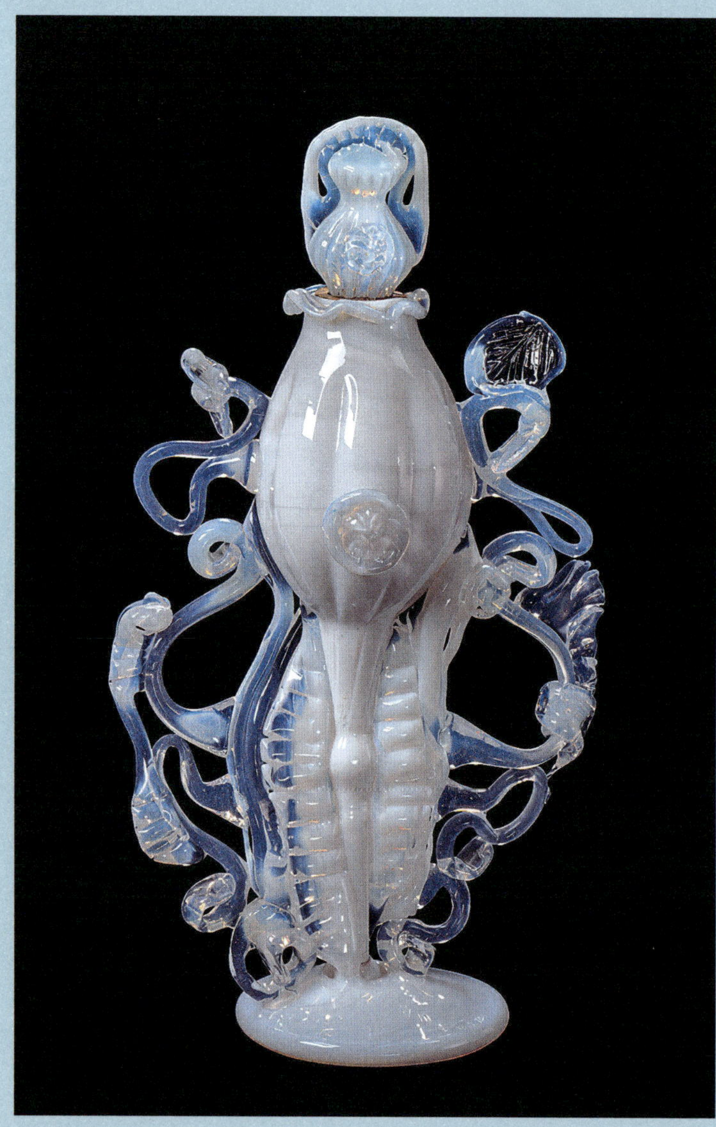

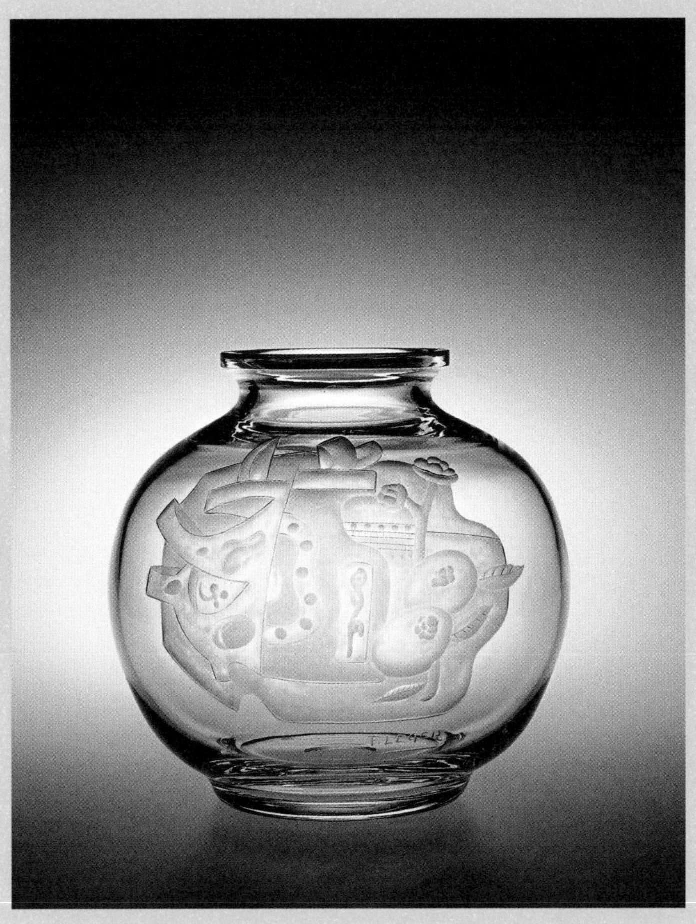

Fig. 5. Stanislav Libenský (Czech, 1921–2002) and Jaroslava Brychtová (Czech, 1924–2020). *Head I*, 1957–58. Radical in its use of glass for abstract sculpture, this work was exhibited in the international traveling exhibition *Glass 1959: A Special Exhibition of International Contemporary Glass* organized by The Corning Museum of Glass.
The Corning Museum of Glass (62.3.132).
Photo: The Corning Museum of Glass.

Fig. 4. Fernand Léger (French, 1881–1955), for Steuben Glass, New York. *Vase with Cubist Composition*, 1939.
The Corning Museum of Glass (2014.4.30, gift of the Ennion Society).
Photo: The Corning Museum of Glass.

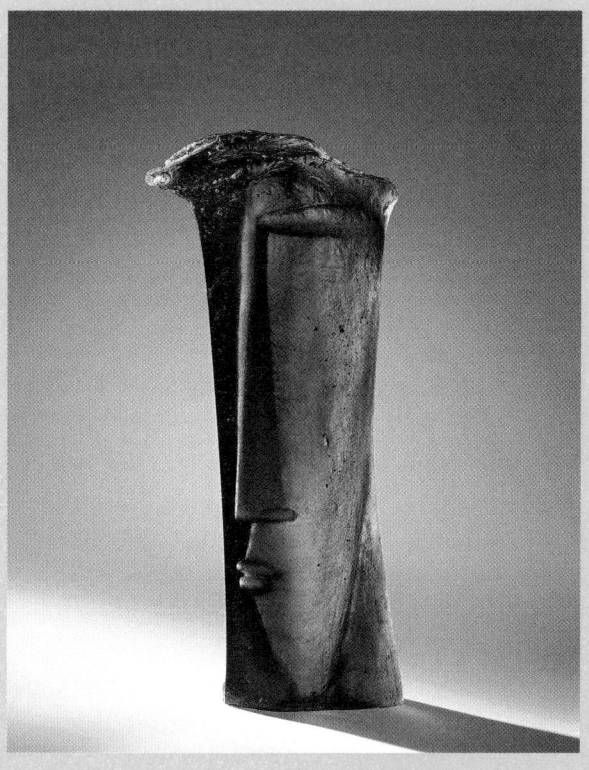

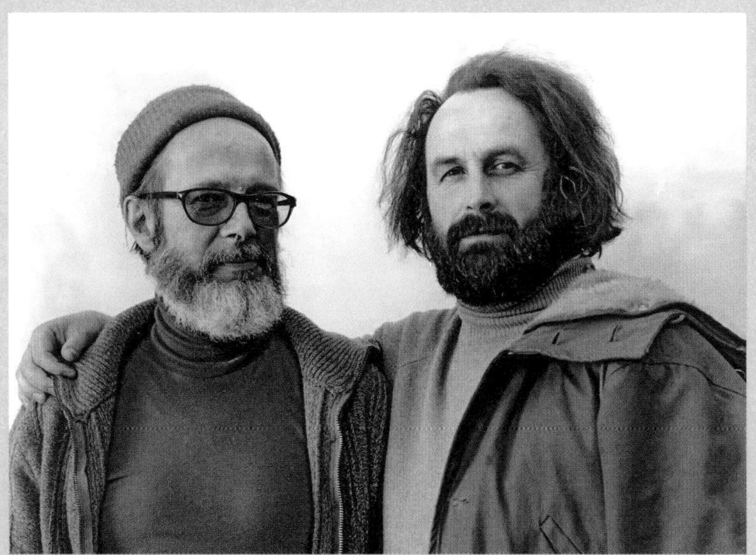

Fig. 6. Harvey Littleton and Erwin Eisch, 1974. Of their first meeting in 1962, Littleton recalled, "I saw Erwin Eisch's work and I realized that he was doing what I wanted to do—play with the glass, make forms that had no other reason for being than that he wanted to make them. Function was something to be used or not used. I knew I had met someone of great importance to what I wanted to do."
Rakow Research Library, The Corning Museum of Glass.

Fig. 7. Dale Chihuly (American, b. 1941). *Pilchuck Pond Installation*, 1971. With the help of his students, Chihuly founded Pilchuck Glass School in Stanwood, Washington in 1971 with Seattle art patrons Anne Gould Hauberg and John Hauberg. Illustrating Chihuly's early interest in glass in landscape, such performative installations distinguished Pilchuck from other American craft schools and programs.
Photo: courtesy Pilchuck Glass School.

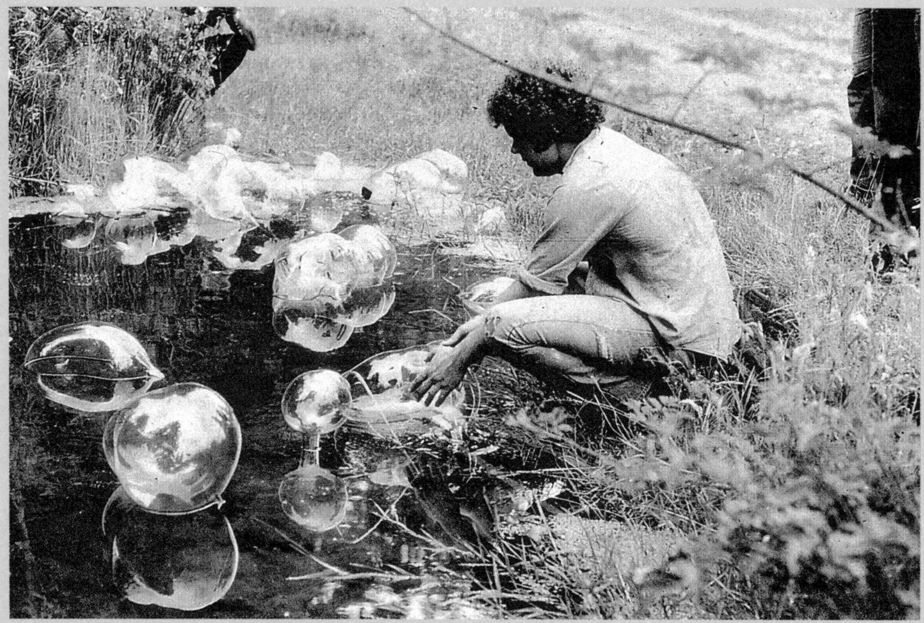

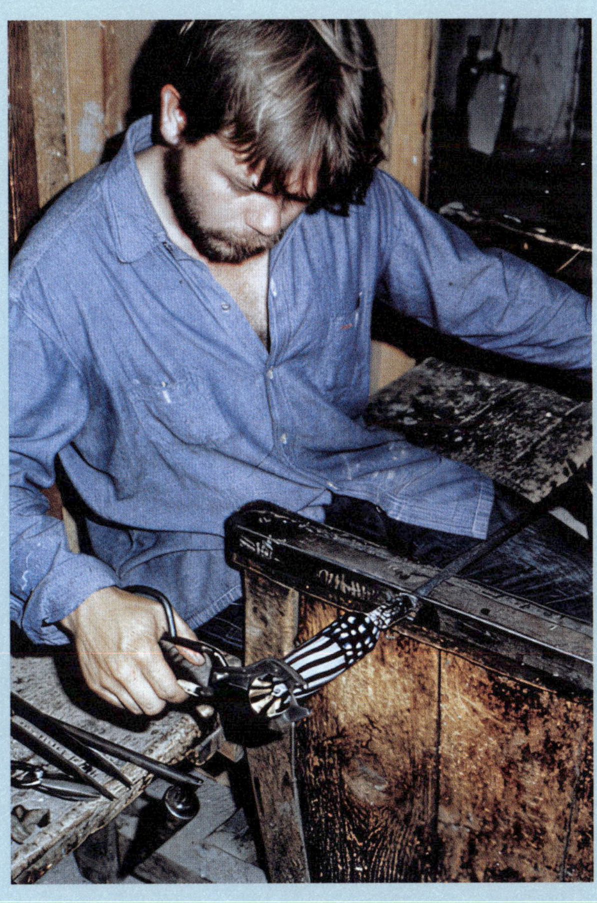

Fig. 8. Richard Marquis (American, b. 1945). *Stars and Stripes Acid Capsule #4*, 1969–1970. Utilizing Venetian techniques to make something quintessentially American, Marquis made a series of his American flag pieces at the Venini glassworks on Murano. The Corning Museum of Glass, Corning, New York (2012.3.34, gift of the artist in memory of Ludovico Diaz de Santillana). Photo: The Corning Museum of Glass. Period photo of Marquis working at Venini: Marvin Lipofsky Collection, Rakow Research Library, The Corning Museum of Glass.

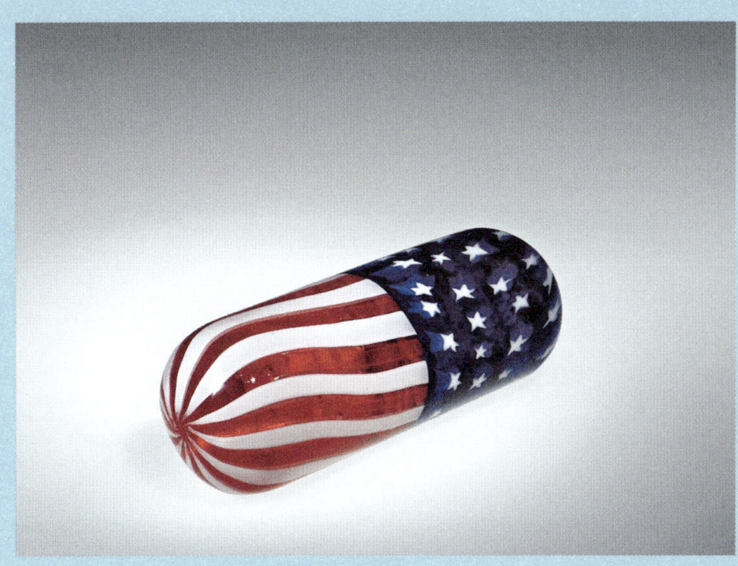

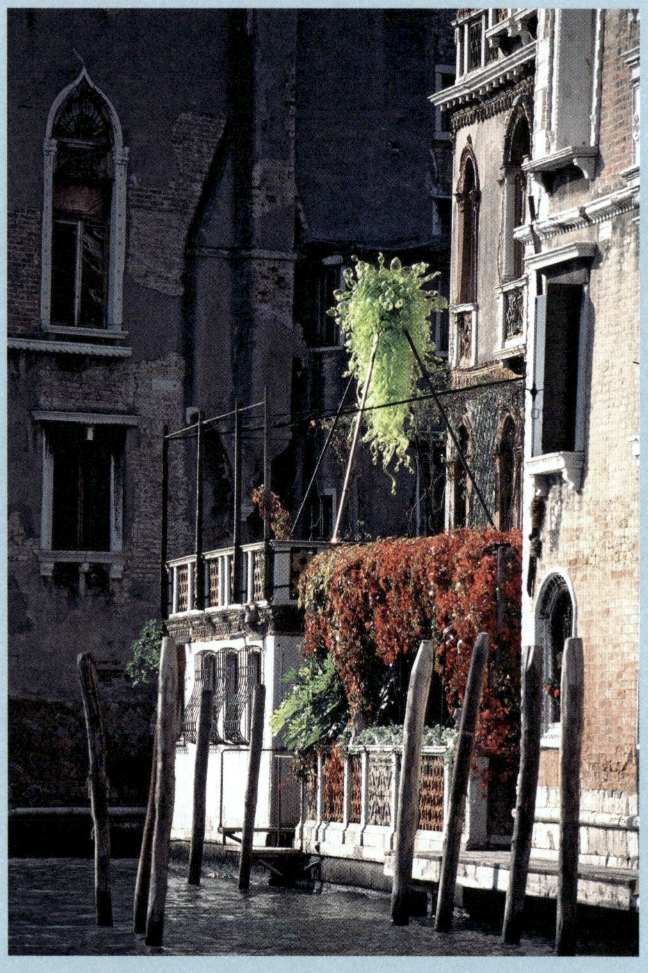

Fig. 9. Dale Chihuly (American, b. 1941). *Palazzo di Loredana Balboni Chandelier*, 1996. Dale Chihuly's extraordinary project *Chihuly Over Venice* demonstrated that glass was capable of as great a scale, complexity, and significance for sculpture as it was for architecture. Chihuly and his teams made 14 architectural-scale glass *Chandeliers* that were installed at sites throughout the city of Venice—in outdoor gardens, on terraces and bridges, in loggias and courtyards, and over cisterns.
© 2020 Chihuly Studio / Artists Rights Society (ARS), New York. Photo: Russell Johnson © Chihuly Studio, all rights reserved. © Dale Chihuly / VG Bild-Kunst, Bonn 2025

Fig. 10. Robert Rauschenberg (American, 1925–2008). *Tire*, designed in 1995–96 and made in 2005. Beginning in the 1990s, contemporary artists wanting to work in glass could more easily access glass studios, such as UrbanGlass in New York (where this was made), to fabricate their ideas.
The Corning Museum of Glass (2007.4.5, gift in part of Daniel Greenberg, Susan Steinhauser, and The Greenberg Foundation, and the F. M. Kirby Foundation). Photo: The Corning Museum of Glass. © Robert Rauschenberg Foundation / VG Bild-Kunst, Bonn 2025

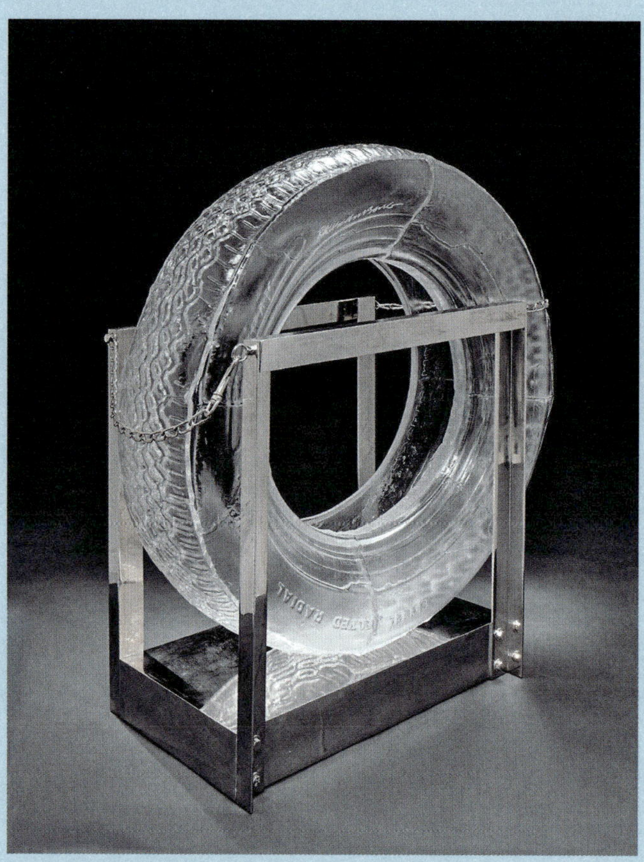

Artists

Niko Abramidis &NE / Philip Baldwin / Monica Guggisberg / Monica Bonvicini / Mark Bradford / Kristi Cavataro / Dale Chihuly / Tony Cragg / Jimmie Durham / Erwin Eisch / Jes Fan / Carlos Garaicoa / Donghai Guan / Jens Gussek / Mona Hatoum / Shirazeh Houshiary / Ann Veronica Janssens / Hassan Khan / Ki-Ra Kim / Namdoo Kim / Yoshiaki Kojiro / Raimund Kummer / Alicja Kwade / Glenda León / Antoine Leperlier / Silvia Levenson / Stanislav Libenský / Jaroslava Brychtová / Jessica Loughlin / Haroon Mirza / Masayo Odahashi / Sibylle Peretti / Laure Prouvost / Colin Reid / Gizela Šabóková / Anri Sala / Masahiro Sasaki / Alejandra Seeber / Eric Sidner / Kiki Smith / Jana Sterbak / Jenna Sutela / Hui Tao / Neringa Vasiliauskaitė / František Vízner / Ursula von Rydingsvard / Janusz Walentynowicz / Qin Wang / Sunny Wang / Pae White / Terry Winters / Ann Wolff

Niko Abramidis &NE

born 1987 in Munich, Germany;
lives and works in Munich and Berlin, Germany

The art of Niko Abramidis &NE engages with economic structures and visions of the future. His drawings, paintings, sculptures, and spatial installations create parallel universes in which he forges fictitious corporate identities and appropriates modes of expression from the financial economy. He uses the medium of glass as a display, as a support for digital images.

It is like entering a small office: you can even take a seat at the "desk." Obviously, someone has already done this before, used the smartphone lying there, and scribbled a few notes on a Post-It. The desk is presented as a locus for creating ideas, negotiations, and strategies, where small items, including a cryptic symbol, appear like objects from some supposed everyday reality. The "chair" is constructed with subversive humor: it looks like a roll of dollar bills on which one sits comfortably; and the "desk" consists entirely of a large-format screen.

This installation, entitled *Agenda Table (Muc-Manila)* (2020), part of a series of works of the same name (since 2018), recreates a desk "in whose steel-welded frame a large-format screen is embedded under a glass plate as a tabletop. Visualizations and aerial photographs of places are displayed on the screen, through which the artist makes global movements of money flows visible. Centers of power, such as central business districts, but also remote places important to financial companies or global trade, are explored and made spatially tangible."[1]

Niko Abramidis &NE studied at the Academy of Fine Arts Munich under Julian Rosefeldt and Markus Oehlen and at the Berlin University of the Arts under Byung-Chul Han. He received a scholarship from the Cité internationale des arts in Paris (2017) and was awarded the ars viva prize for visual arts in 2019. He had his first solo exhibition at the Salzburger Kunstverein in 2023. PGH

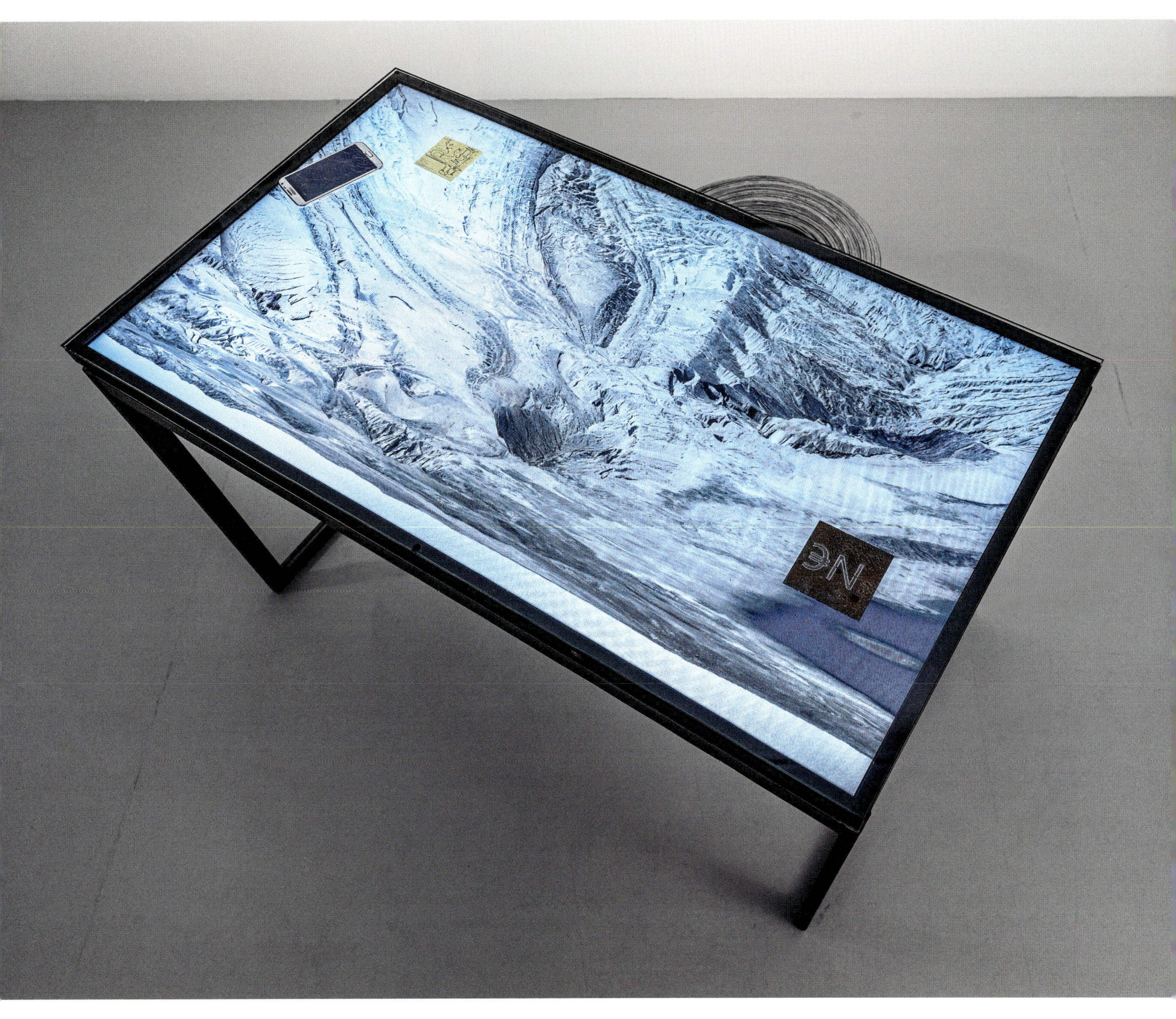

Agenda Table (Muc-Manila), 2020
Steel, screen, glass, steel plate, smartphone dummy,
drawing on Post-It and Google Earth video loop (27'13")
125 × 80 × 72 cm

Philip Baldwin
Monica Guggisberg

born 1947 in New York, USA
born 1955 in Bern, Switzerland
Both live and work in Wales, UK

The boat series has a prominent position in Philip Baldwin and Monica Guggisberg's oeuvre.[1] Boats symbolize the journey of life which every person must take, but also the means of transport by which we navigate our way through existence. *First Memories,* a 150-centimeter-long metal boat, is loaded with colorful bottle-like objects that protrude from the vessel like a bunch of flowers from a vase, each one pointing in a different direction. It seems like people from different countries have crowded themselves into the boat as they undertake an uncertain voyage. Where are they traveling to? Who are these "passengers" who have been thrown together? Their memories and stories are the only cargo contained within these hollow structures. The nineteen empty objects made of glass are each unique, having been freely formed from the glassmaker's blowpipe and then further worked while cold using what is known as the battuto technique (Italian for "beat" or "tap").

Guggisberg and Baldwin's more than forty years of artistic collaboration began in Sweden when they were assistants at the renowned and pioneering Stenhytta Studio run by Ann Wolff. In 1982 they opened their first studio together in Switzerland. They later lived and worked in France before moving to Wales. Their approach has always been based on master craftsmanship. The works are influenced both by Swedish overlay methods and by traditional Italian cold-working techniques. Color, light, and varied surface patterns give the works their artistic significance.[2] AC

First Memories, 2010
Blown-glass vessel with
cold-worked surface
139.7 × 34.9 × 40 cm

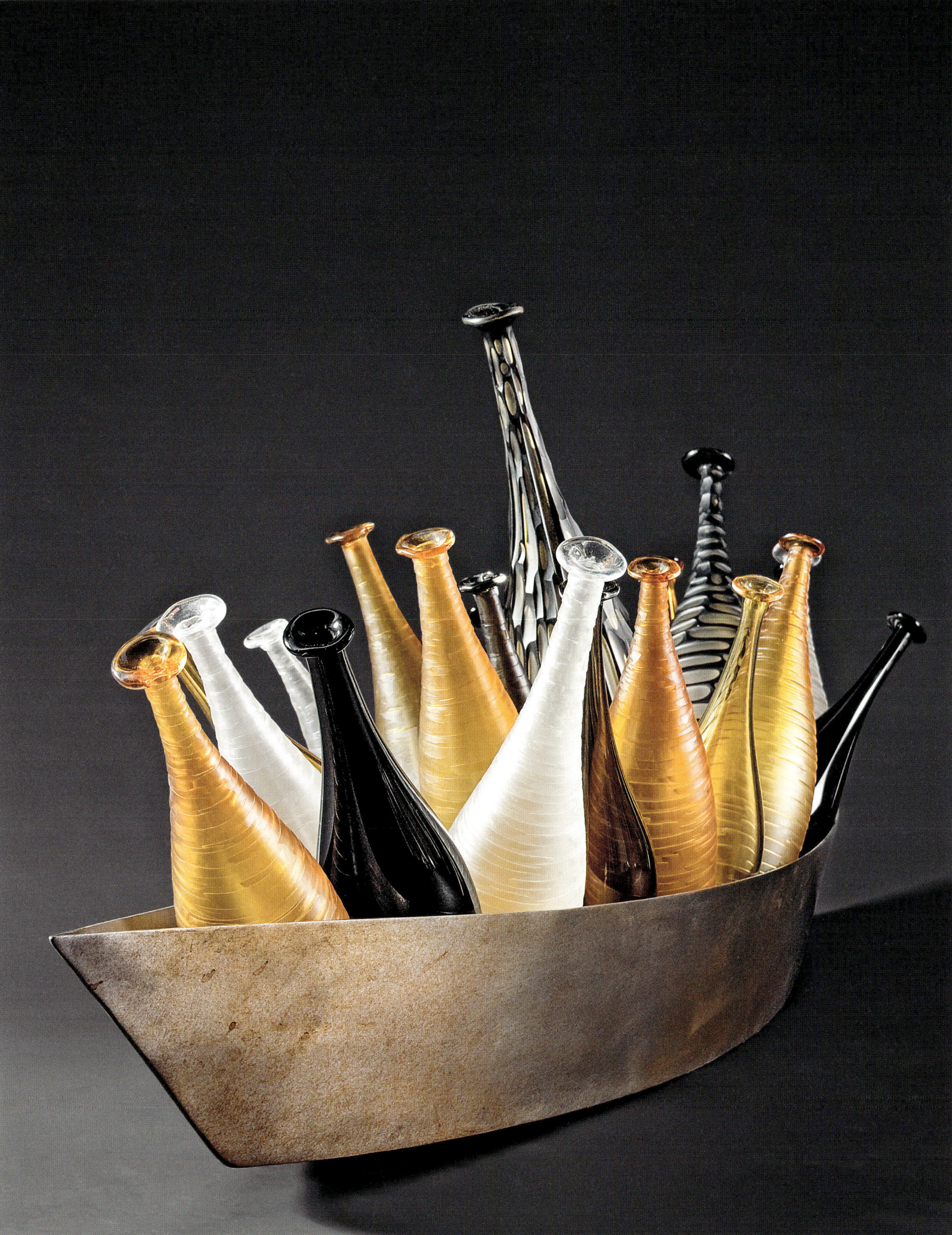

Monica Bonvicini

born 1965 in Venice, Italy;
lives and works in Berlin, Germany

In her multifaceted artistic practice, Monica Bonvicini explores the relationships between architecture, power structures, gender, and space. This award-winning artist (Golden Lion at the Venice Biennale, 1999; Preis der Nationalgalerie für junge Kunst, Staatliche Museen zu Berlin, 2005) has presented multimedia exhibitions of drawings, sculptures, and videos in major museums around the world. She uses materials with "libidinous surfaces," such as mirrors, latex, leather, and steel—as well as glass—to create sculptures that, despite their poetry, beauty, and intimacy, are provocative and sometimes disturbing. Gender roles and the subtle mechanisms of power are foregrounded, as the works express themselves through lust and violence, desire and submission.

Her own hands are cast in solid clear glass, holding a curved belt, as though ready to give a beating (*In My Hand,* 2019)—a reference to her piece *A Choir of Five* (2018), in which the performers create harsh rhythmic noises using leather belts.[1] The violent gesture of holding a belt, a sign of domination now manifested in glass, has a combative connotation. In *Fleurs du Mal (pink)* (2019)—the title an allusion to the "offensive" and often banned poems by Charles Baudelaire—shows pink, deflated, sapless, and powerless phallic objects hanging on a steel construction that recalls Marcel Duchamp's *Bottle Rack* (1914): an image of broken masculinity, with the spikes evoking "the notion of frustrated male flesh" (Julia Wilson). Similarly, hand-blown glass objects hang from hooks in her work *Pendant.*

Bonvicini uses humor and irony to attack cultural symbols of masculinity, interrogating social conventions and disrupting areas traditionally dominated by men. PGH

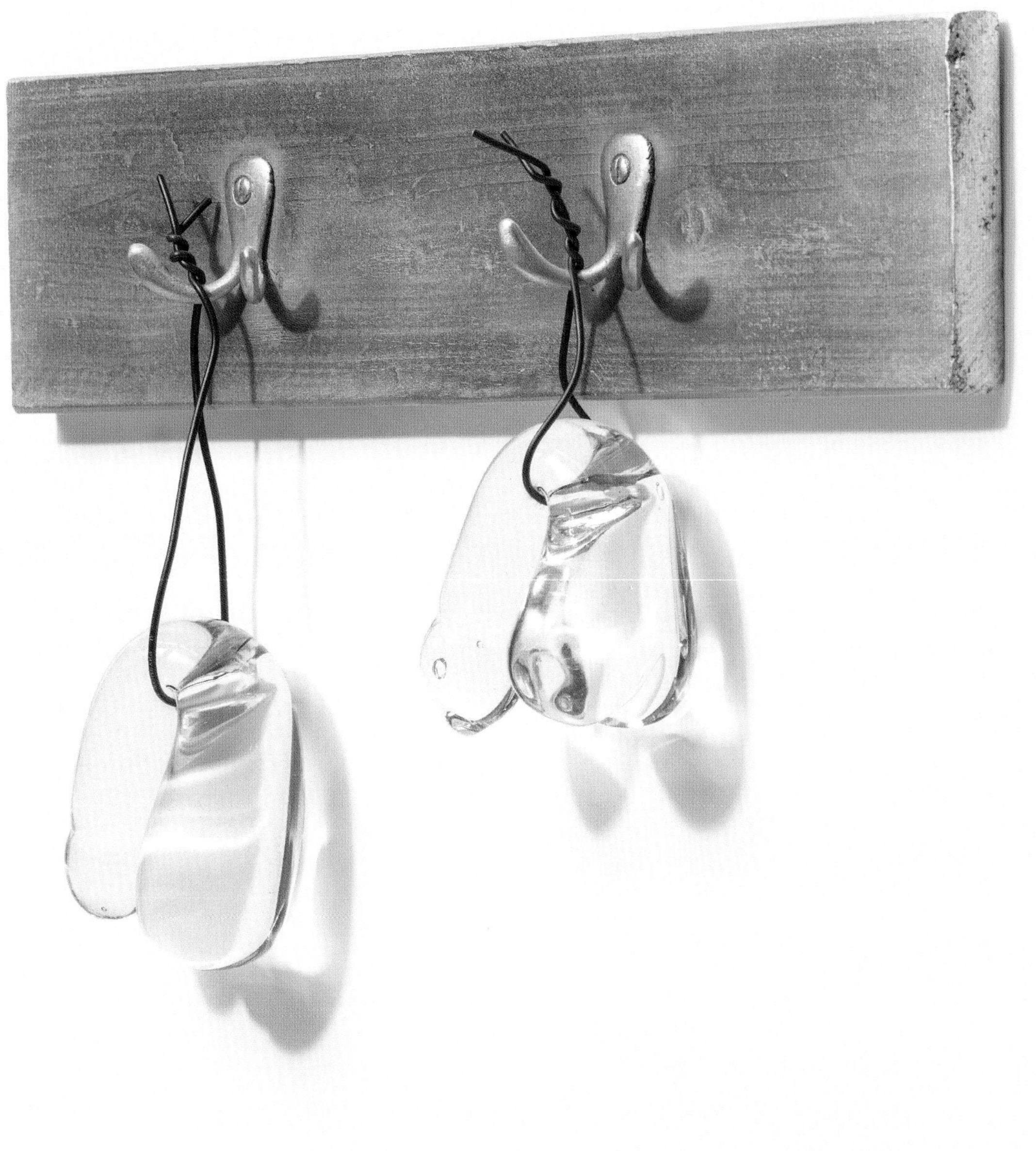

Small Pendant (2), 2021
Glass, cable, cast aluminum
26 × 39 × 6 cm

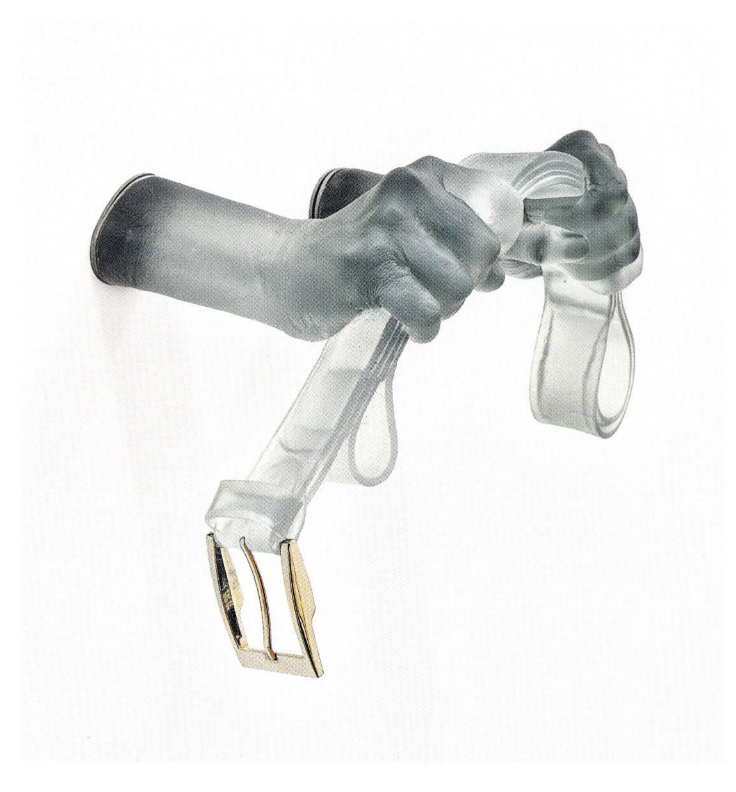

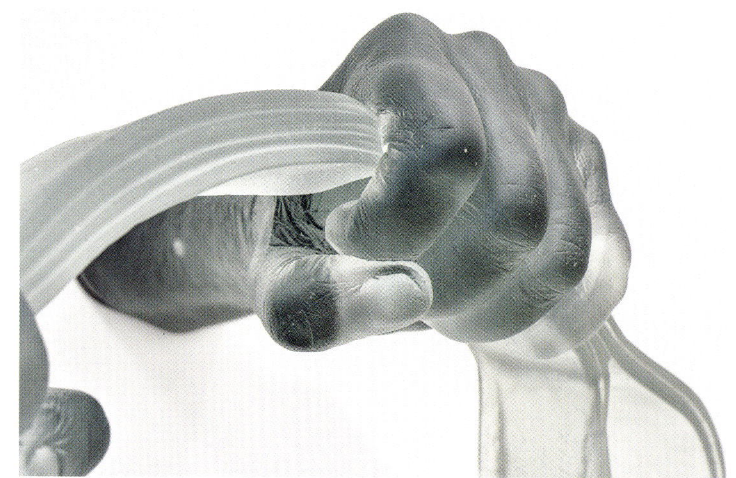

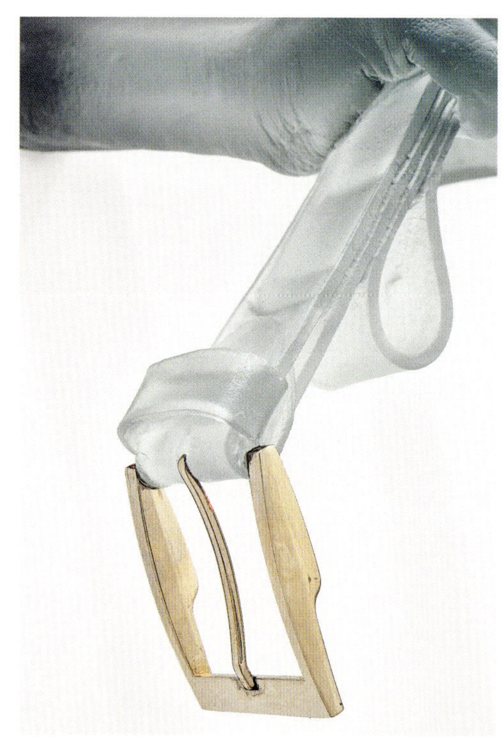

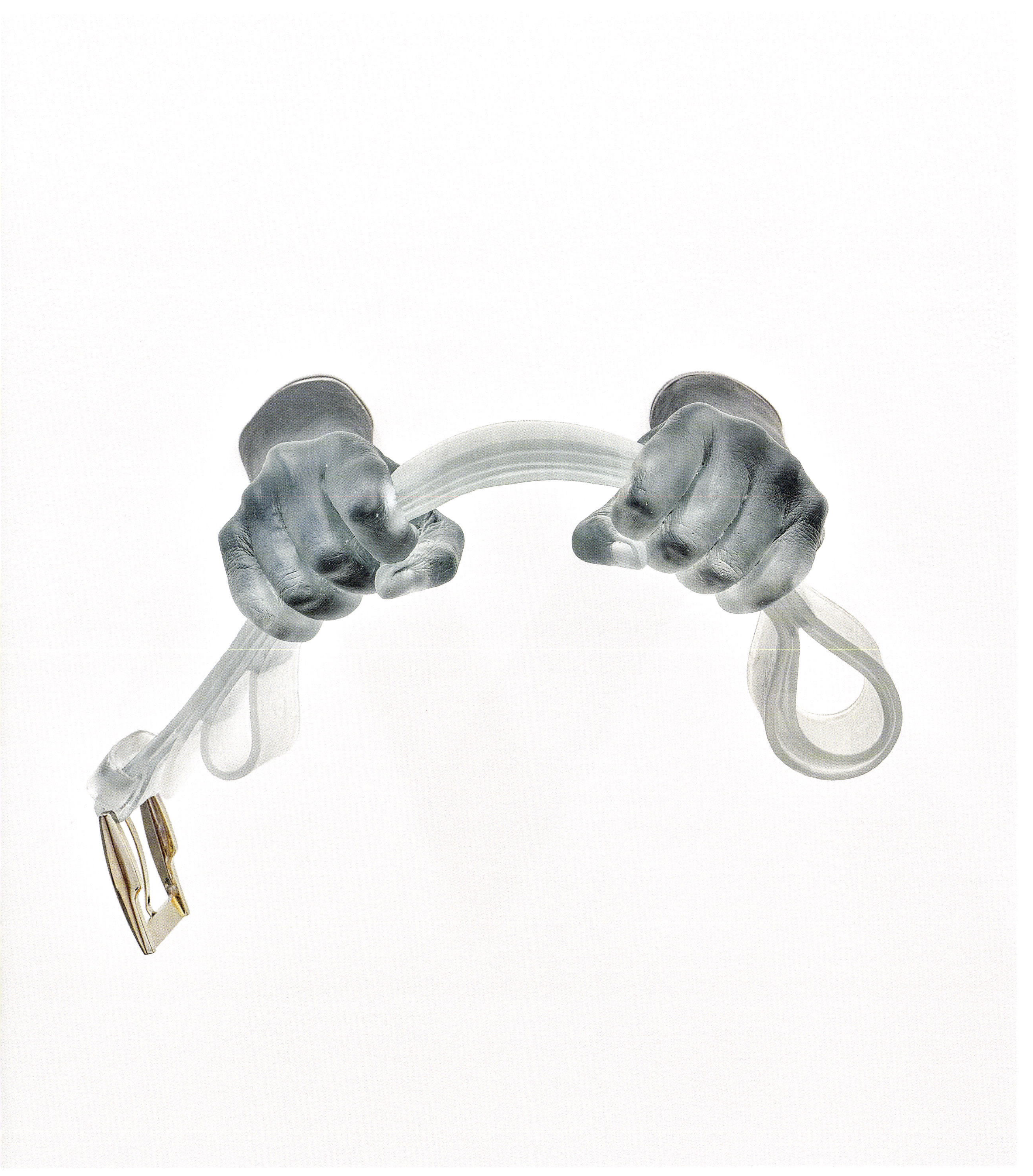

In My Hand, 2019
Glass, metal
35 × 20 × 20 cm

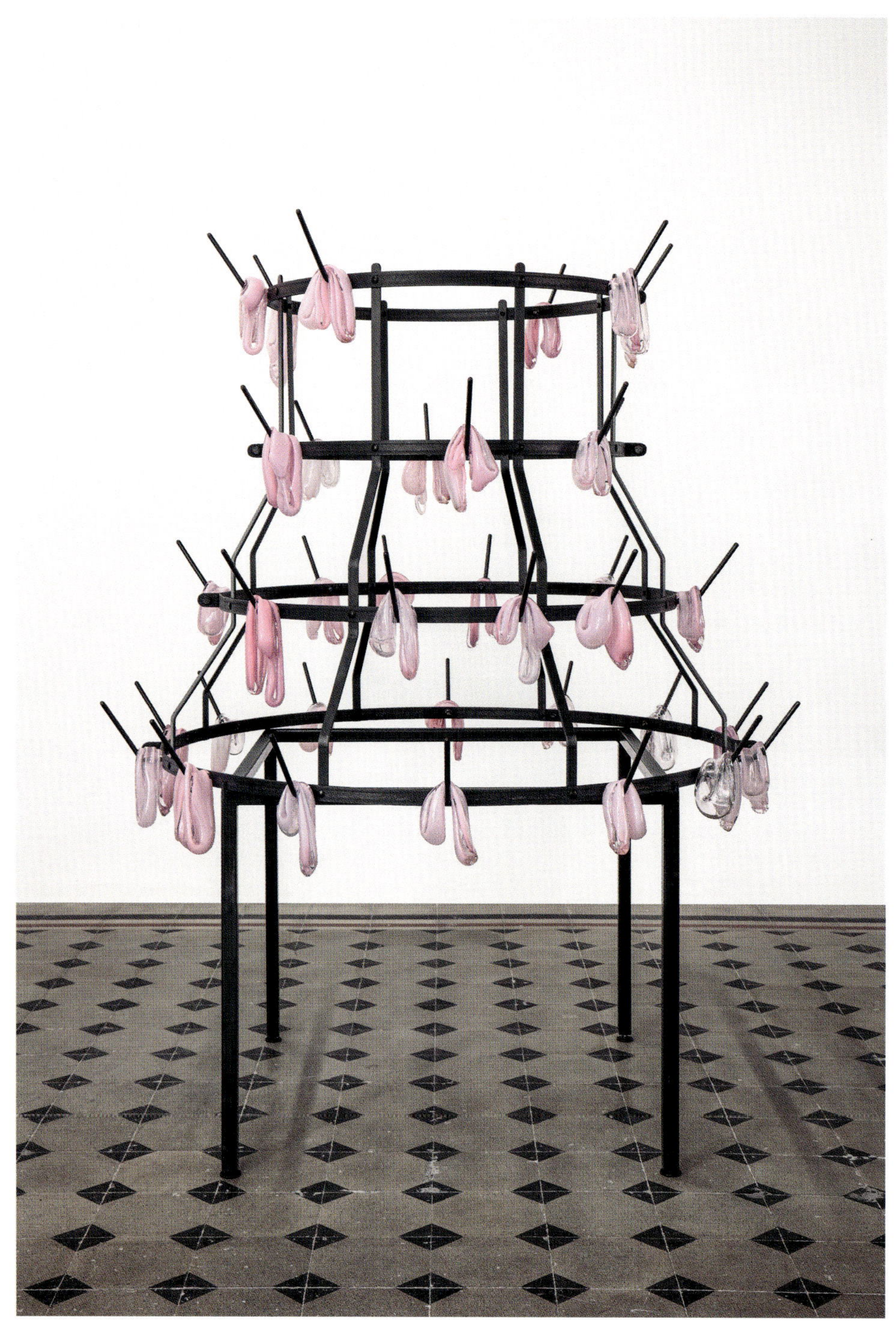

Fleurs du Mal (pink), 2019
Steel, hand-blown glass
Approx. 170 × 150 × 150 cm

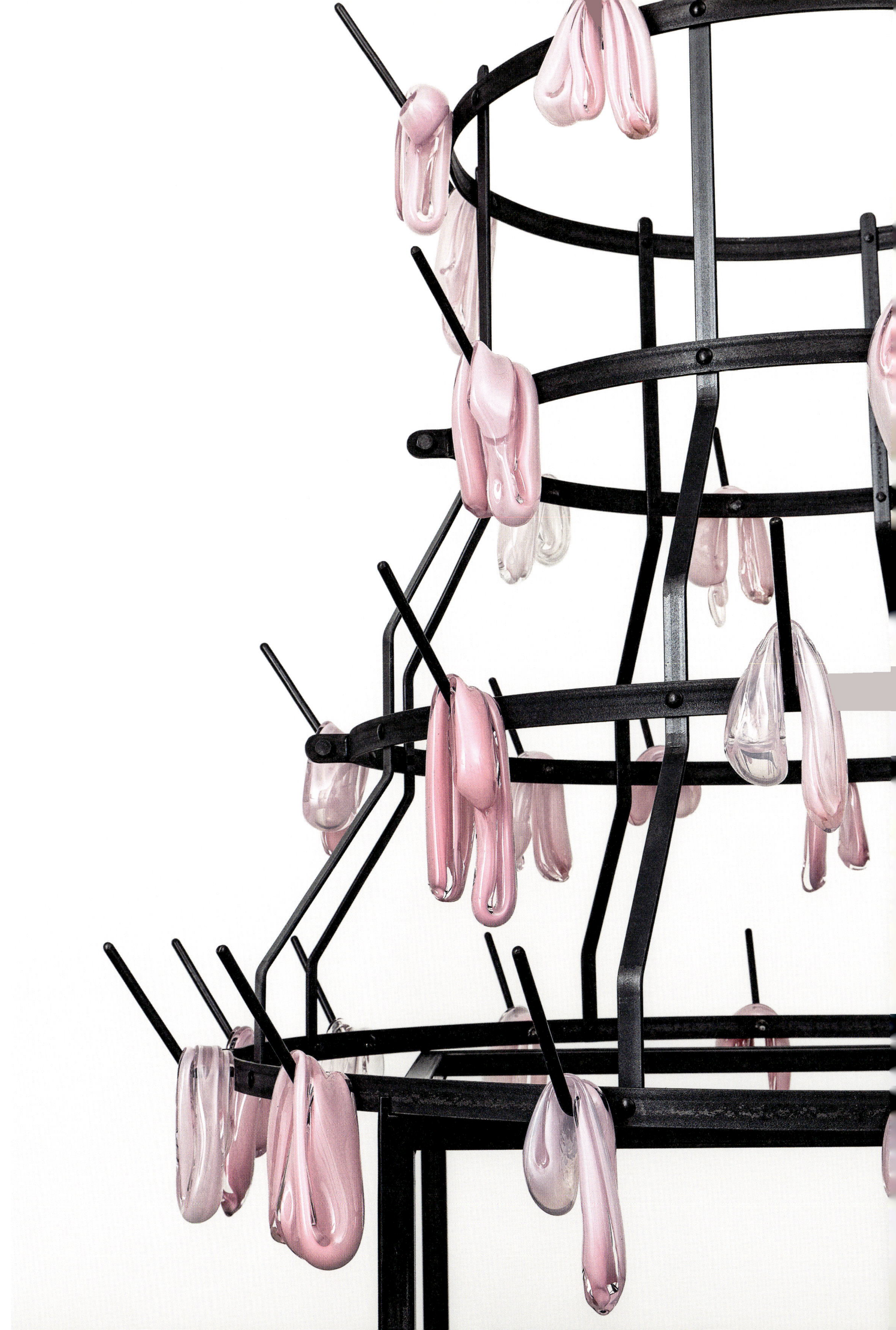

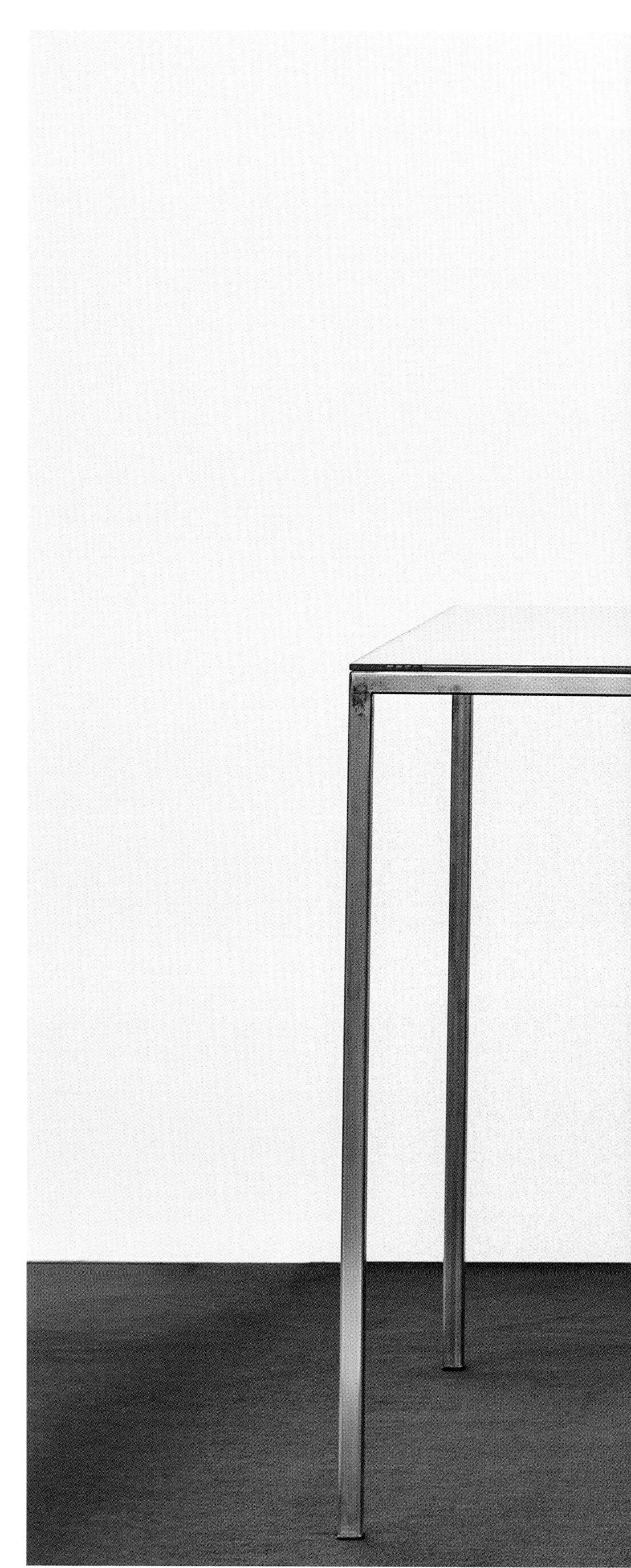

Bonded, 2017
Glass, metal, mirror, table
Sculpture: 84 × 47 × 47 cm
Table: 70 × 100 × 60 cm

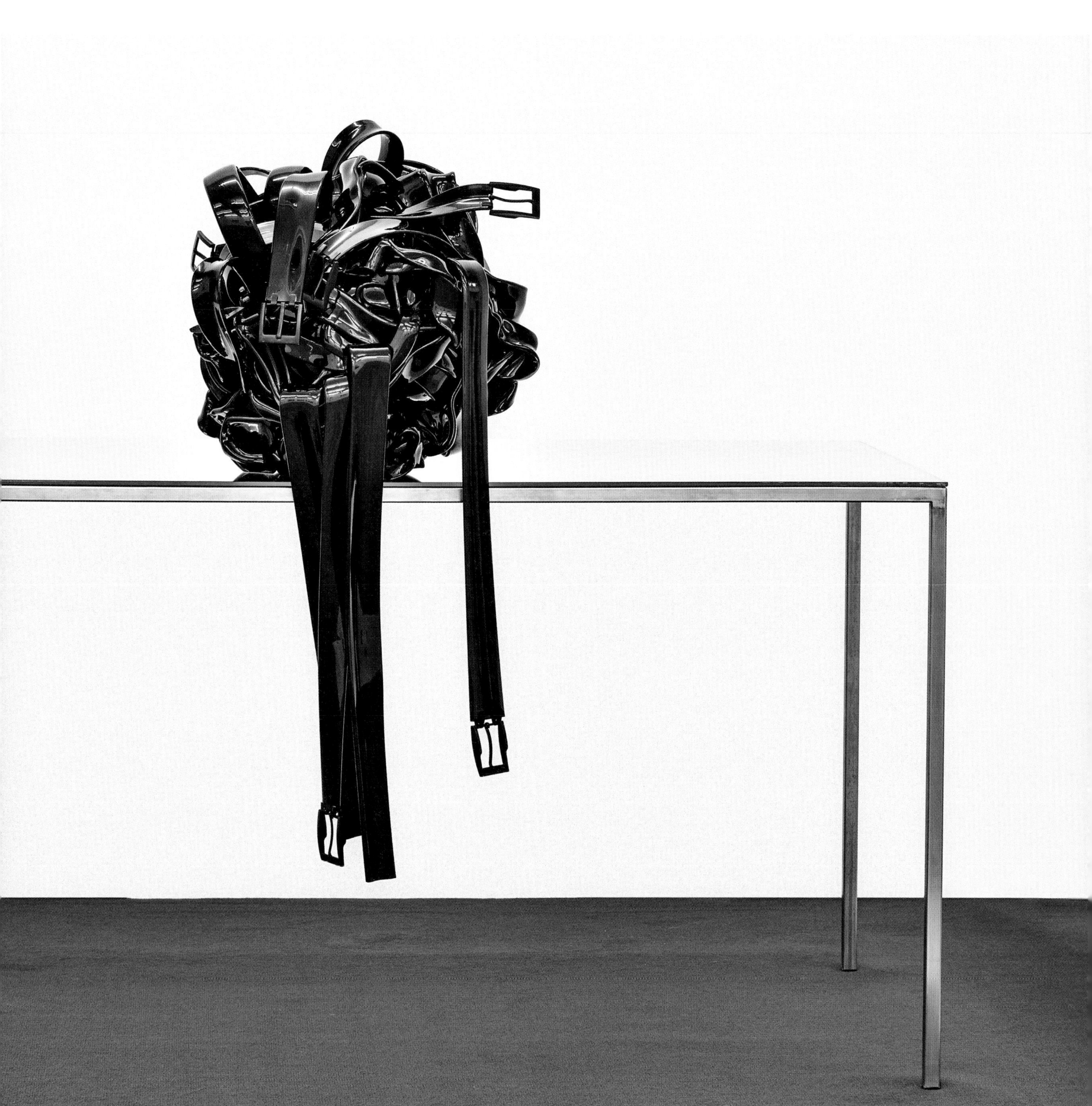

Mark Bradford

born 1961 in Los Angeles, USA;
lives and works in Los Angeles, USA

World-renowned American artist and activist Mark Bradford has been a driving force in critically addressing the status of his country's vulnerable populations and its prison system.

In 2016, Bradford partnered with Rio Terà dei Pensieri, a nonprofit organization in Italy supporting local prisoners. Rio Terà encourages incarcerated people to work for honest wages by manufacturing hands-on products. Male prisoners in Venice, for instance, embellish garments using silk screens and produce PVC bags to be sold online and through the Malefatte store in the heart of the San Polo district.

Borsa, 2024
Murano glass
66 × 17.8 × 33.3 cm

In 2017, Bradford represented the United States at the Venice Biennale. While his gigantic pulp canvas *Tomorrow Is Another Day* (now at MoMA, New York) spoke of failures and fissures in American history, Bradford wholeheartedly engaged locally. Teaming up with Rio Terà, he aimed to draw attention to the underbelly of Venice, of this biannual stronghold of art-world glitz and affluence. In the ongoing *Process Colletivo*, he created a direct and permanent link between the two. On the occasion of the 2024 Venice Biennale, Bradford created a limited edition of 30 *Borsa* sculptures to commemorate this socially engaged project.[1]

Given its large size, double handles, and open top, a tote bag can be used for almost anything. Historically made from cotton or hemp, it evolved over the last forty years from a simple carrier to a lifestyle signifier: first used by avid book-readers and intellectuals, it became the preferred bag for the ecologically aware and for farmers' market regulars, before Dior disciples came to relish its iconic toile de Jouy. While other luxury *maisons* such as Balenciaga, Givenchy, and Louis Vuitton followed suit, the tote has now turned into a marker of the global art glitterati—and into a marker of the Venice Biennale. But Bradford topped it all: he took such a bag and added layers of meaning. By using glass, he alluded to centuries-old Venetian tradition and craftsmanship. The pink rubino hue speaks of a Renaissance aristocracy and dazzling Venetian wealth. However, Bradford also incorporated the Serenissima's underbelly: *Borsa* references the PVC bags made at the men's prison, and the tallies he engraved on its front allude to the length of the prisoners' incarceration: one tally per day. Tallies can be also found in glassblowers' hotshops. Chalked onto the doors of the annealers, they keep track of time and temperature while the glasswork cools down. Only a precisely monitored, well-structured cooling process will prevent deformation, stress, or thermal shock. As much as Bradford's *Borsa* is about Venice, its Biennale, and its prisoners, it is also about (social) structure, time, and freedom—as well as about their preciousness and their fragility. Just like the glass tote, all three can deform, melt down, shatter, and break. To prevent disaster, Bradford's leitmotif surfaces once again: give respect—to people, to places, to (hi)stories and even to things—so that they may thrive.

The collaboration between Mark Bradford, Rio Terà, Berengo Studio, and Hauser & Wirth is exemplary: intellectual sharpness, glassblowing mastery, and serious blue-chip thrust transform far-sighted aspirational communal altruism into a global must-have. JG

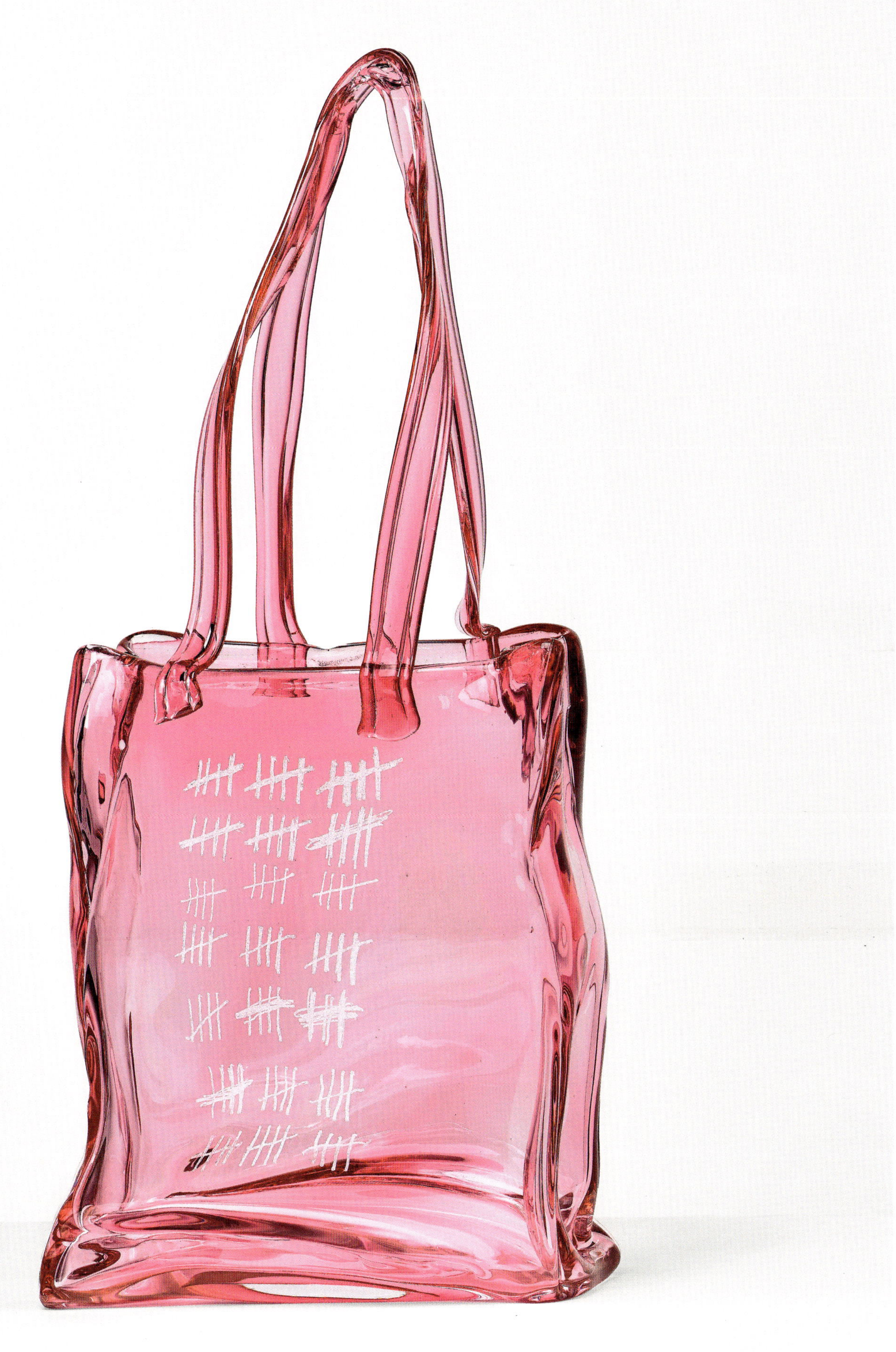

Kristi Cavataro

born 1992 in Connecticut, USA;
lives and works in New York, USA

The gridded structure of Kristi Cavataro's fascinating arrangements of three-dimensional geometric forms made of colored glass is easily reminiscent of machines. Yet the young artist is bringing old techniques back to life, "breathing new life into an ancient medium: stained glass."[1] Freeing stained glass from its traditional place in windows and lamps, she builds tubular forms that create a reality of their own. Each work consists of a grid of rectilinear pieces of glass, which Cavataro cuts and grinds by hand and then welds together using Louis Comfort Tiffany's well-known traditional method (plywood armatures, which she later removes, serve as temporary supports during the production process). The hollow forms that result sometimes merge into a seamless whole; in other cases, one serpentine module nestles into another to form an evocative architectural construction. These forms are usually around one meter high and are made by hand in a painstaking process of cutting, bending, and soldering individual glass tiles into intricate cylindrical compositions. Cavataro is inspired by minimalist and post-minimalist sculpture, as she says, and her interest in seriality and modular construction in particular derives from this: "Once I figure something out with form, or shape, or geometry, or material, it opens so many doors and I want to go through all of them."[2] The artist, who has lived and worked in the South Bronx since 2015, says of her work, "I'm not trying to make a thing that is easily nameable. They're not illustrations of a thing. They *are* the thing."[3]

Cavataro created her first glass sculptures in 2018 during a residency at Lighthouse Works on Fishers Island, New York. She had had no formal training in glass; up to that point, she had focused mainly on more conventional sculptural processes, such as mold-making and casting. In her first solo exhibition, her most recent works in glass were shown at the Ramiken gallery in New York in 2021. A few months later, Cavataro was the youngest artist to participate in the group exhibition *Greater New York* at MoMA PS1, where her pieces were highly praised by critics in journals ranging from *The New Yorker* to *Art in America*. PGH

Untitled, 2019
Stained glass
86.4 × 53.3 × 22.9 cm

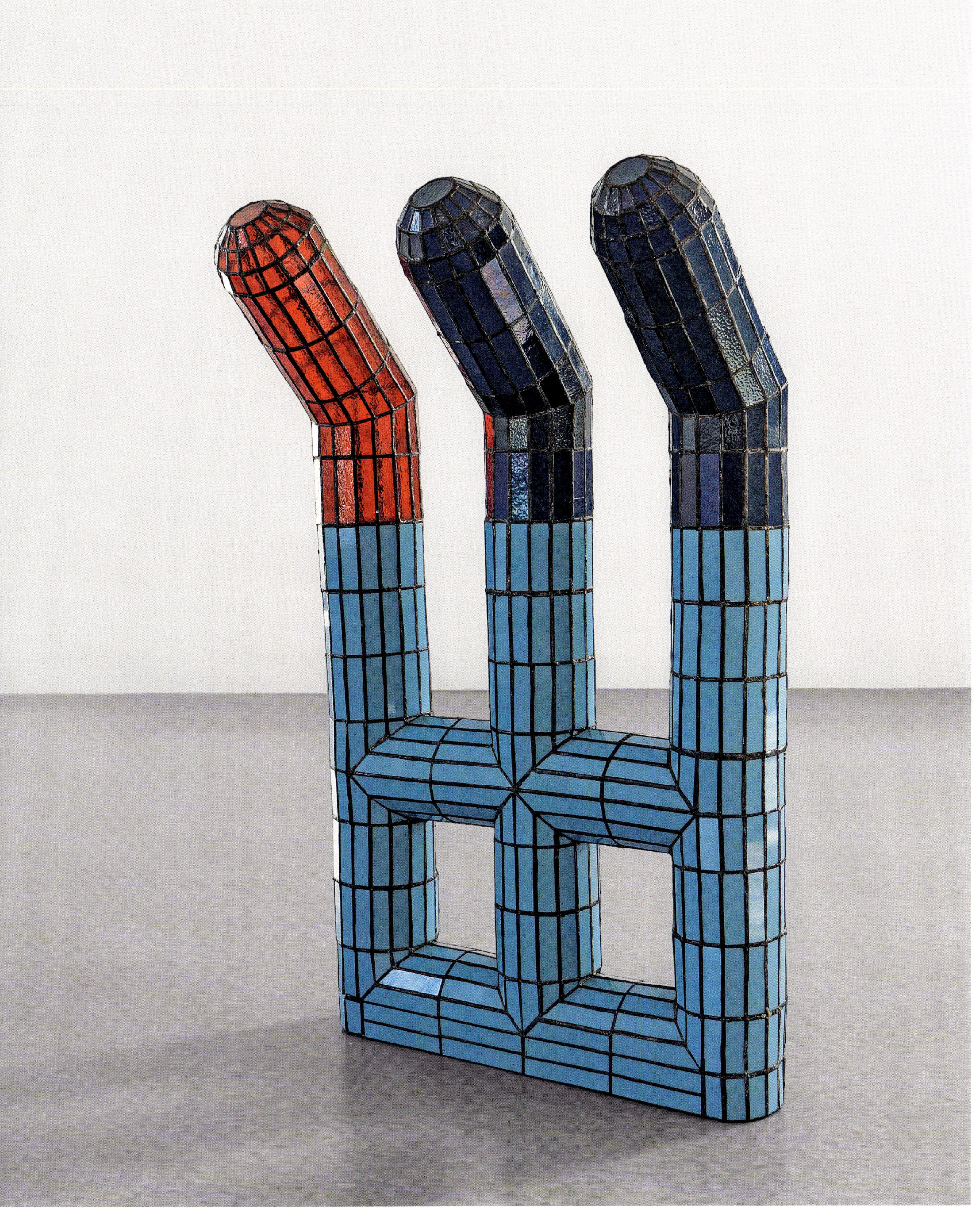

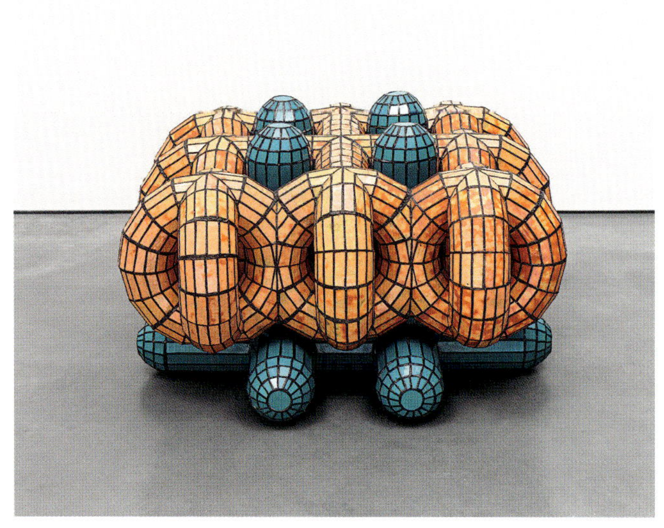

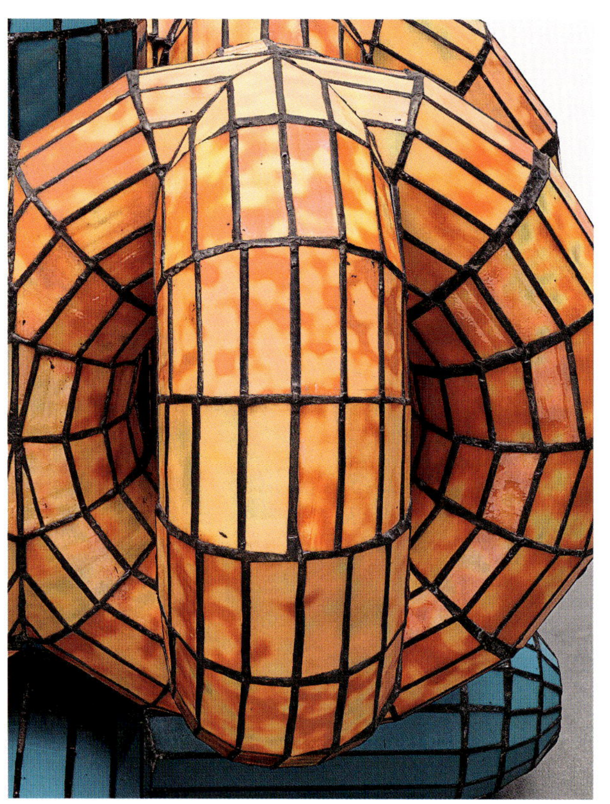

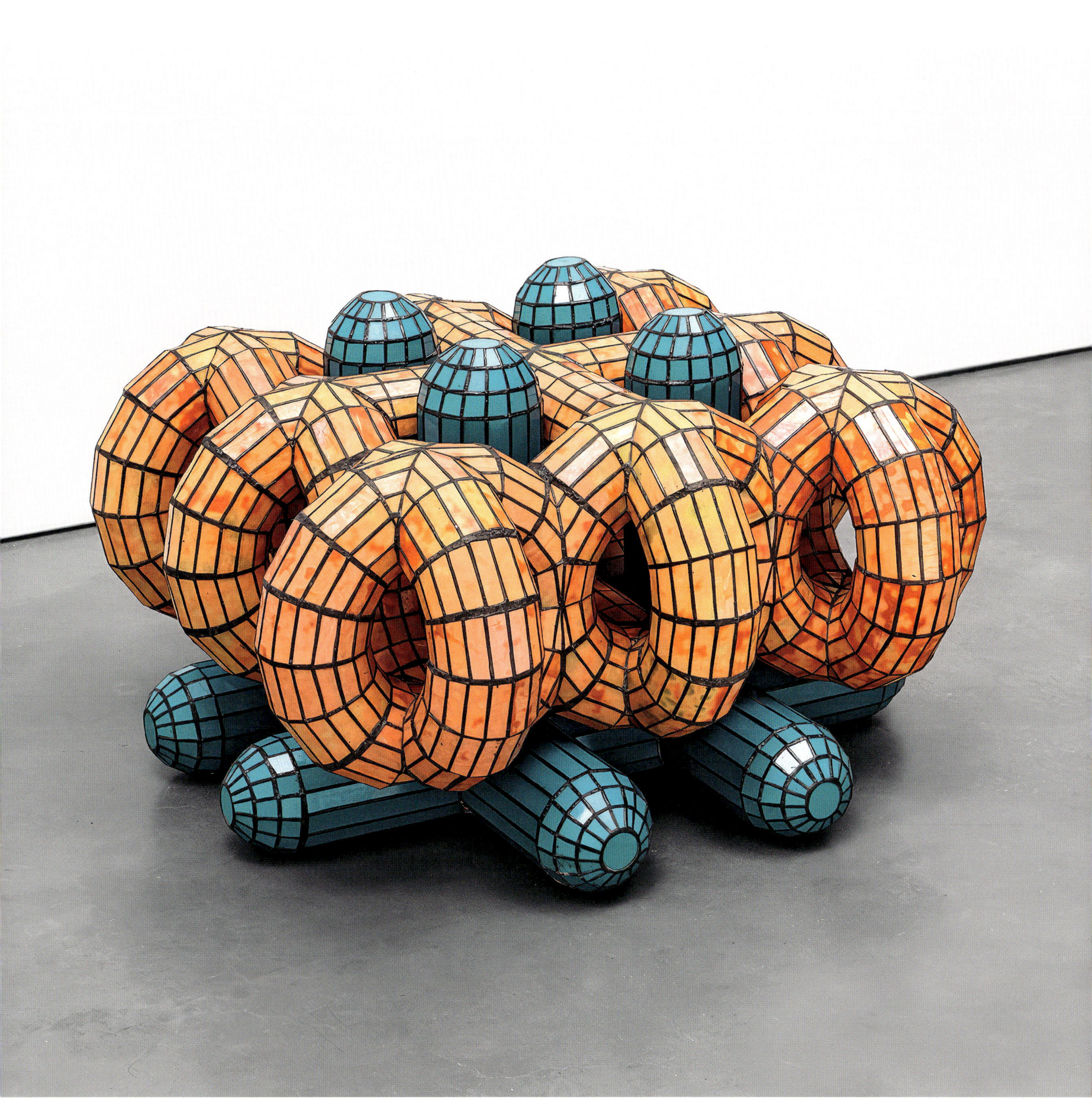

Untitled, 2022
Stained glass
59.7 × 94 × 94 cm

Dale Chihuly

born 1941 in Tacoma, Washington, USA;
lives and works in Seattle, Washington, USA

Both a master and a rock star of glass, Dale Chihuly is a pioneer of fantastical glass forms who turned blown glass into large-scale sculptures and grand installations. Chihuly started the now world-famous Pilchuck Glass School outside Seattle as a hippie commune in 1971, and soon afterward came to oversee his own Renaissance-style studio operation, with 150 experts working in his own hotshop. The flamboyant virtuoso prides himself in having his own film and publishing companies to record his work.

In the late 1990s, Chihuly was invited to conceive a year-long open-air exhibition in the old Citadel of Jerusalem to mark the arrival of the new millennium. With 17 large-scale installations built from more than 10,000 pieces of glass and weighing 43 tons, *Chihuly in the Light of Jerusalem 2000* came to be the artist's biggest, most sensational project. Over one million visitors flocked to see it.

Jerusalem Cylinder, 2000
Mold-blown glass, chunks of crystals applied hot
59 × 17 × 17 cm

To commemorate this epochal outdoor exhibition, Chihuly made several medium-sized *Jerusalem Cylinders* in various colors, modeled after their large-scale equivalents exhibited below the Crusader Hall on the outer Western Wall of the Citadel. First and foremost, the *Jerusalem Cylinders* are technical masterpieces. "I have spent my life as an explorer searching for new ways to use glass and glassblowing to make forms and colors and installations that no one has ever created before," Chihuly says.[1] In his famous baskets, sea forms and persians, he used fire and heat, gravity, movement and centrifugal force to make glass as thin as possible, pushing it to the edge of collapsibility.

Chihuly's *Jerusalem Cylinders* are, by contrast, extraordinarily heavy and robust. "I always wanted to do a series of blown objects with chunks of crystal on them," the artist stated. The technical challenge lies in attaching large, rugged pieces of solid glass to the cylinders and reheating them without losing their sharp edges. Then there is the equilibrium to maintain, to keep the cylinder standing while carrying massive, irregularly placed crystals. Working with up to 15 experienced glassblowers at any one time, Chihuly conceded that these cylinders were "perhaps the most difficult and complicated pieces I've ever made."[2]

In addition to its technical mastery, this particular *Jerusalem Cylinder* reverberates with the specific context in which it was made. The blue may allude to the azure in Israel's national colors, while the rough chunks of crystal speak of the gigantic slabs of stone that form the massive walls of the Citadel. Viewed up close, Chihuly's clear chunks of glass are covered with what seems to be a thin layer of grayish sand. In that, they may refer to Chihuly's *Jerusalem Wall of Ice*, which he had erected outside the Jaffa Gate in the Citadel's southern moat. The artist had imported 24 blocks of clear Alaskan ice and stacked them up to form a 60-foot-long, 20-foot-tall wall of ice, which melted in just two days into the dust of the parched ground. It was to symbolize the hope for a thawing of tensions in the region, for dissolving barriers and divisions between the Jewish and the Arab worlds. The dust makes the core of the conflict palpable: it conveys the opposing views on connection to the land, soil, and territory. JG

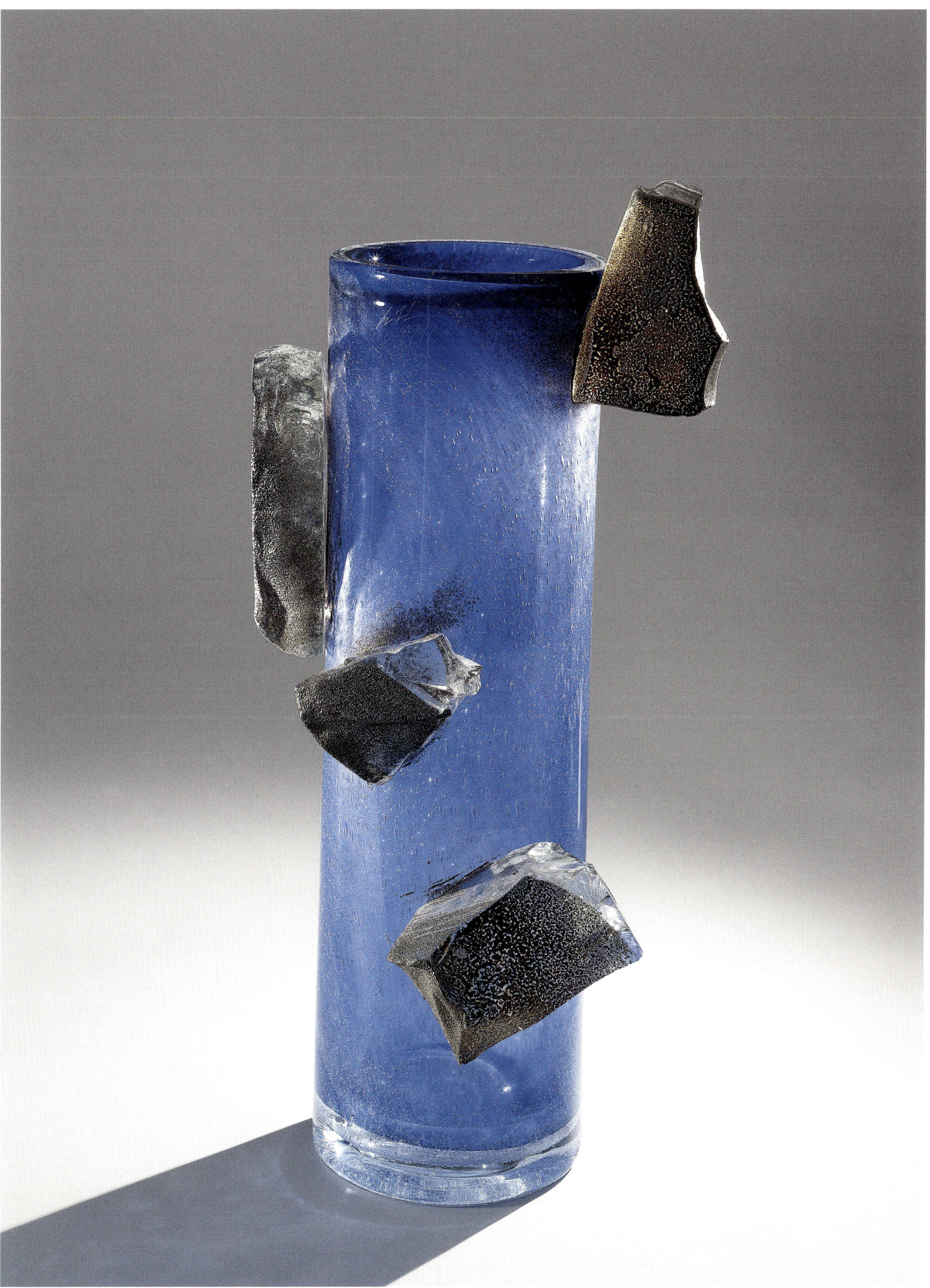

Tony Cragg

born 1949 in Liverpool, UK;
lives and works in Wuppertal, Germany

British artist Tony Cragg graduated from the Royal College of Art in London in 1977 and has lived in Germany since 1979. Winner of the Turner Prize in 1988, he represented the United Kingdom at the 43rd Venice Biennale the same year. He initially worked with found objects, arranging them into installations on the wall or floor, before discovering his passion for materials in the 1990s. A "radical materialist," as he describes himself, as well as a master of perfection, he embraces the language of each material. He uses wood, stone, bronze, polished stainless steel, and glass, all with their own specific properties, meanings, and effects. Cragg's unmistakable sculptures are often twisted, swirling, and tumbling columns, totem-like and futuristic at the same time.

Cragg has worked with glass from the very beginning, initially with commercially manufactured glass vessels such as vases, bottles, or bowls, stacking them on glass plates to create large objects and combining familiar objects to create new forms. He then began to experiment with transparency and glass as a material. The two works shown here, which he created in Murano, belong in this context. The sculpture *Untitled* (2015), in which cuboids of clear glass are piled on top of each other, draws from the language of abstraction while at the same time including anthropomorphic elements: is this a couple, as if held together in affection? The two *Listeners* (2015) also represent a sensorium: hearing, listening, transmitting, receiving, paying attention. As the artist says, "Making a new form gives us a new word, gives us a new term, gives us a new emotion. Sculpture expands the possibilities of our own horizon and allows us to expand our imagination."[1] PGH

Untitled, 2015
Glass
47 × 26 × 27 cm

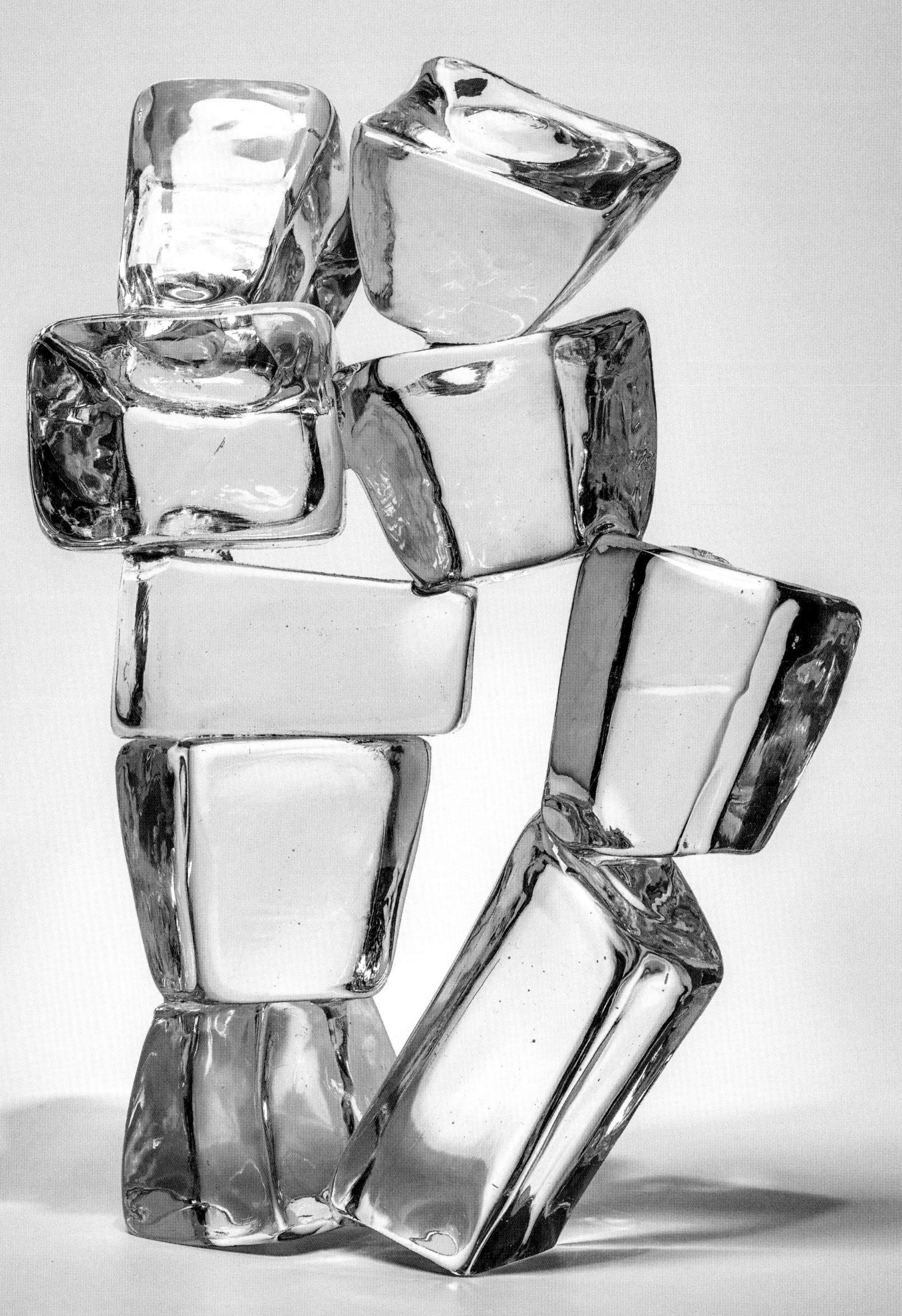

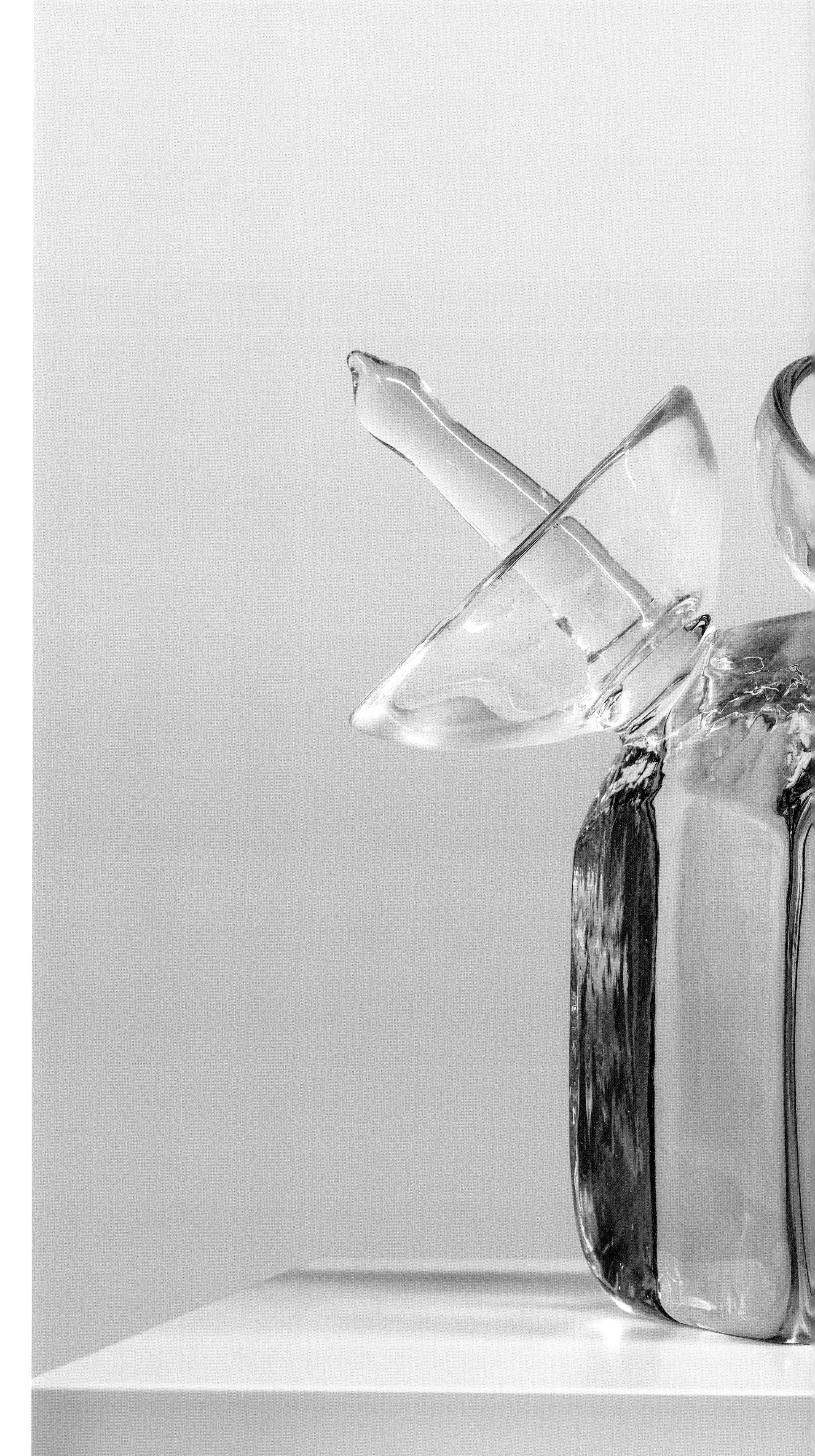

Listeners, 2015
Glass
37 × 35 × 21 cm /
36 × 40 × 18 cm

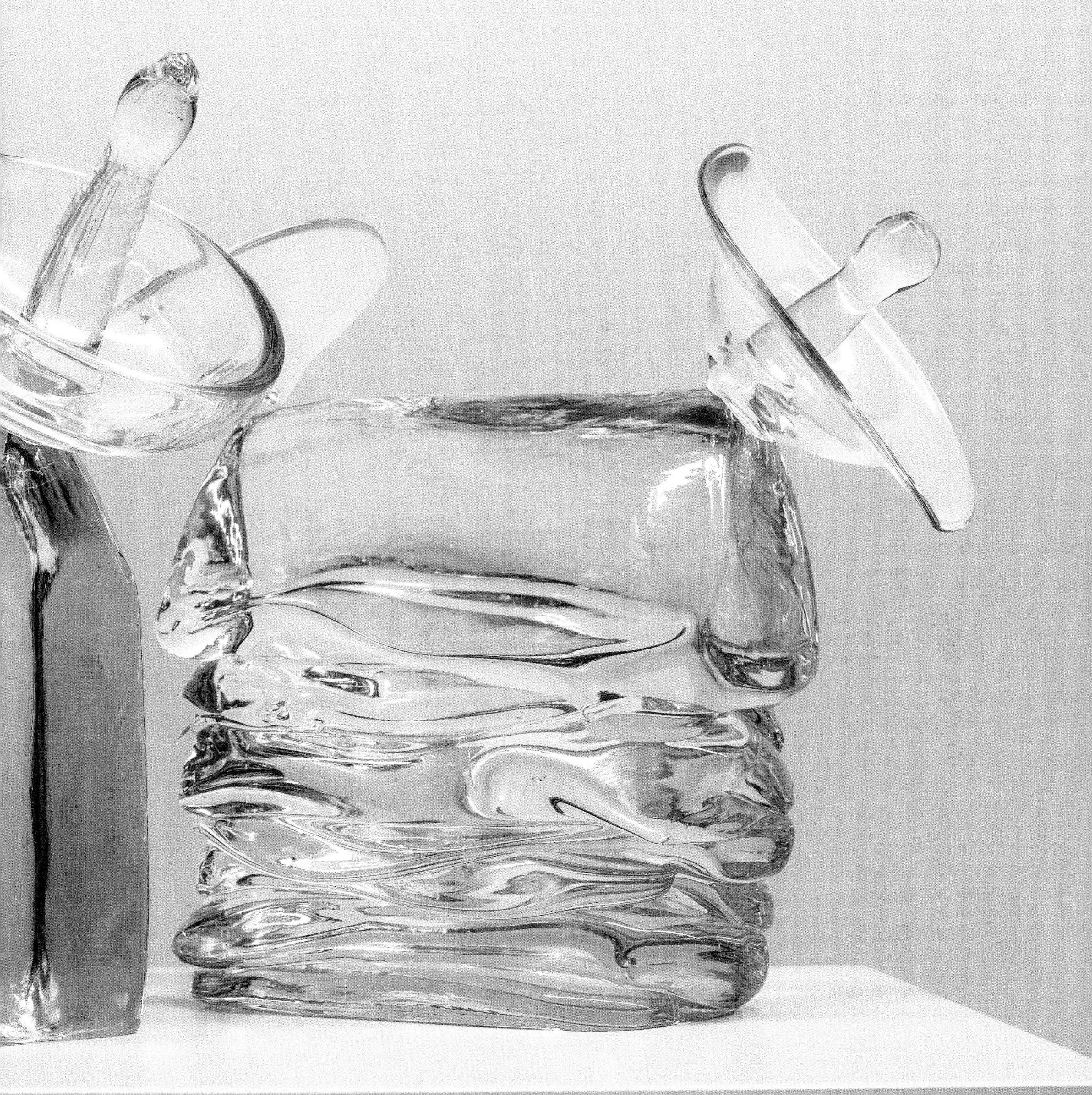

Jimmie Durham

born 1940 in Washington, Arkansas, USA;
died 2021 in Berlin, Germany

An outdoor glass work, *Verre en plein air 1* (2017), was the result of Jimmie Durham's first experiment with glass as an art medium. An artist, poet, and activist in the American civil rights movement, as well as a campaigner for the rights of indigenous peoples, Durham was invited by CIRVA in Marseille for a residency lasting several weeks. He took the opportunity to fully explore the material: "Glass is never really solid, it is in a state of flow that does not flow in our universe. One scientist described it as flowing more slowly than the universe operates. ... For me broken glass shows the true qualities of glass. It vibrates. It scares us. To encounter broken glass is like meeting a dangerous wild animal. It has a constant energy; energy that cannot fit into our world." The artist "wanted to see how to return to some essentiality of glass. I wanted to show these strange qualities of both flowingness and the willingness to dangerously break."[1] He then set the variations of red glass that emerged in his working process in a gate-like steel construction, as though they were amorphous panes. Placed in the middle of a room, they offer surprising views of color and form.

Verre en plein air 1, 2017
Steel structure with glass
165.5 × 87 × 89.5 cm

Durham, who studied art in Switzerland, settled in Europe in 1994 after living in Mexico for several years. His work has been shown at the documenta (1992 and 2012) and the Venice Biennale (2001, 2003, 2005, and 2011). With sculptures, installations, paintings, drawings, performances, videos, and photographs, he has created a multifaceted oeuvre that is "critical, humorous and profoundly humanistic," as stated in the citation for the Golden Lion for Lifetime Achievement at the Venice Biennale in 2019. PGH

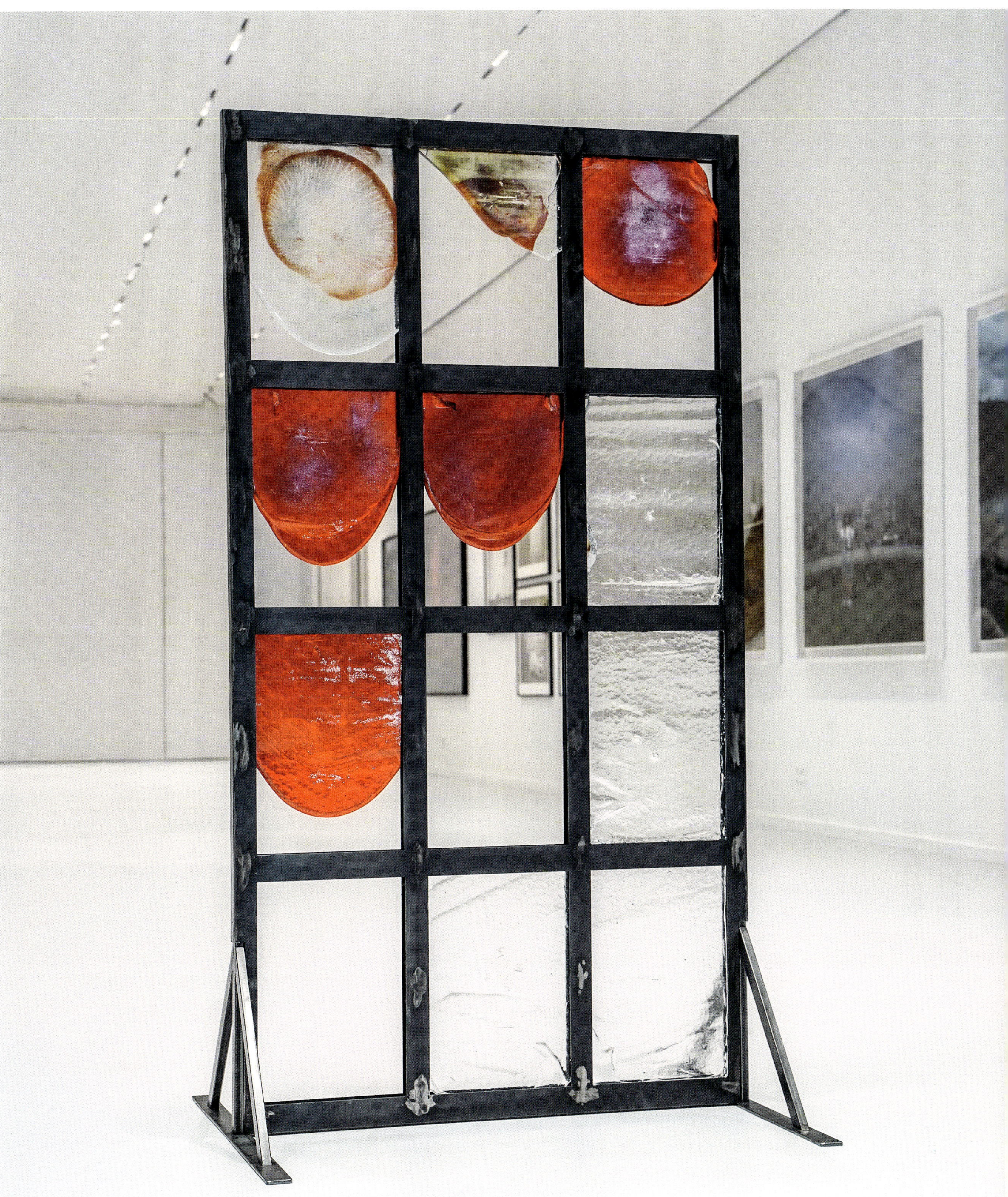

Erwin Eisch

born 1927 in Frauenau, Germany;
died 2022 in Zwiesel, Germany

This blown, painted, and engraved series of portraits was created beginning in the mid-1970s. In their expressiveness, they are more than portraits, as they display—critically and humorously—Erwin Eisch's convictions and worldview. In the *Buddha Heads* series, identical head shapes molded into one form have become individual: Eisch distorts them, blows them out further, manipulates them with tongs, and expands them with hot glass. It is not only in his handling that he interrogates our accustomed way of seeing, but also in the stories he tells and the ambiguous messages captured by the glass. Eisch negates the typical properties of glass, such as transparency; instead, the material becomes a sculptural carrier of his artistic statement. In contrast to other portrait heads, the Buddhas are elongated and thus emphasize the spiritual nature of Buddha. *Der Bruch ist die Sünde* (The break is the sin, 1997), from his series of self-portraits, addresses both the fragility of the material and the expectations placed on the artist.[1]

Eisch was an artist, teacher, and critical citizen. Born into a family of glassmakers, he trained as a glass engraver at the Munich Art Academy, studying glass design (1949–52) and later sculpture (1956–59). He and his future wife, Gretel Stadler, were founding members of the SPUR group. In 1959, they split from the group and founded the RADAMA group with Max Strack. Disillusioned with the art world, Eisch turned his back on city life and returned to the rural Frauenau district in Bavaria, where he began experimenting with glass. In 1962, he met Harvey Littleton, the founder of the studio glass movement, and became himself a driving force of the movement.[2] AC

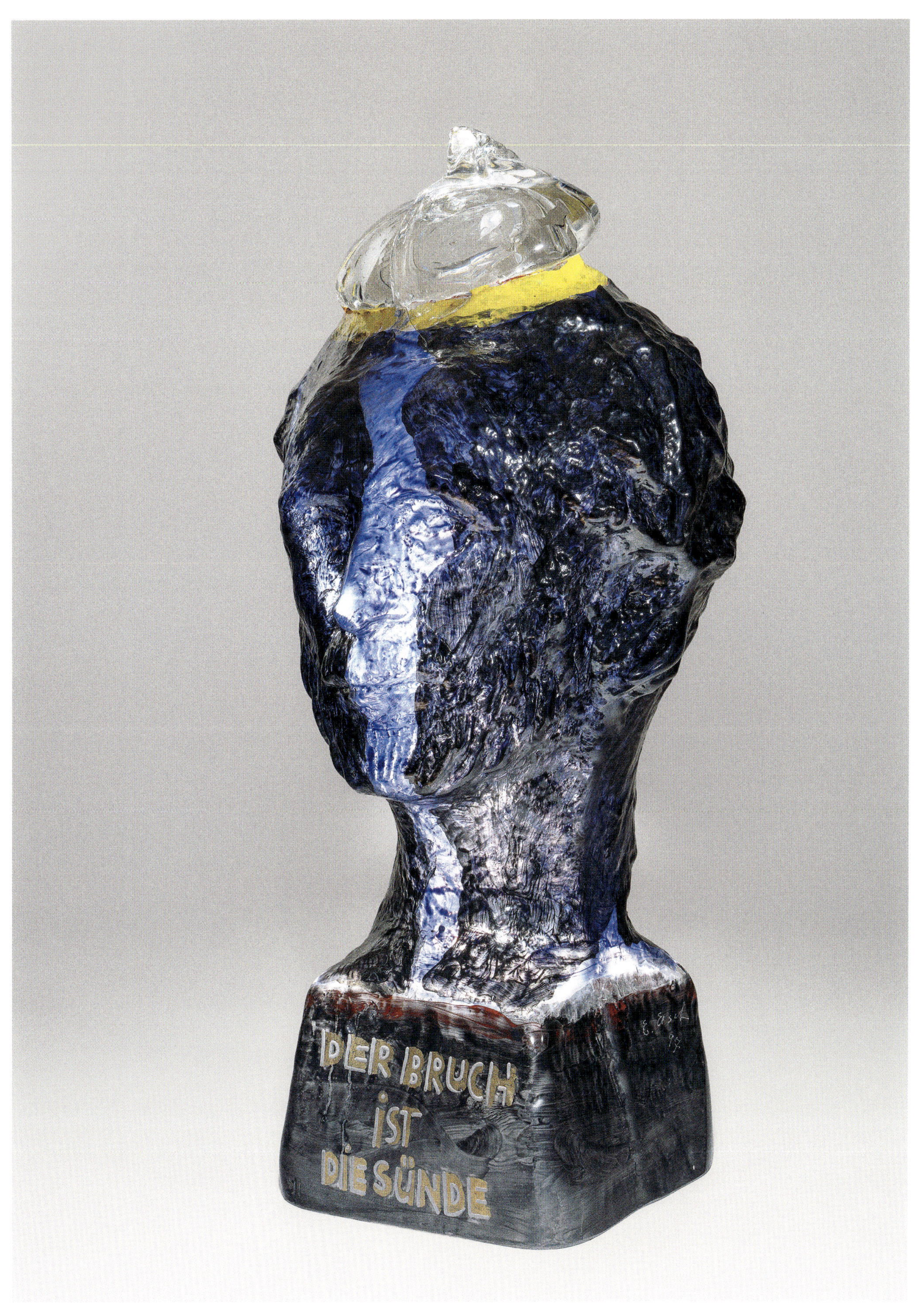

Der Bruch ist die Sünde, 1997
Mold-blown glass, painted
58 × 26 × 30 cm

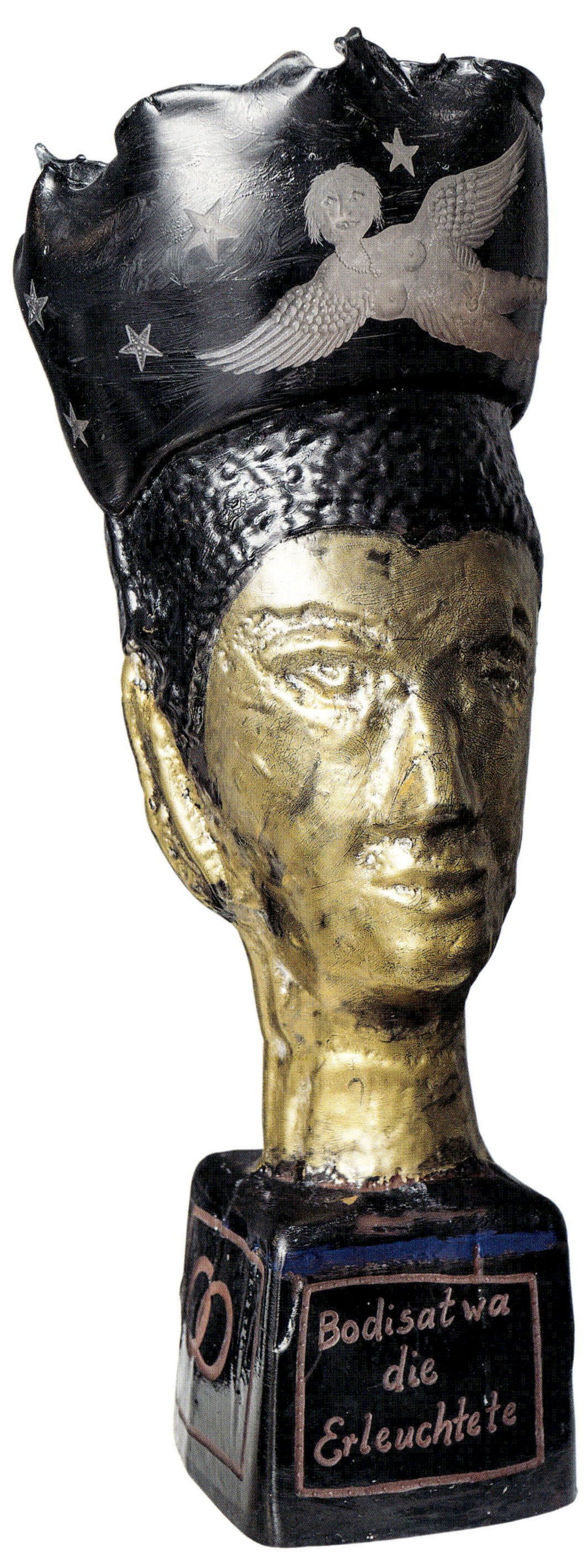

Bodisatwa, die Erleuchtete, 1985
Mold-blown glass, painted, engraved
54 × 24 × 24 cm

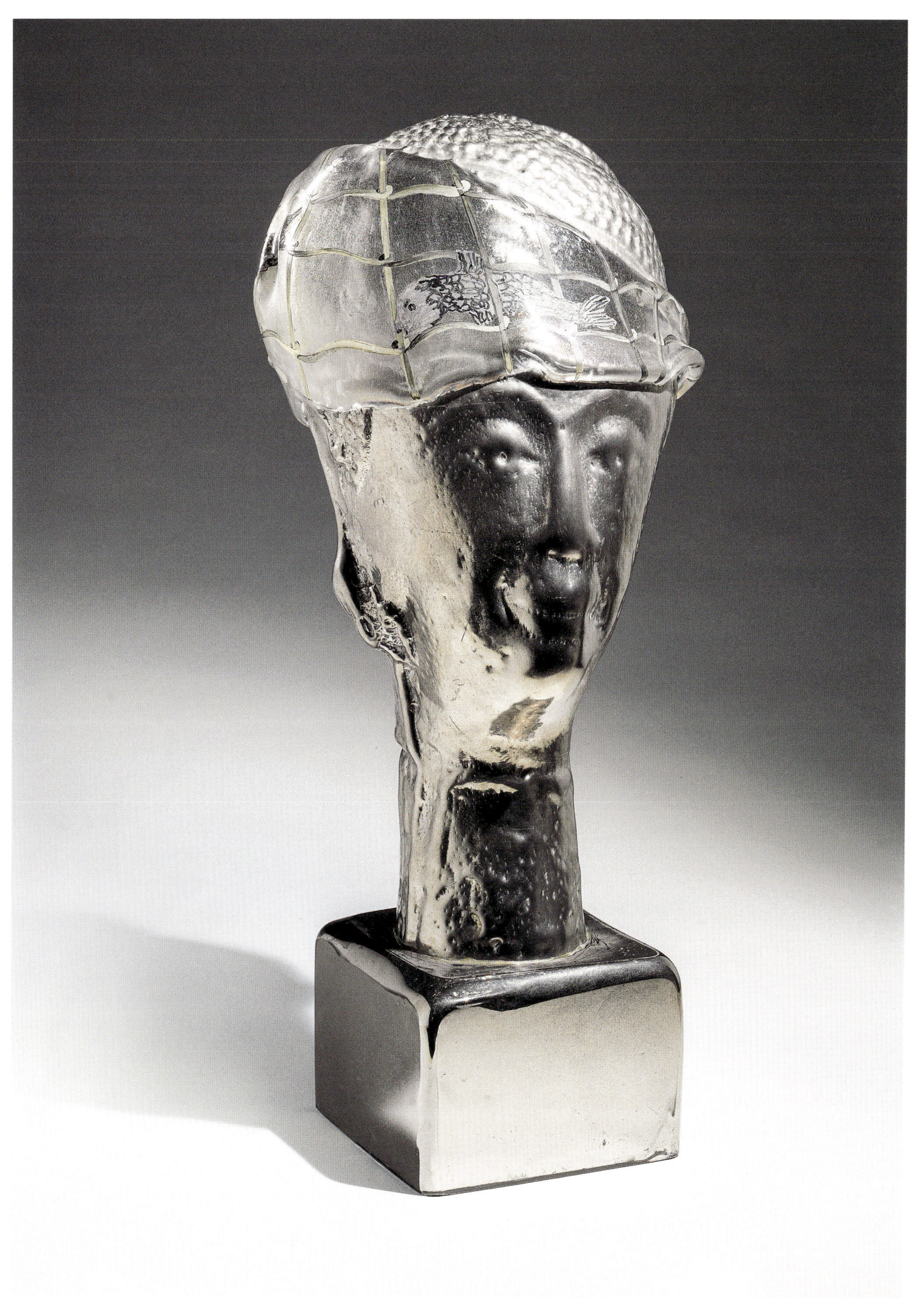

Buddha, 1982
Mold-blown glass, mirrored, painted
50 × 24 × 22 cm

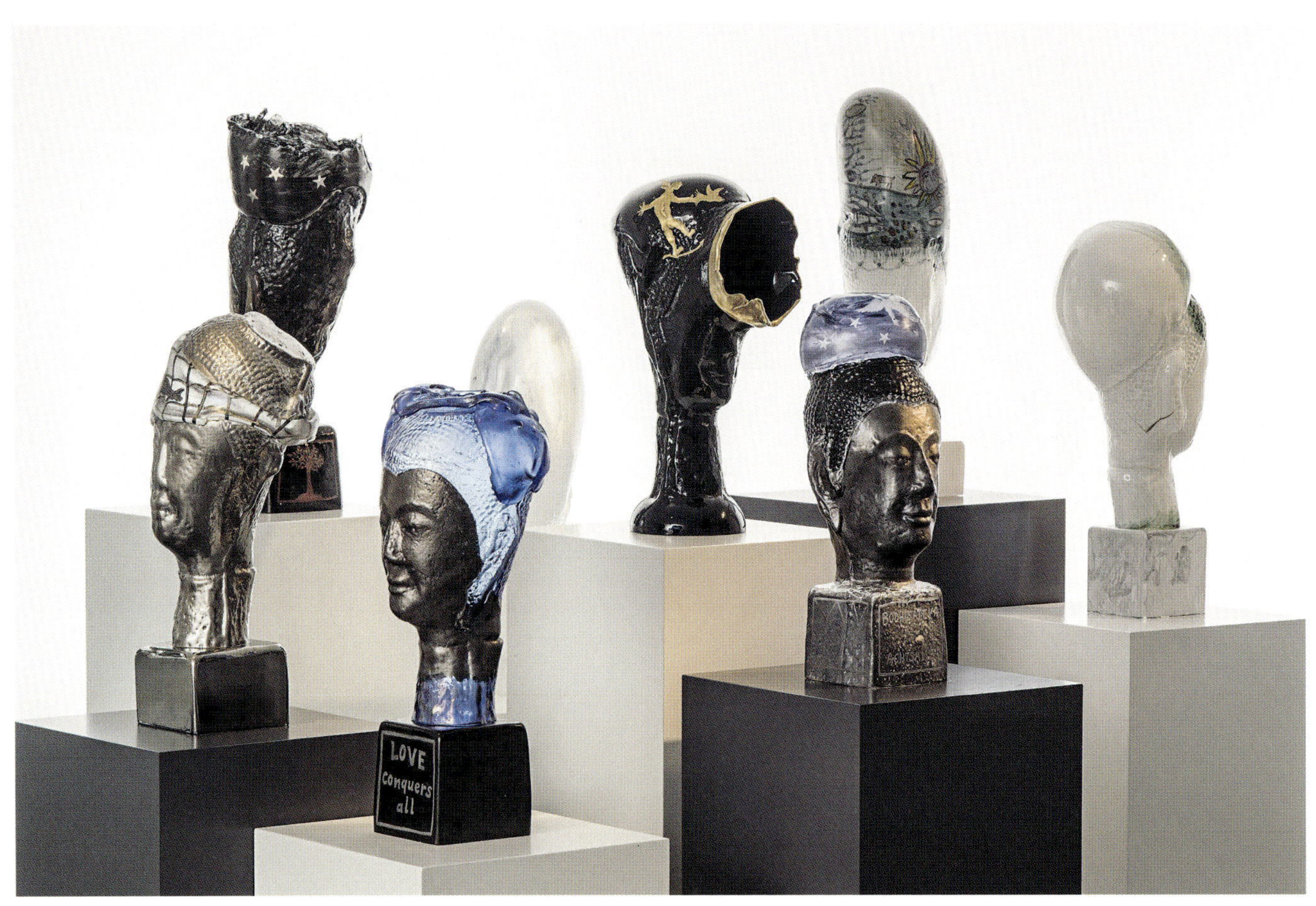

Buddha Heads
Installation view
Alexander Tutsek-Stiftung

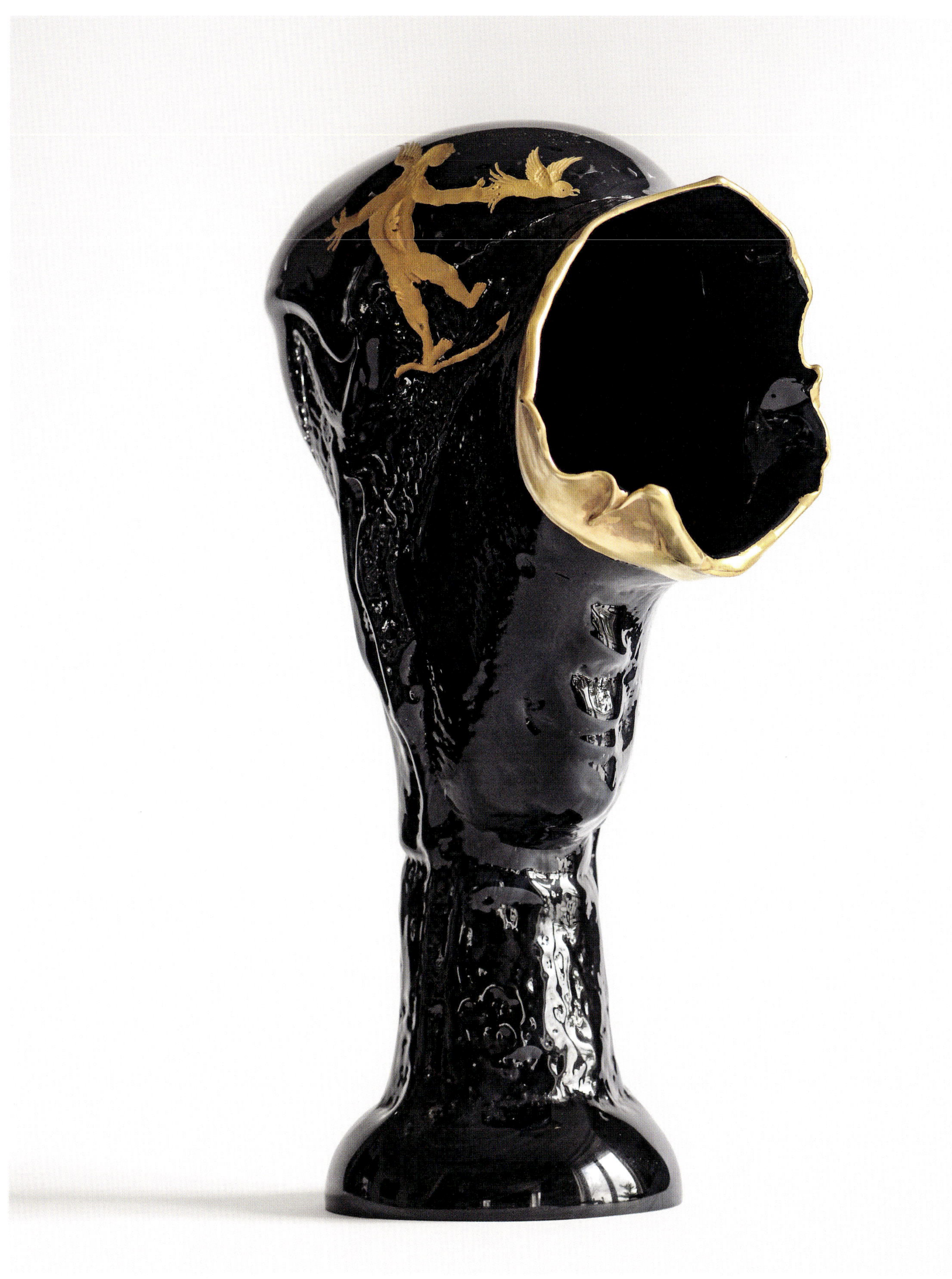

Die Einsicht, 1989
Mold-blown glass, engraving, gold leaf
47 × 30 × 24 cm

Jes Fan

born 1990 in Scarborough, Canada;
lives and works in Brooklyn, New York, USA
and Hong Kong, China

Jes Fan is a trained glassmaker who earned a BFA in glass from the Rhode Island School of Design. But how does this artist work with the medium, and what other materials are chosen to combine it with? Fan's studio must be a sort of laboratory: the artist's sculptures employ fungi, bacteria, and hormones to explore the intersections of biology, identity, and creativity. The inclusion of organic elements such as sex hormones, blood, and urine represents a unifying theme in Fan's oeuvre. The artist experiments with the biological characteristics that characterize the formation of identity, and thus the construction of the gender-specific body. Fan's aim is to interrogate binary notions of origin, gender, and identity.

The piece *Networks (for Expansion)* (2021) is made of borosilicate glass, used industrially to produce bottles and other containers, and consists of tubular systems that Fan has injected with hormonal substances. The work was featured in the 2021 exhibition *Soft Water Hard Stone* as part of the Fifth New Museum Triennial at the New Museum, New York, where it attracted a lot of attention. Fan's artistic approach is that "I'm not interested in the technique, but in the process." Taking a cue from the title of the 59th Venice Biennale, *The Milk of Dreams* (2022), Fan examined udders for an installation in the Arsenale. PGH

Networks (for Expansion), 2021
Borosilicate glass, silicone, *Phycomyces* zygospore liquid culture
116.8 × 61 × 127 cm

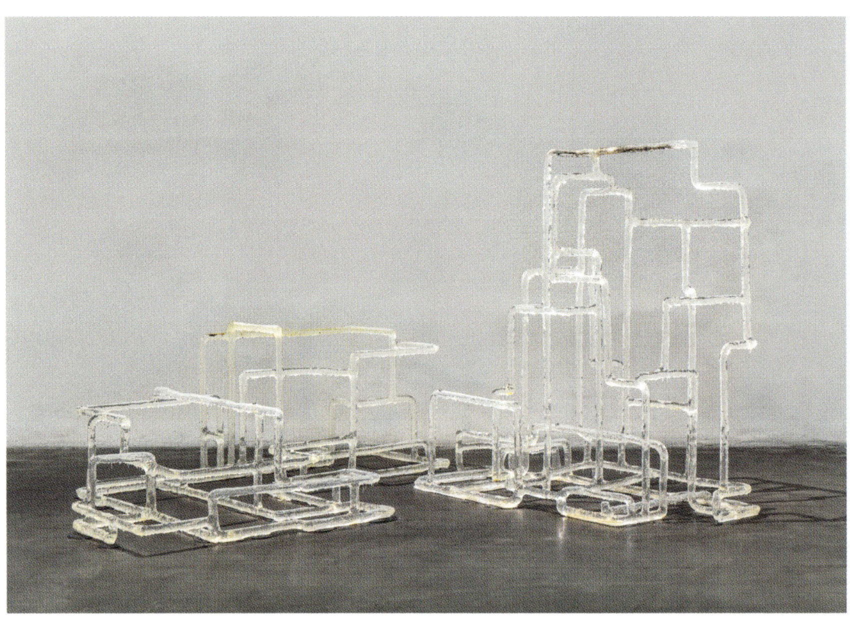

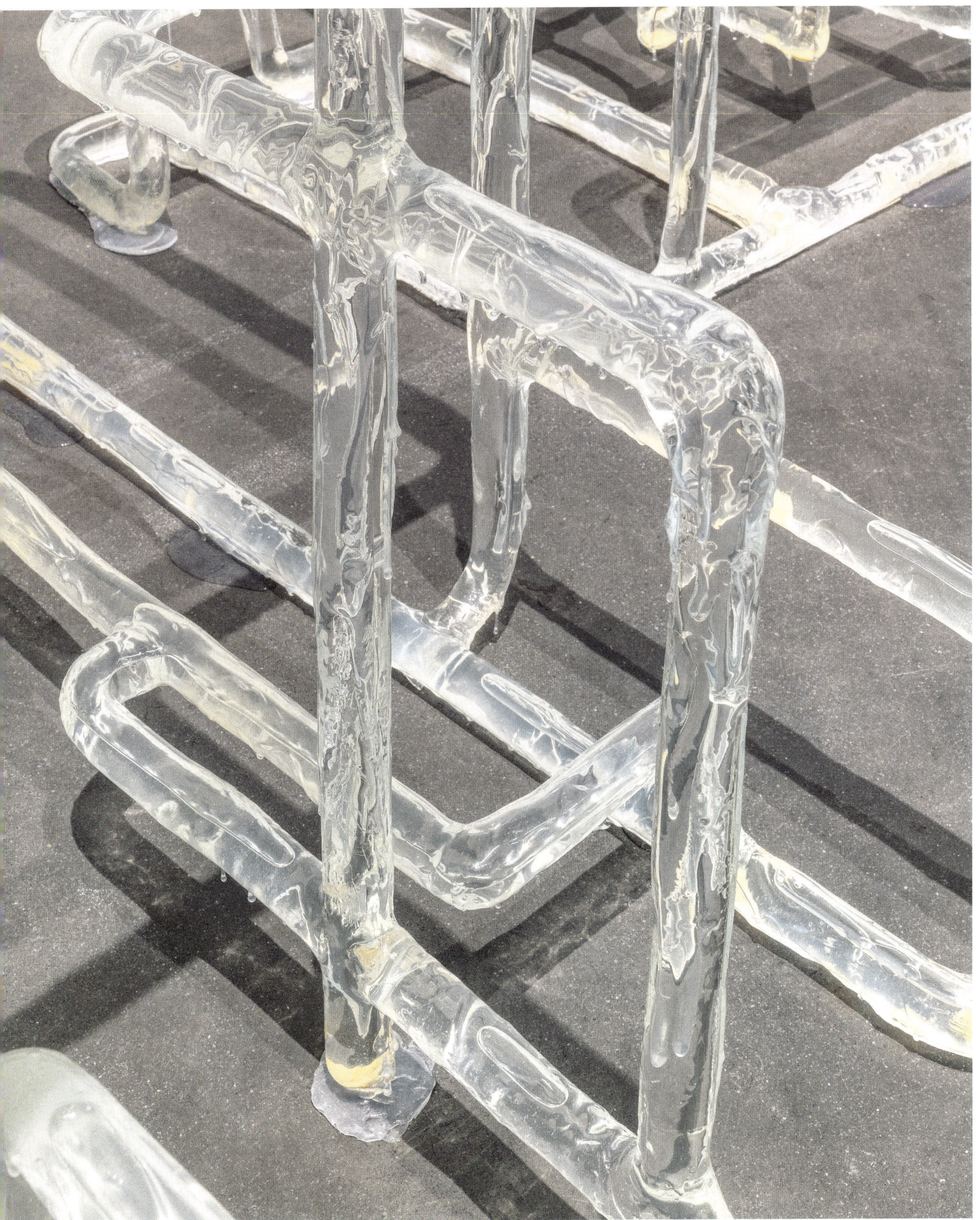

Carlos Garaicoa

born 1967 in Havana, Cuba;
lives and works in Havana, Cuba and Madrid, Spain

In its form and materials—glass and steel—this large "table" by Carlos Garaicoa merges nature and culture: it is a "homage to the freedom of nature's flowing and organic forms ... as well as the geometric-mathematical structure of crystals and of architecture itself," as the artist says. The installation could be an opening to discuss the rituals of giving and taking or free exchange in a functional community. But the title of the work itself, *Fragile Garden*, which is clearly inspired by the use of delicate Murano glass and its beguiling colors, hints at the vulnerability of a harmonious social order. The impressive glass table, with its massive crystal "cutlery" and delicate plant forms in glass, invites a multitude of associations, from the Garden of Eden to the negotiating table; across its surface, Garaicoa has spread out his metal rods like magical lances "floating at varying distances above the abyss."[1] The material and the form recall a series of tables by the Italian Arte Povera artist Mario Merz (1925–2003), who piled them up with fruits and vegetables: *Tavola spirale* (Spiral Table, 1982), "symbolizing a locus of the human need for fulfillment and interaction."[2]

Garaicoa himself emphasizes formal aspects of the work: "The work contrasts the natural, mathematical and physical structure of glass with the freedom of drawing and the free forms created with this material. I try to capture the spontaneity and intervention of the handcraftsmanship, playing with the most fickle and unpredictable forms that drawing and artistic thought can produce against the immovable, mathematical and scientific perfection of the material itself."[3]

Through a multidisciplinary approach that incorporates architecture, urbanism, and history, Garaicoa addresses questions of culture and politics in his works, using a variety of materials and media. He has participated in numerous biennials, including Havana (1991, 1994, 1997, 2000, 2003, 2009, 2012, 2015), Shanghai (2010), São Paulo (1998, 2004), Venice (2009, 2005), Johannesburg (1995), Liverpool (2006), and Moscow (2005), as well as *documenta 11* (2003) and *14* (2017). PGH

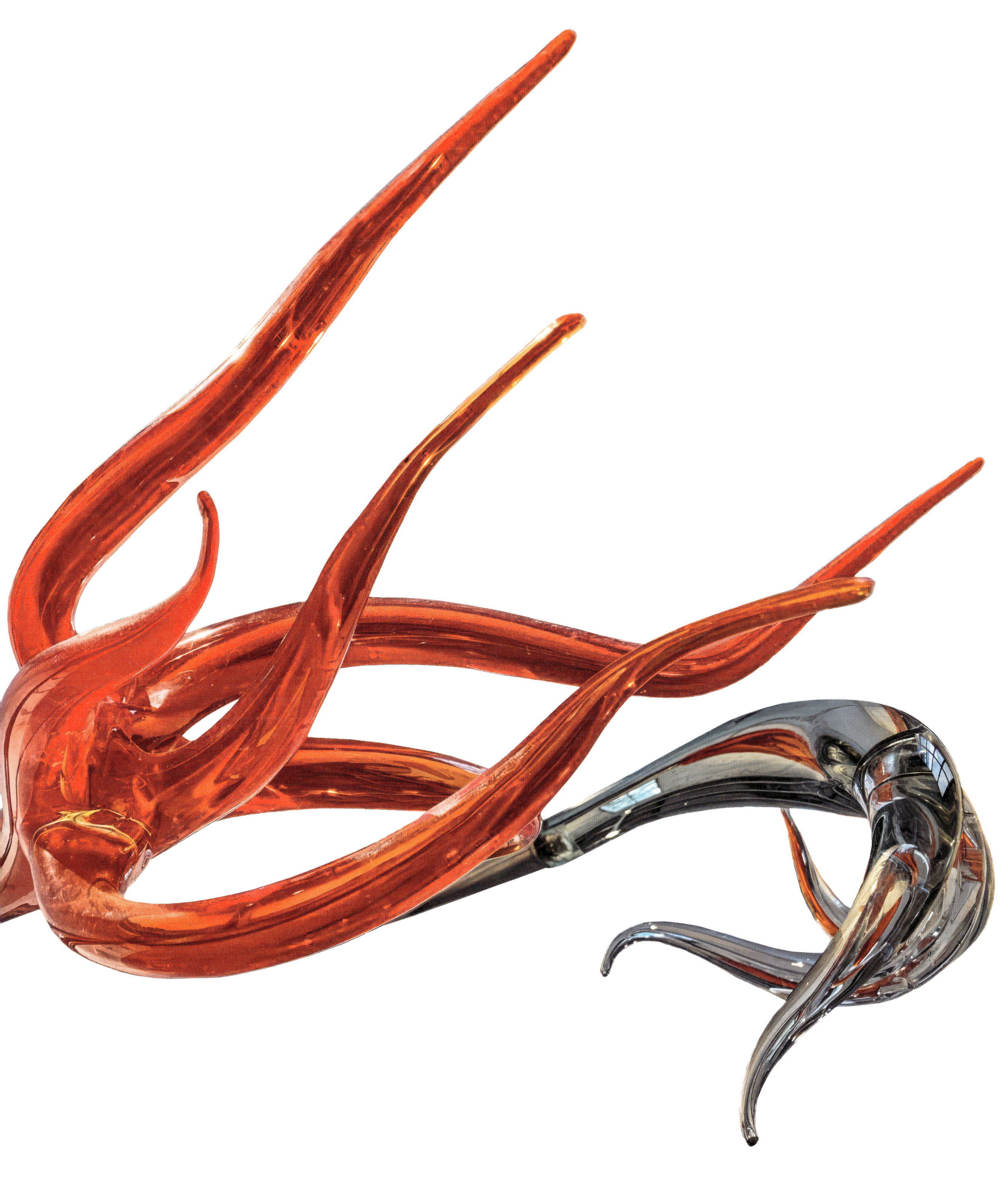

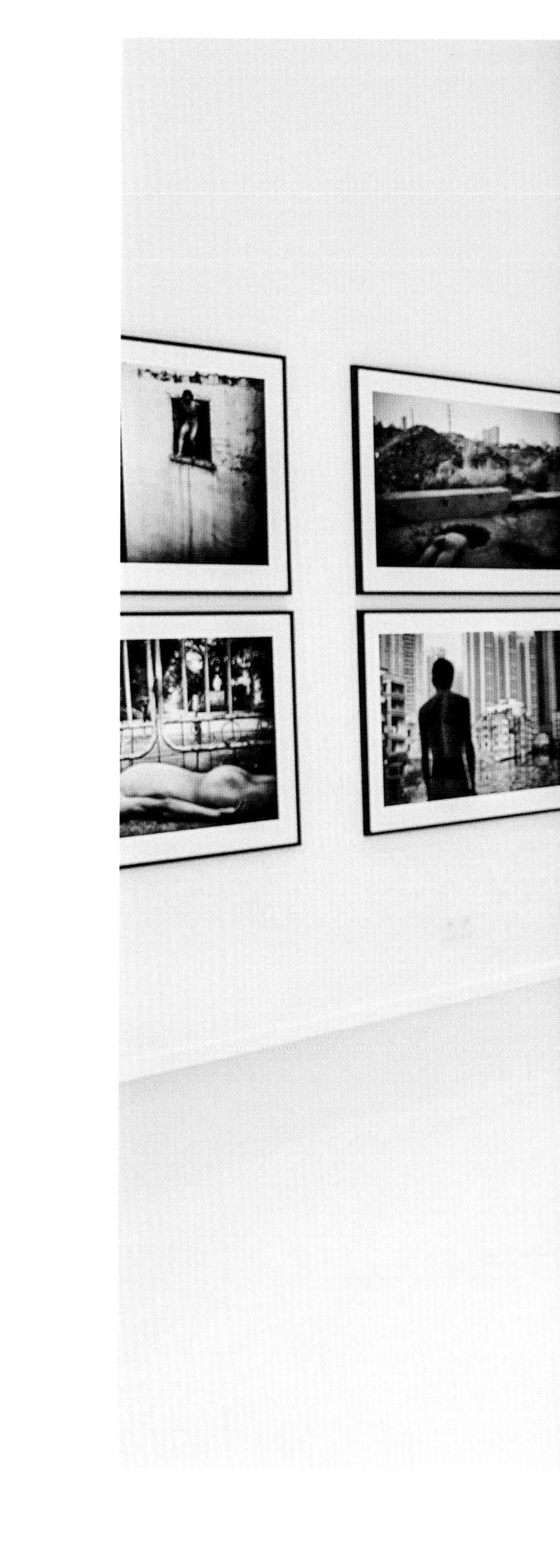

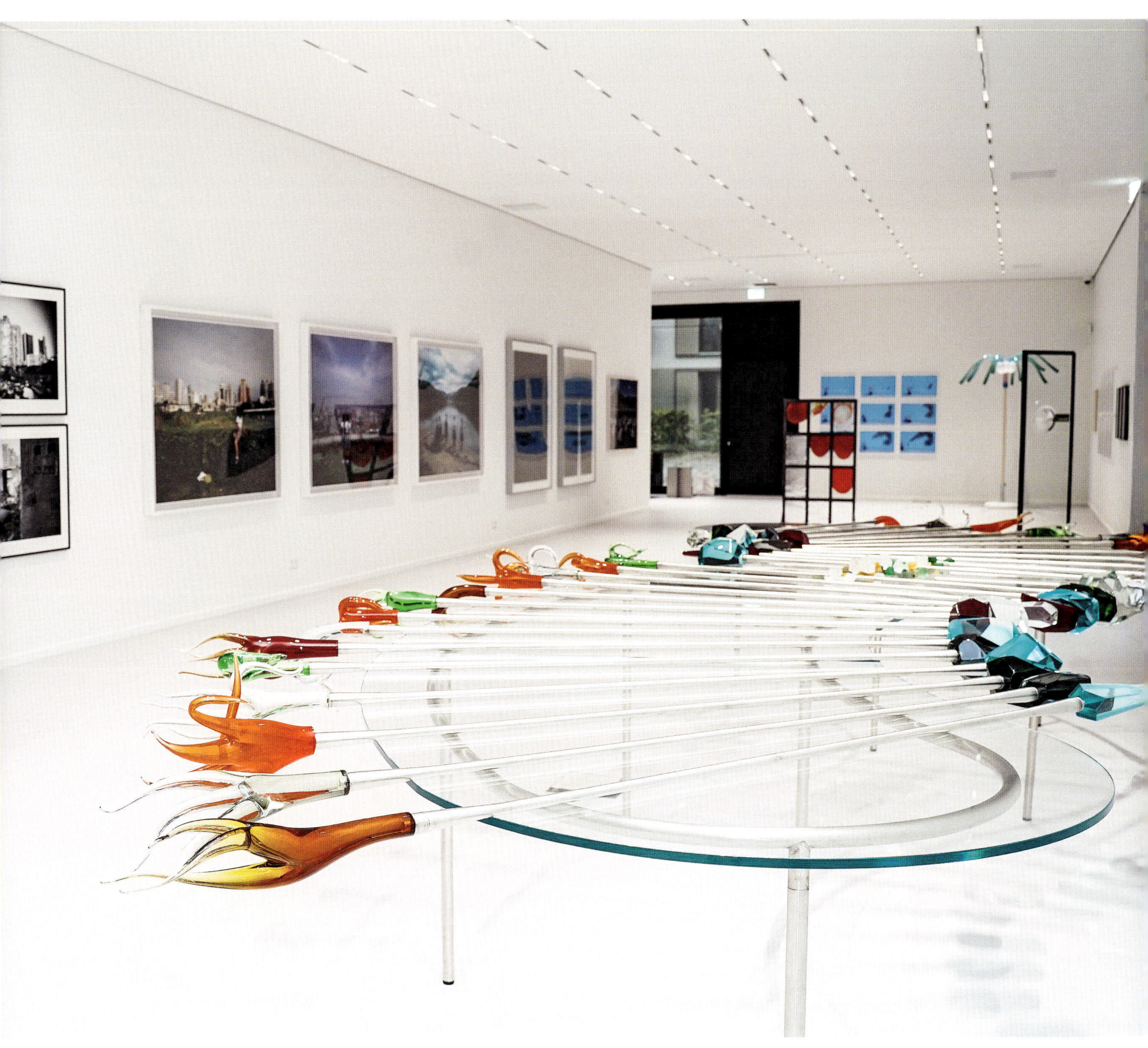

Jardín Frágil (Versión I) / Fragile Garden (Version I), 2019
Murano crystal, metal, glass
25 + 5 blowpipes, each 200–220 cm
Overall: approx. 90 × 230 × 620 cm

Donghai Guan

born 1966 in Mudanjiang, Heilongjiang Province, China;
lives and works in Beijing, China

Donghai Guan's distinctive body of work is about the combination of tradition, power, and strength. In his glass pieces, he attempts to describe a certain "situation" and is thus continually searching for forms and colors that he can use as elements for assembling and abstraction. Thematically and aesthetically, he draws on the Chinese tradition—since, in his eyes, that which is primal has the greatest and most imperishable power.

His *City Gate* series is influenced by the motifs and subjects of traditional Chinese ceramic art and painting. The ancient city gates that he portrays bear typical architectural details, and the workmanship is reminiscent of Chinese bronzes and jades. These rough and robust gates are brimming with power and dignity, Donghai Guan's main intention in his artwork. However, he does not always portray power and strength in a positive light: "An ancient city gate is closely related to its function as a guarding facility to separate, protect, and reject, which eventually make it a symbol for the overwhelming conservative power which kills human nature and wipes out individuality."[1]

This explains the fixed and fearful expressions on the faces looking out of his city gates, inspired as they are by depictions of people in ancient Chinese art.

Regime (2006) also focuses on the themes of power and the strength of systems in relation to the individual. Four heads with topknots, lined up in a row and with an iron expression on their faces, are firmly attached to a railway track, gripping the track with their runners like a magnetic levitation train. The only thing that distinguishes them from each other and expresses their individuality is the different coloring of their runners and, on their faces, the primary colors red, blue, yellow, white, and black. The individual subordinates himself to the system and to certain rules in order to ride the modern track and serve the common good.

Donghai Guan is a tenured professor at the Academy of Arts and Design at Tsinghua University in Beijing, China, and director of the Glass Art Studio there. He has studied in both China and the UK and graduated from the School of Art and Design at the University of Wolverhampton, UK, with a master's degree in glass. KW

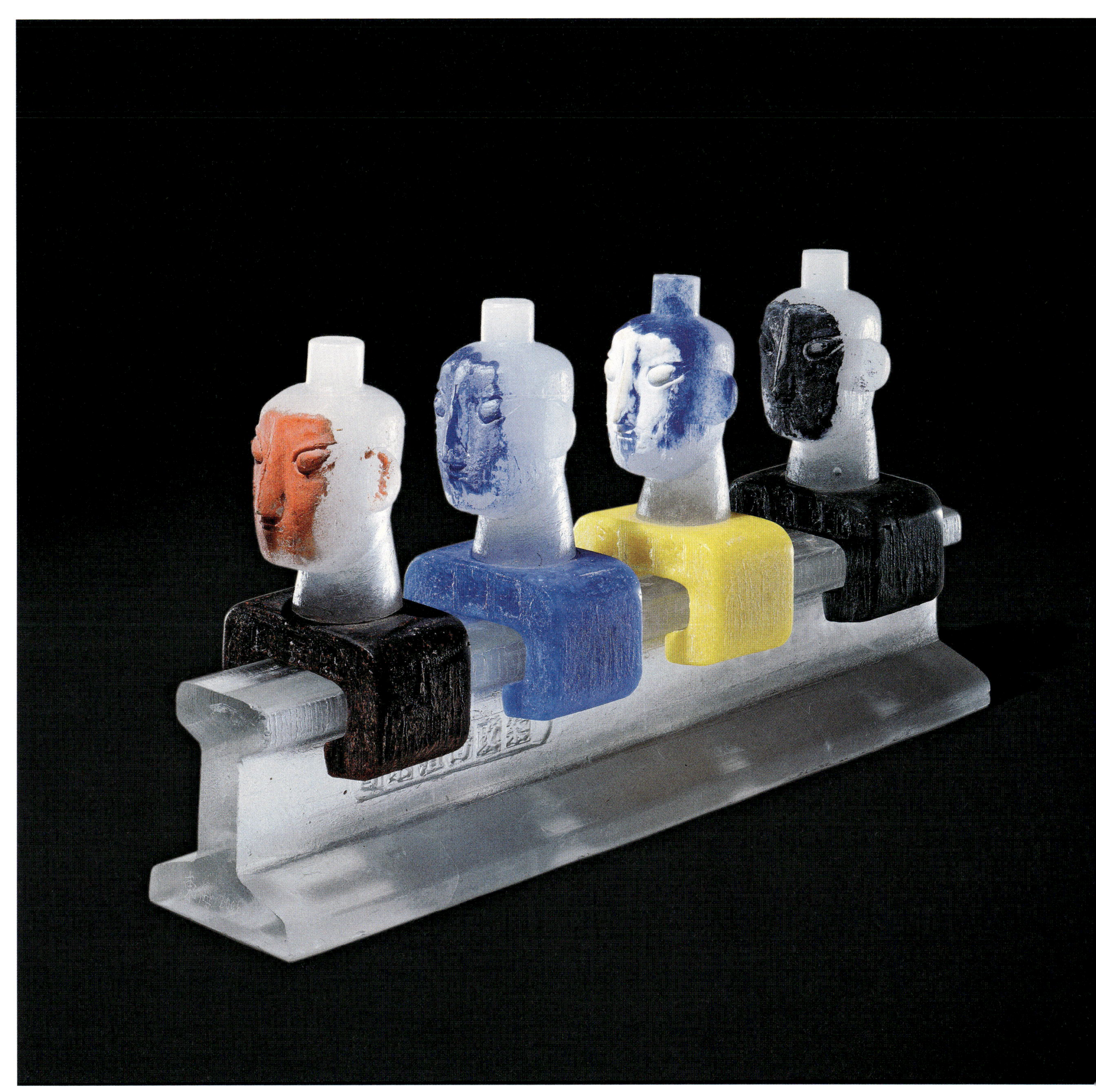

Regime, 2006
Cast glass
25 × 11 × 49 cm

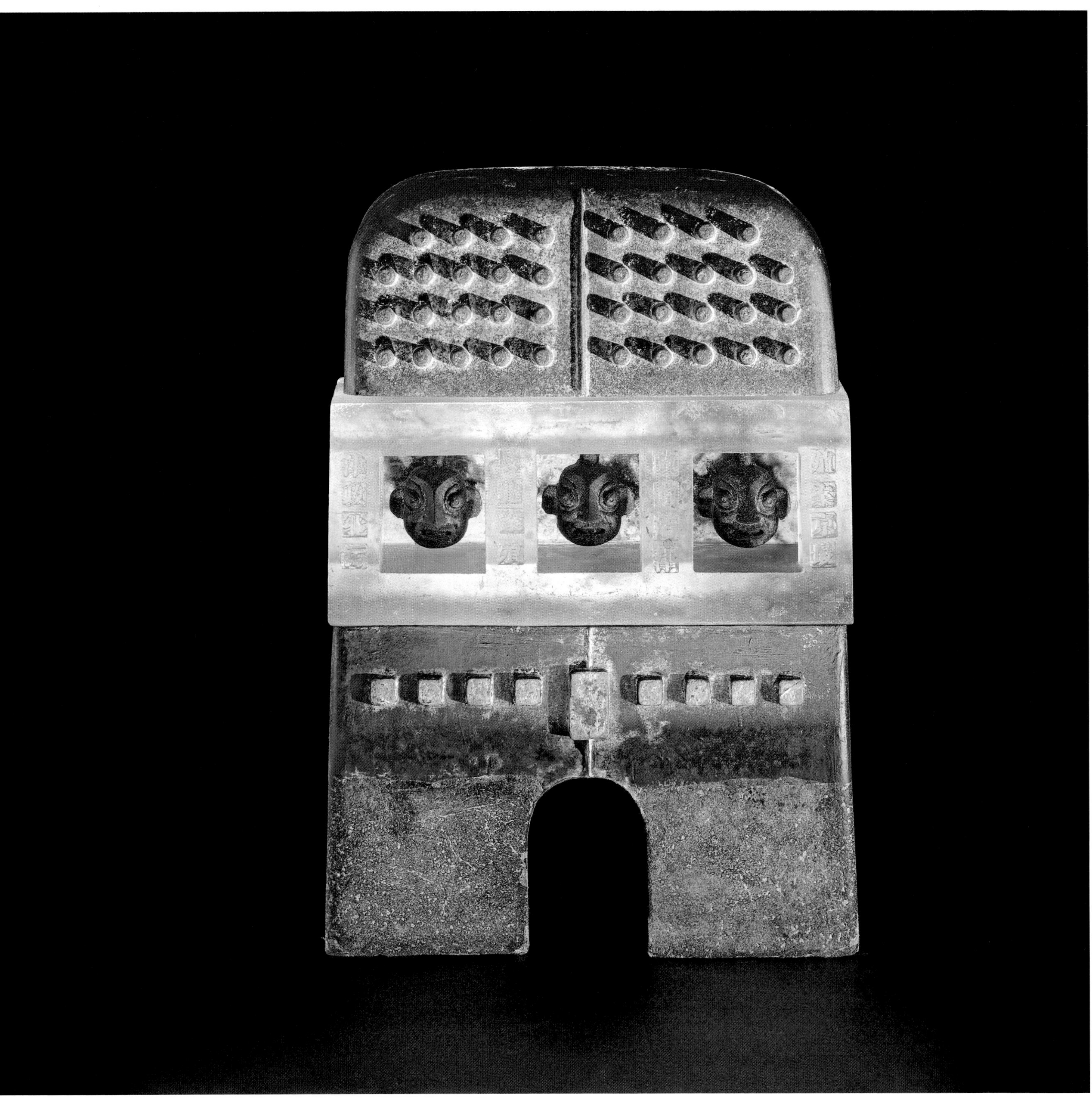

City Gate #7, 2006
Cast glass with bronze detail
47 × 32 × 13 cm

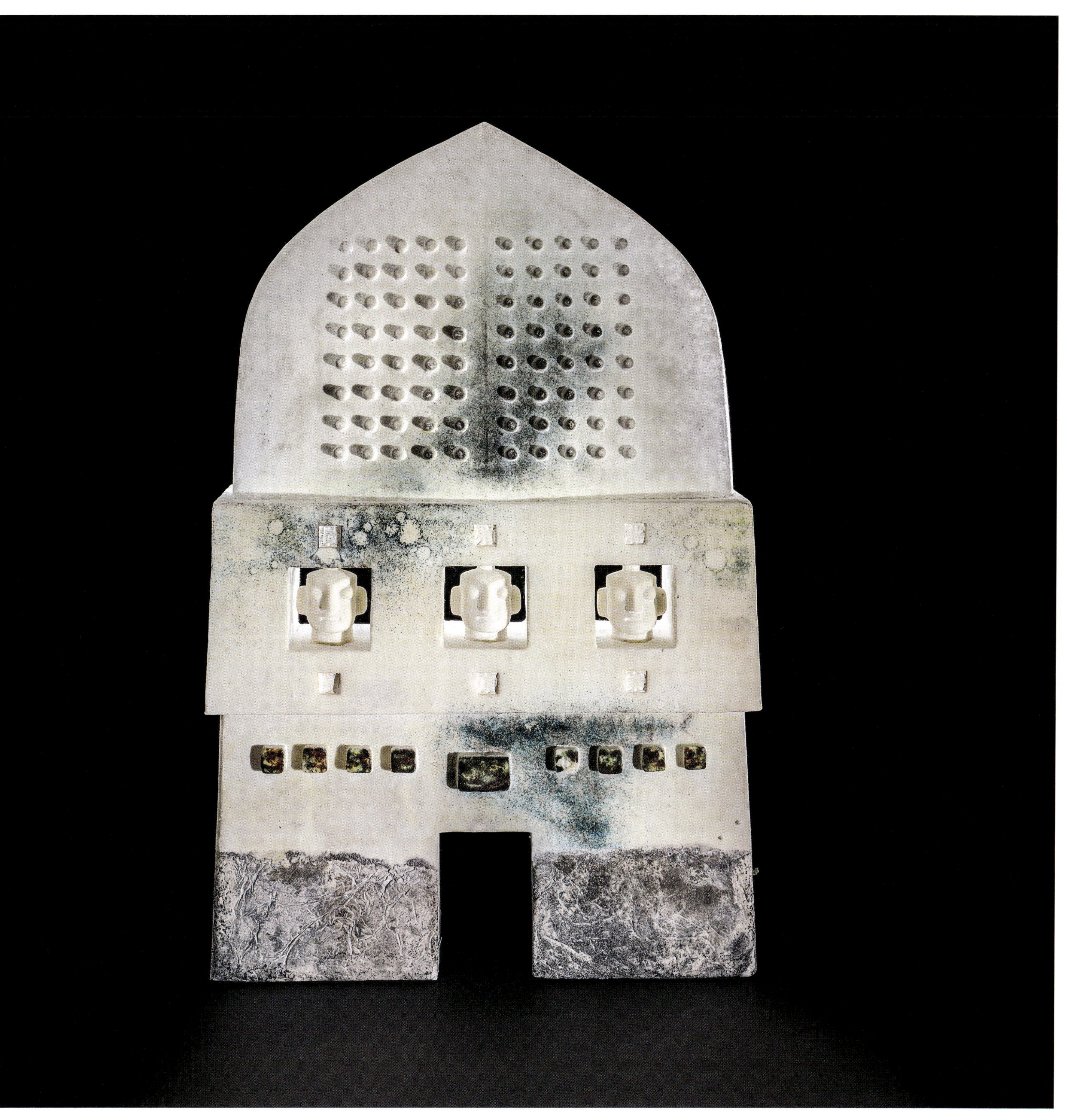

White City Gate, 2008
Cast glass
60 × 38 × 10 cm

Jens Gussek

born in Glauchau, Germany;
lives and works in Bad Ems, Germany

Jens Gussek is an exceptionally thoughtful, sensitive artist. He merges blown or fused glass with easily recognizable imagery or found objects from everyday life. His sleek and captivating installations resonate with profound meaning. Despite being firmly rooted in reality, Gussek imbues his works with an overriding sense of mystery, a kind of magical realism, in which ships tug gigantic bubbles and flowers bloom on the tips of icebergs.

The search for meaning is a leitmotif within Gussek's artistic oeuvre. Alluding to the existentialist philosophy of Gabriel Marcel, the viewer—like the artist—is a "homo viator," a pilgrim in search of meaning, love, and hope. We all are on the move, physically and intellectually; we are constantly exploring physical space and symbolism. We can be nautical passengers, as in Gussek's *Dreams Behind Me*, or mountaineers as in his *The Blue Flower* (both 2007).

The Blue Flower, 2007
Blown glass, wood
Object: 62 × 48 × 32 cm
Wood: 68 × 36 × 11 cm

Despite their apparent fragility, the glass balloons in *Dreams Behind Me* exude an inherent might. It does take a battleship reinforced with solid steel to pull them along. Indeed, do they not seem potentially more powerful than the naval vessel in front? Could they not rise any minute, like a triplet of hot-air balloons, and lift the ship out of the ocean to float away through the air? Gussek's personal image for the body and the self is a ship: "A ship is like a self-portrait," he says. As the title suggests, the delicate bubbles of blown glass are the dreams—fragile fantasies, too many and too large to all be held in our brain. "We can't store them all," Gussek concedes: "Tethered to a disproportionately small vessel [that] is illogically distant from its cargo of big dreams."

Gussek's *The Blue Flower* plays both in title and motif on the foremost symbol of Romanticism: a blue flower denoting yearning—usually a painful yearning for love, or for the unattainable, for contemplative solitude, or for far-off places. The yearning and the pursuit of the "blue flower" is ongoing. In his installation, Gussek imbues his tiny flower with a powerful presence. It grows delicately atop a monumental block of rock and ice, its stands in full bloom in the high-altitude death zone of the frozen mountain. Gussek masterfully captures the icy feel and wintry shimmer by overlaying glass of varying thickness. His blue flower—be it love or yearning in general—is jubilant amid its life-defying surroundings. The powerful attraction it holds for the "homo viator" and his restless quest is symbolized by the sturdy litter of solid wood that needs strong men to lift it and carry it along. As onlookers, we follow the artist through his phantasmagorical imagination and magical realism. Mystery, longing, and awe: to today's technological world, which focuses on functions and solutions, Gussek's art is a refreshing and necessary antidote: "Life is not a problem to be solved, but a mystery to be lived." JG

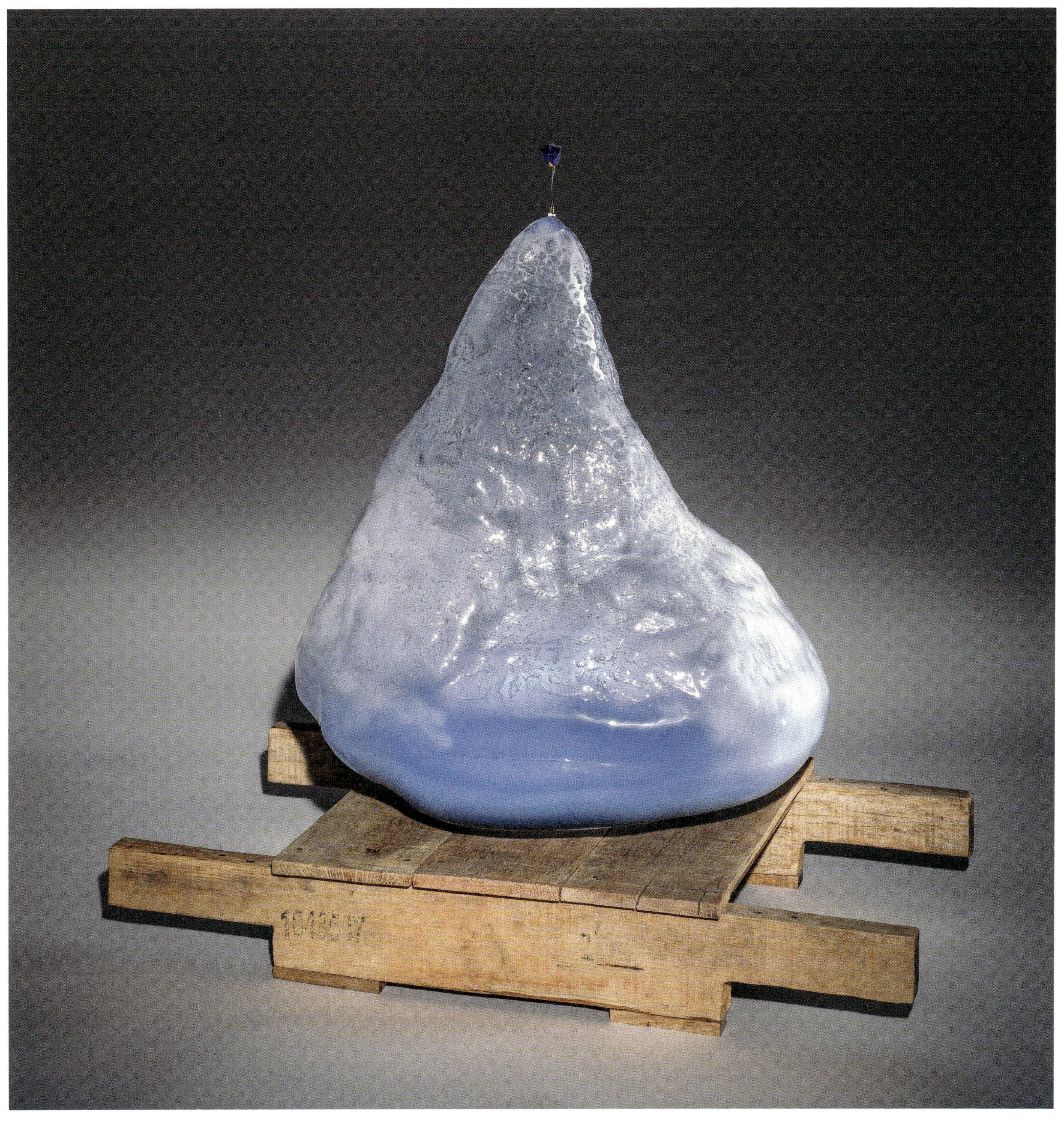

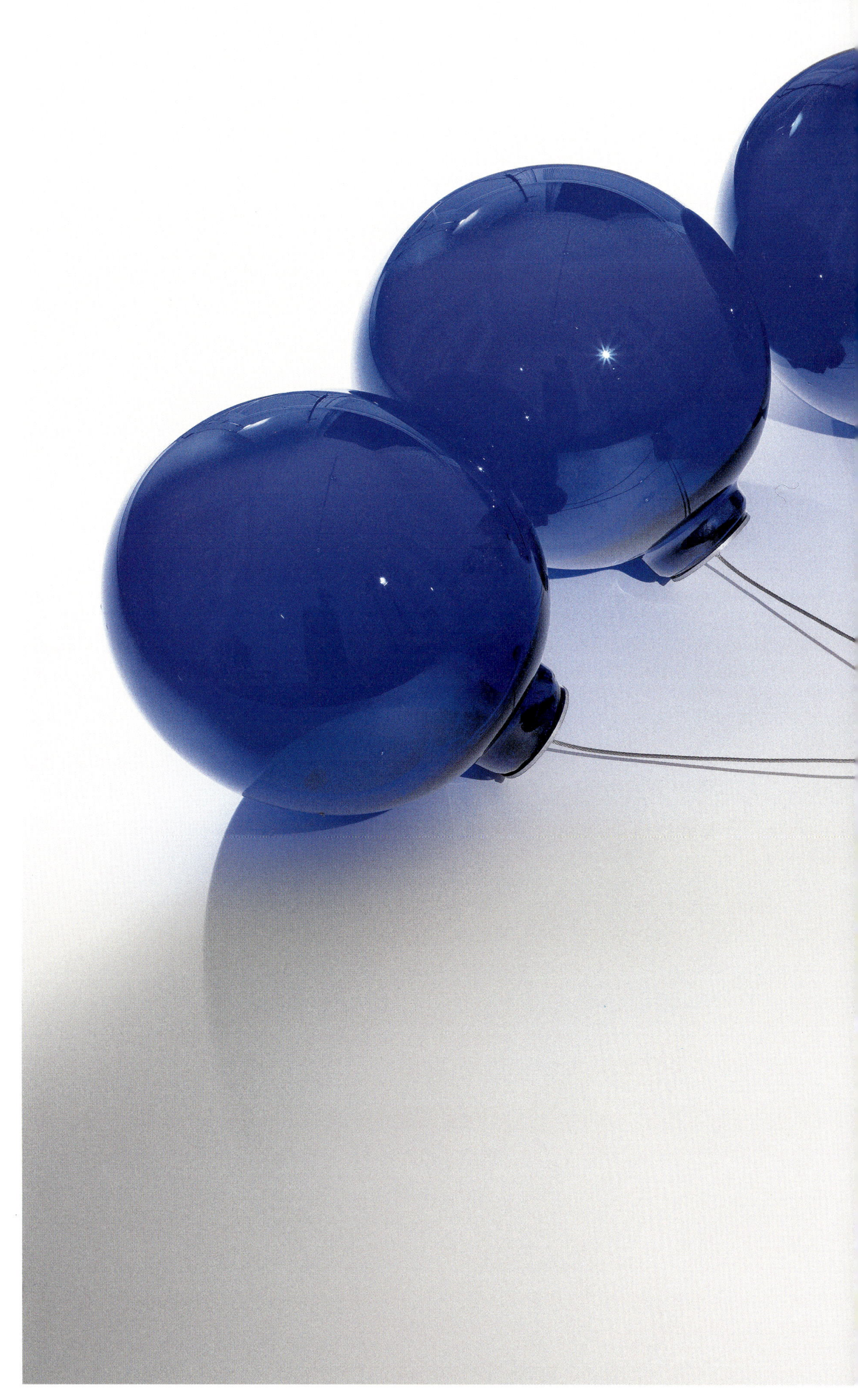

Dreams Behind Me, 2007
Blown glass
180 × 130 × 35 cm

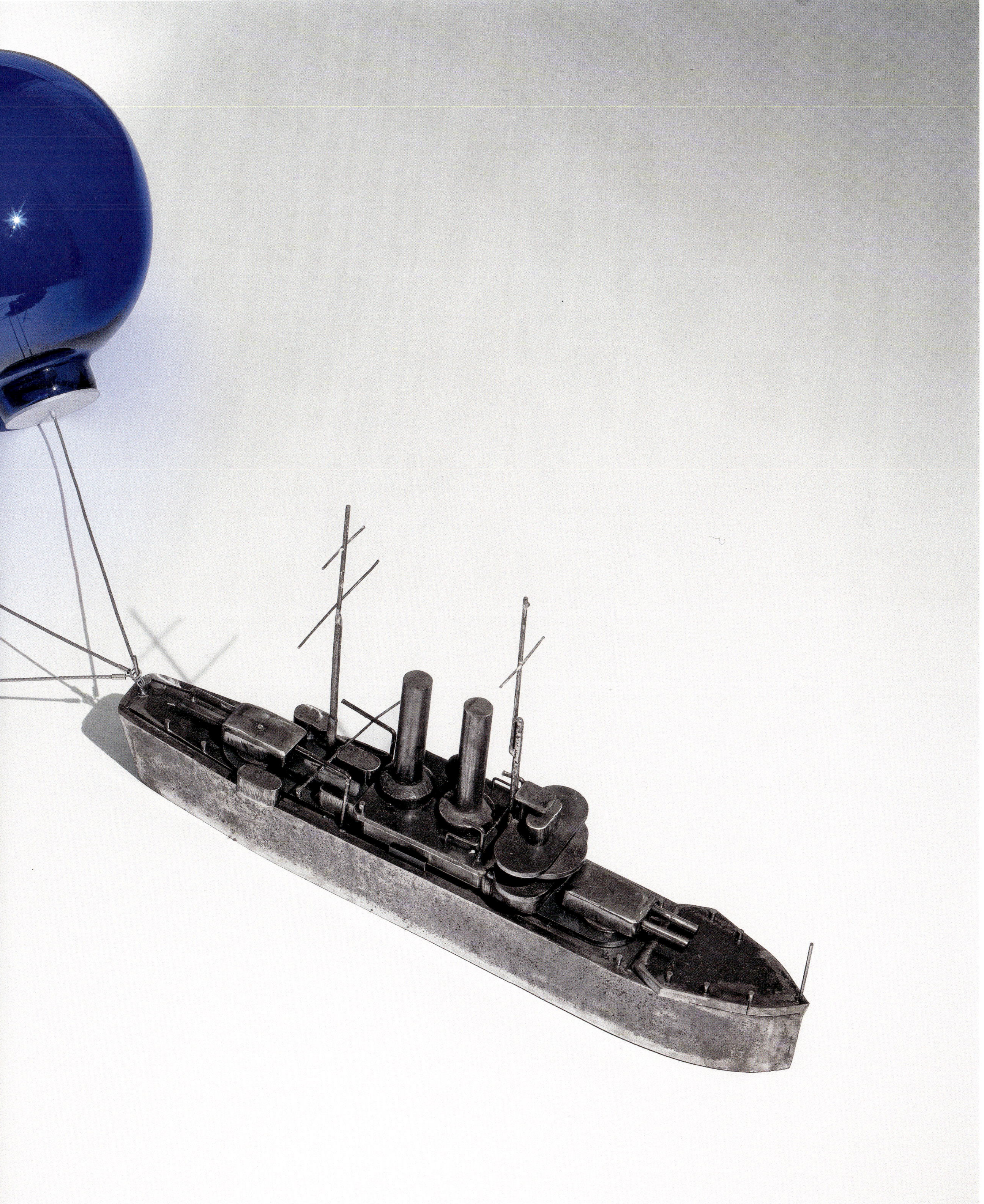

Mona Hatoum

born 1952 in Beirut, Lebanon;
lives and works in London, UK

The British-Palestinian artist Mona Hatoum was on a short visit to London in 1975 when the Lebanese Civil War broke out and prevented her from returning to her family home in Beirut. She remained in the British capital and attended the Byam Shaw School of Art and the Slade School of Fine Art. She has lived and worked in London ever since.

Hatoum's poetic and political art is realized in a diverse and often unconventional range of media that includes performance, video, photography, sculpture, installation, and works on paper. Her work deals with issues of displacement, marginalization, exclusion, and systems of social and political control. She often uses furniture and familiar everyday objects which she transforms in such a way that they become alien or even threatening, making the viewer reflect on a suspicious and hostile environment. Since the mid-'90s, glass has often featured in her creations, as in the clear glass marbles that she first used for her installation *Marbles Carpet* (1995). This initiated a series of installations in which large expanses of clear marbles are spread across the floor in the shape of a world map, turning the ground into a destabilized surface that is both seductive and treacherous.

Korb V, with its two blood-red hand-blown glass forms resembling undefined creatures huddling together, is also reminiscent of bodily organs. This work arouses contrasting emotions in the viewer, such as attraction and repulsion. The basket evokes warm associations with the familiar domestic object normally used to gather apples or leaves. The association with body shapes seems uncanny, almost grotesque, as they seem to be trapped within a steel cage. *Drowning Sorrows (cachaça)* (2014) is a floor-based sculpture in which bottles that have been cut in half at various angles are arranged in a circular pattern on the floor. The bottles appear as if they are bobbing on the surface of a body of water. As the title suggests, they look as if they are part-floating, part-drowning.

"I'm working with feelings of displacement, disorientation, estrangement—when the familiar turns into something foreign or even threatening. It's about shattering the familiar to create uncertainty and make you question things that you normally take for granted. I suppose this is what critical awareness is about."[1]

Turbulence (black) (2014) is another floor-based work consisting of thousands of differently sized black glass marbles that have been amassed in the shape of a circle. The circle appears like an indefinable black hole, as if the solid floor could be sinking. Although minimal in its material elements, this cluster of glass marbles suggests a force field. Its organic, turbulent surface is nevertheless contained within the perimeter of its circular form. It is both beautiful in its multiple reflections, yet threatening in its blackness—a vision of a turbulent world?

"I think your personal experience shapes the way you view the world around you. With fifteen years of civil war in Lebanon and conflict in the Middle East ever since I can remember, there is nothing very uplifting about it and this inevitably filters through my work. So, yes, there is darkness but there is lightness as well. There are often two sides to each piece, not just one meaning. Duality and contradictions exist in most of the work: darkness and light, heaviness and humor, beauty and danger."[2] PGH

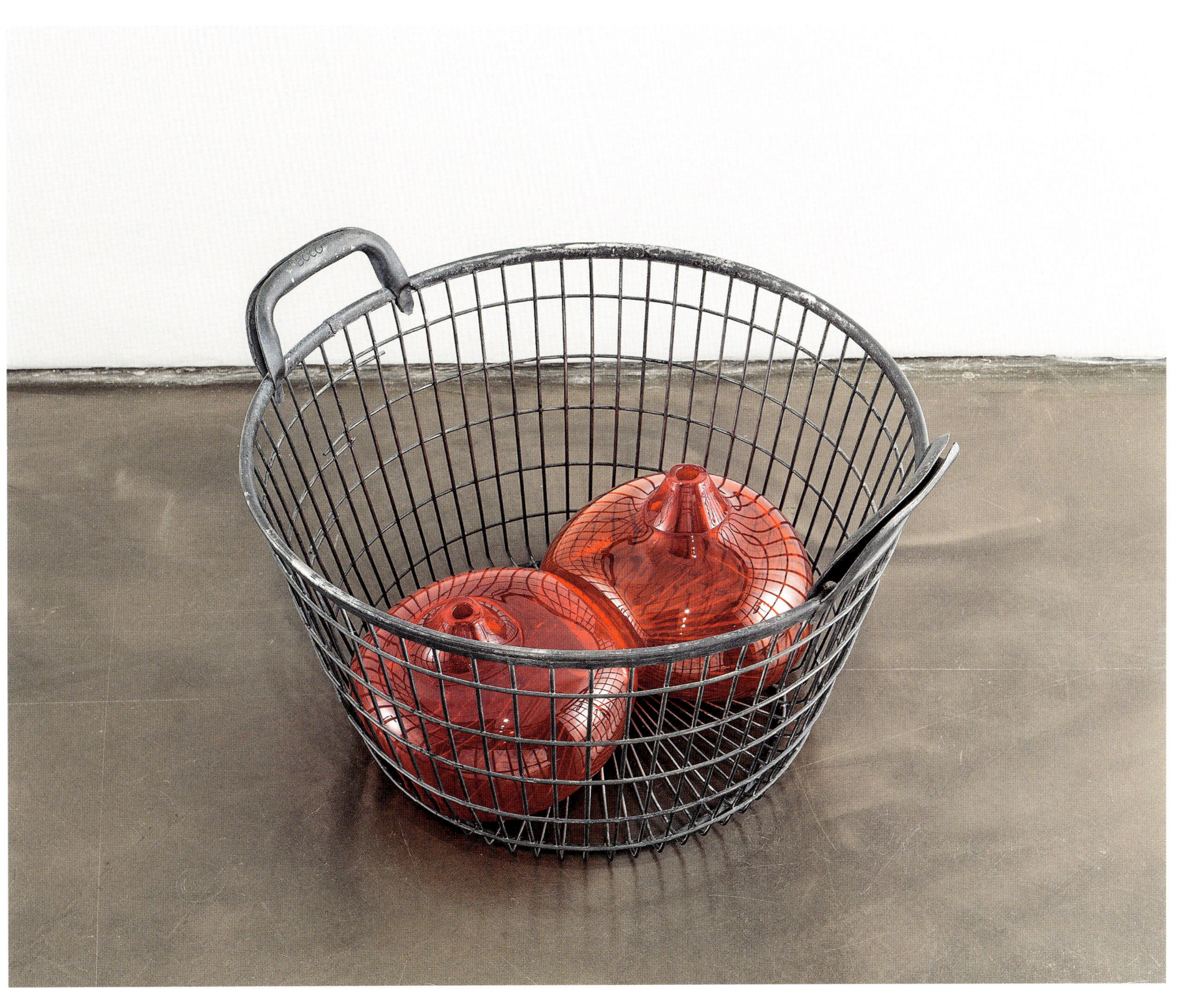

Korb V, 2014
Hand-blown glass and steel
33 × 49.5 × 45 cm

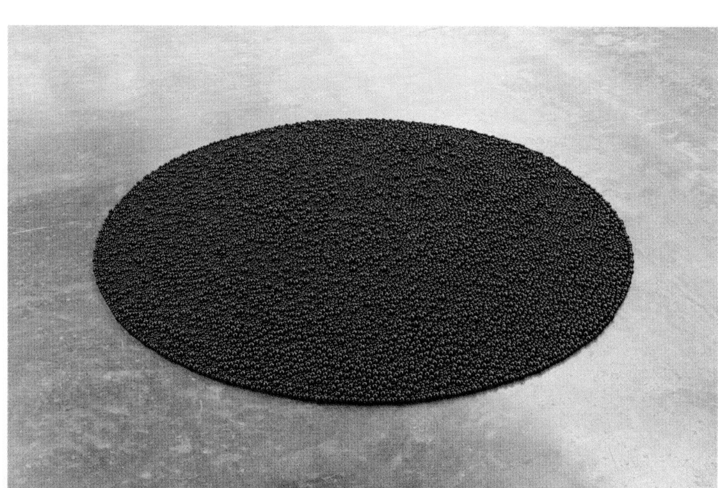

Turbulence (black), 2014
Black glass marbles
3 × 250 × 250 cm

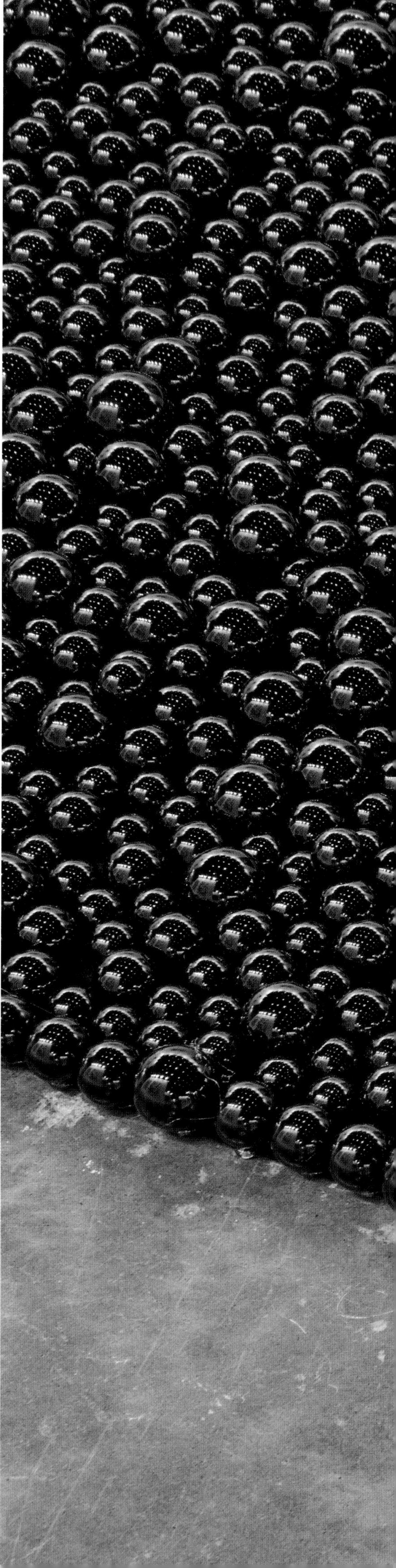

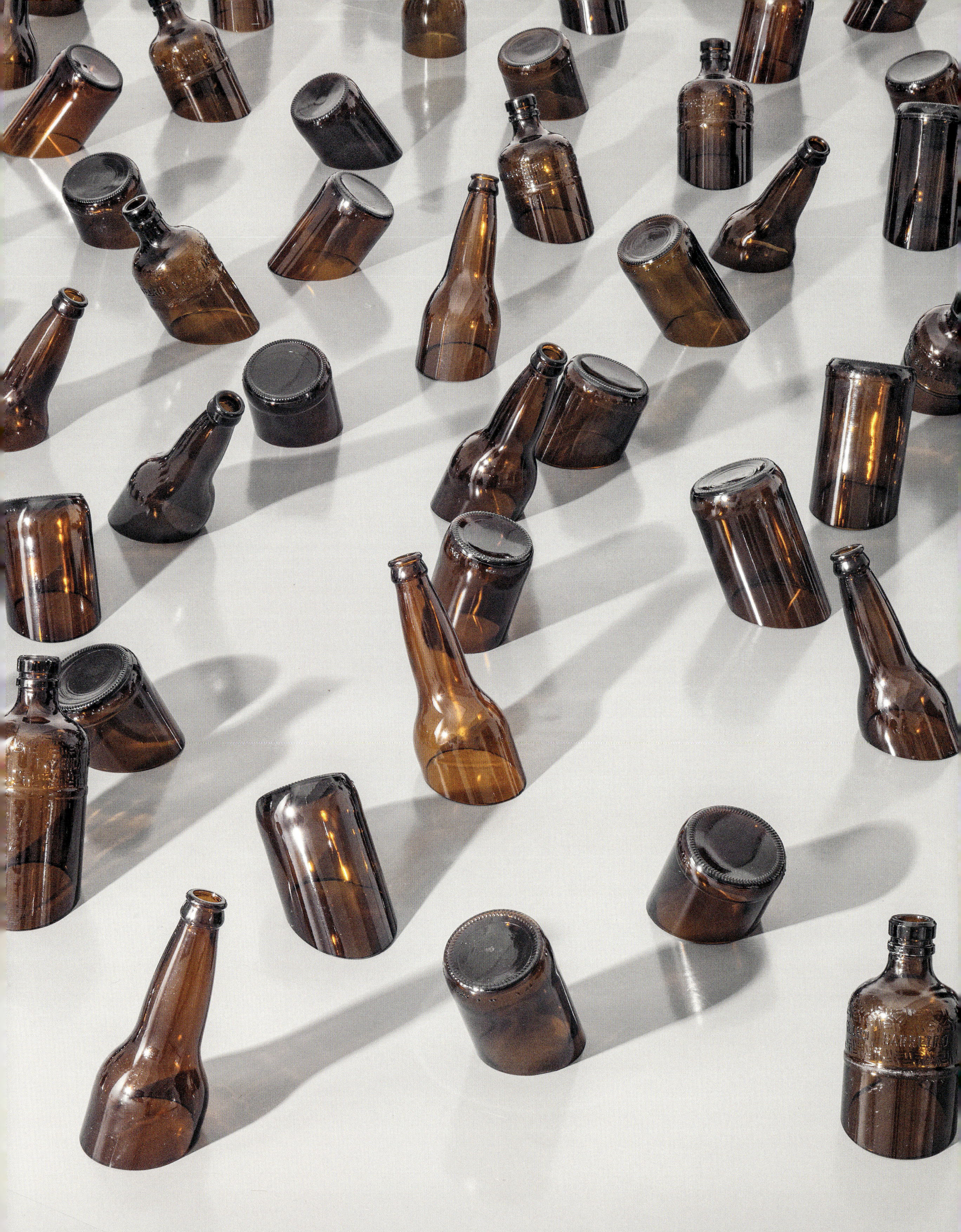

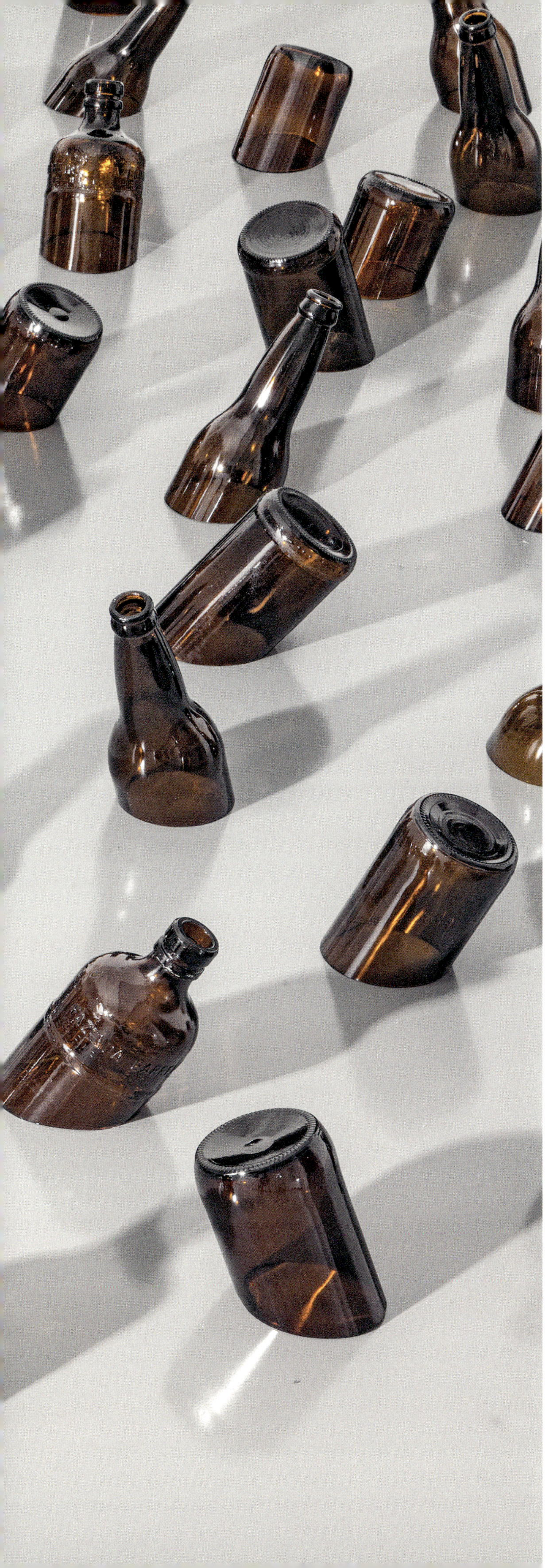

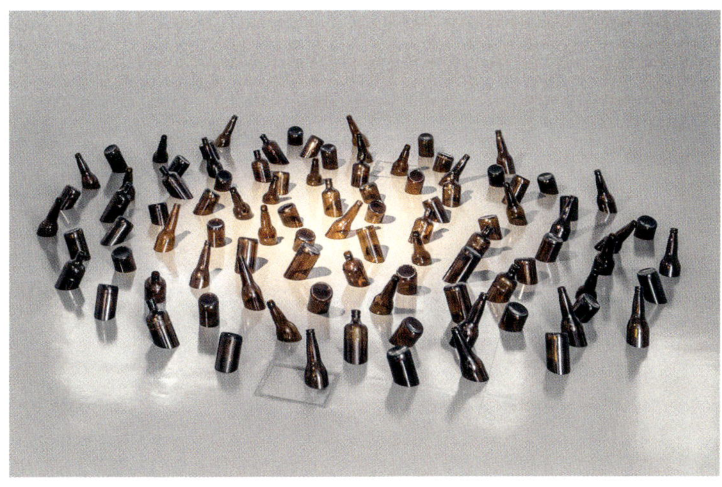

Drowning Sorrows (cachaça), 2014
Cut glass bottles
15 × 200 × 200 cm

Shirazeh Houshiary

born 1955 in Shiraz, Iran;
lives and works in London, UK

Shirazeh Houshiary explores spiritual principles in the context of abstract forms. Her work encompasses painting, installations, architecture, and film and is represented in collections such as the Tate Modern, London; the Centre Georges Pompidou, Paris; and the Solomon R. Guggenheim Museum and the Metropolitan Museum of Art, both in New York. Glass is an important material for Houshiary. She transformed the East Window of St Martin-in-the-Fields in Trafalgar Square, London, into a spectacular abstraction: a work of monochrome glass composed in horizontal and vertical lines around a central opening that allows the light to flow through.

Like this window, which combines religious elements with complex architecture in its structure, Houshiary's sculpture also approaches a metaphysical reality beyond mere form and surface. "I really want to get to the core of what I don't know," says the artist.[1] In its dynamic structure, twisted in on itself and open at the top, formed of glass bricks in light shades of black and gray and shiny polished steel, a body appears to move in space and rise up from the floor: this is *Alar* (2016–17), the wing. The Murano glass bricks, row after row, layer after layer, ascend with elegance and grace—as in the paired works *Aura* and *Twilight* (2019): each vertical plane of glass bricks mirrors the original form at its base, rotated step by step to the maximum degree the form allows before the resulting helical shape becomes unstable. "The universe is in a process of disintegration," says Houshiary. "Everything is in a state of erosion, and yet we try to stabilize it. This tension fascinates me and it's at the core of my work."[2] PGH

Alar, 2016–17
Glass and mirror-polished stainless steel
145 × 118 × 118 cm

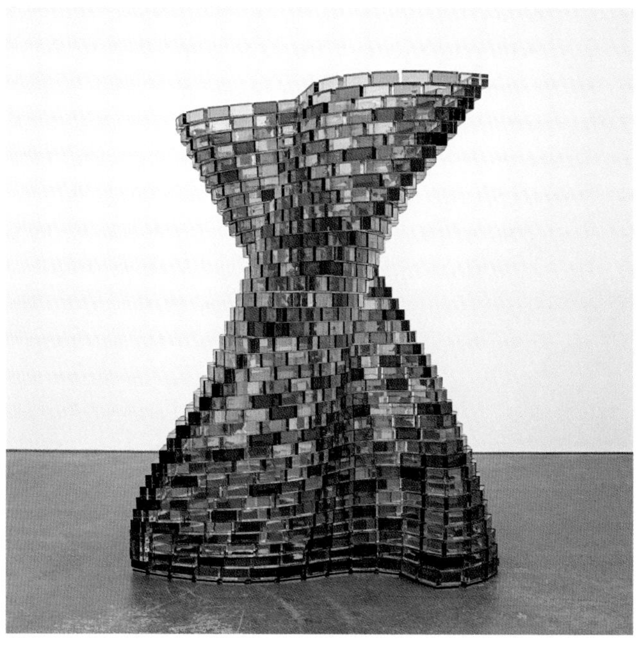

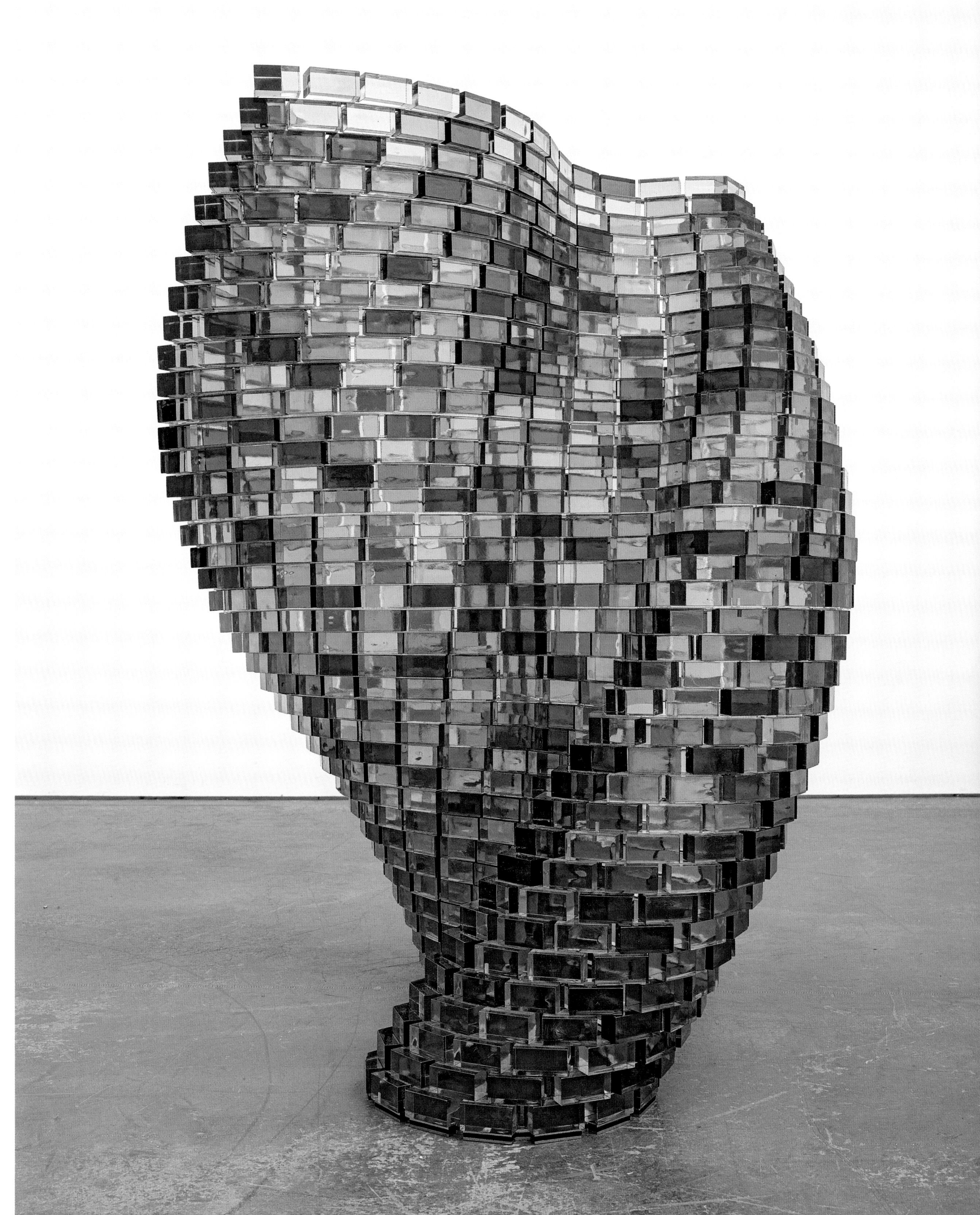

Ann Veronica Janssens

born 1956 in Folkestone, UK;
lives and works in Brussels, Belgium

Her most important artistic material is immaterial: light. As Belgium's representative to the 48th Venice Biennale in 1999, Ann Veronica Janssens filled space with light and thick fog to create a spectacular experience. Glass, in its transparency, became a natural medium for this multidisciplinary artist, and she has collaborated with scientists to investigate the material's qualities and physical phenomena. Janssens' installation at La Chapelle Saint-Vincent au Cimetière in the French town of Grignan (2012–13) is an impressive example of how, when colored blocks are placed before the windows, glass can transform a space into a backdrop of continuously changing colors. "I became fascinated by glass casting techniques" while developing that project, she says.[1] Her works are minimalist in form and emotionally charged through the color and consistency of the glass, as in her object-like floor works (*16 Pink Blocks,* 2016, and *16 Aquatic Blocks,* 2017). Simplicity and clarity are what make Janssens' work so calm and charming, and yet, "I don't want my work to be seductive and some of it is quite rough."[2]

Magic Mirror CL9E166,
2021–22
Dichroic composite glass
120 × 120 × 1.8 cm

Magic Mirror CL9E166 (2021–22) was composed from three layers of glass. The middle pane, made of "crash glass," has been shattered into thousands of pieces. In its fragile state, it is securely sandwiched between the two outer panes. Although fixed to the wall at a slight angle, resting on two brackets, the piece appears to be in motion: the colors shift through the dichroic film laid between the panes, while the numerous shards reflect light in varying ways, creating additional forms and nuances of color. Janssens emphasizes the performative quality of her works in glass, static though they may be: "there is a kind of performance and movement encapsulated within the glass panel."[3] This is sensed by the viewers, too, who see their own movements reflected in the surface. "I share with the visitors an experience of instantaneity, of a present time that offers a present and unstable light."[4] PGH

Hassan Khan

born 1975 in London, UK;
lives and works in Cairo, Egypt

Egyptian artist Hassan Khan articulates his ideas in many different media; he works with choreography, music, performance, sound, video, and his own texts as well as sculptural installations. Khan, who was awarded the Silver Lion for "most promising young artist" at the Venice Biennale in 2017, is interested in the conceptual and communicative role of art. Many of his works are dedicated to culture and the language of everyday life. *The Knot,* a work made of glass and steel from 2012, was prominently exhibited in Kassel, Germany, at *documenta 13* (2012). It forms part of a series of works by Khan—singular sculptures and interventions in the architecture of a space—that aesthetically transform a functional object, such as part of a balcony structure (*The Twist,* 2012), a column (*Brass Column,* 2007), and a railing (*Banque Bannister,* 2010).

The Knot (2012) is a replica of a knot, made in a simple fashion, a "primary gesture," as Hassan Khan has put it: a banal shape, but not if the "rope" is made of glass, an unusual and indeed nonfunctional material for a knot. Transformed into a precise sculptural form, the object becomes an ornament. It possesses value, attracts notice, and opens new dimensions of meaning. The flexible has become fixed, contrary to reason, irrational; the cord connects nothing, coming out of a void and returning to the void. The "figure-eight knot," in its formulation, in the beauty and fragility of glass, and in the manner of its production and presentation, thus suddenly conveys narrative and symbolic elements from mythology and legend, where the knot is a form of magic, a "knot of life," such as the complex Gordian knot that Alexander the Great simply cut open. One might also associate this work with the knots in our mind that we try to undo, or the emotional ties that bind all energies. "You can learn from banal objects.... There is a first layer and something underneath it," says Hassan Khan. PGH

The Knot, 2012
Glass sculpture and
stainless-steel stand
10 × 72 × 6 cm /
120 × 92 × 40 cm

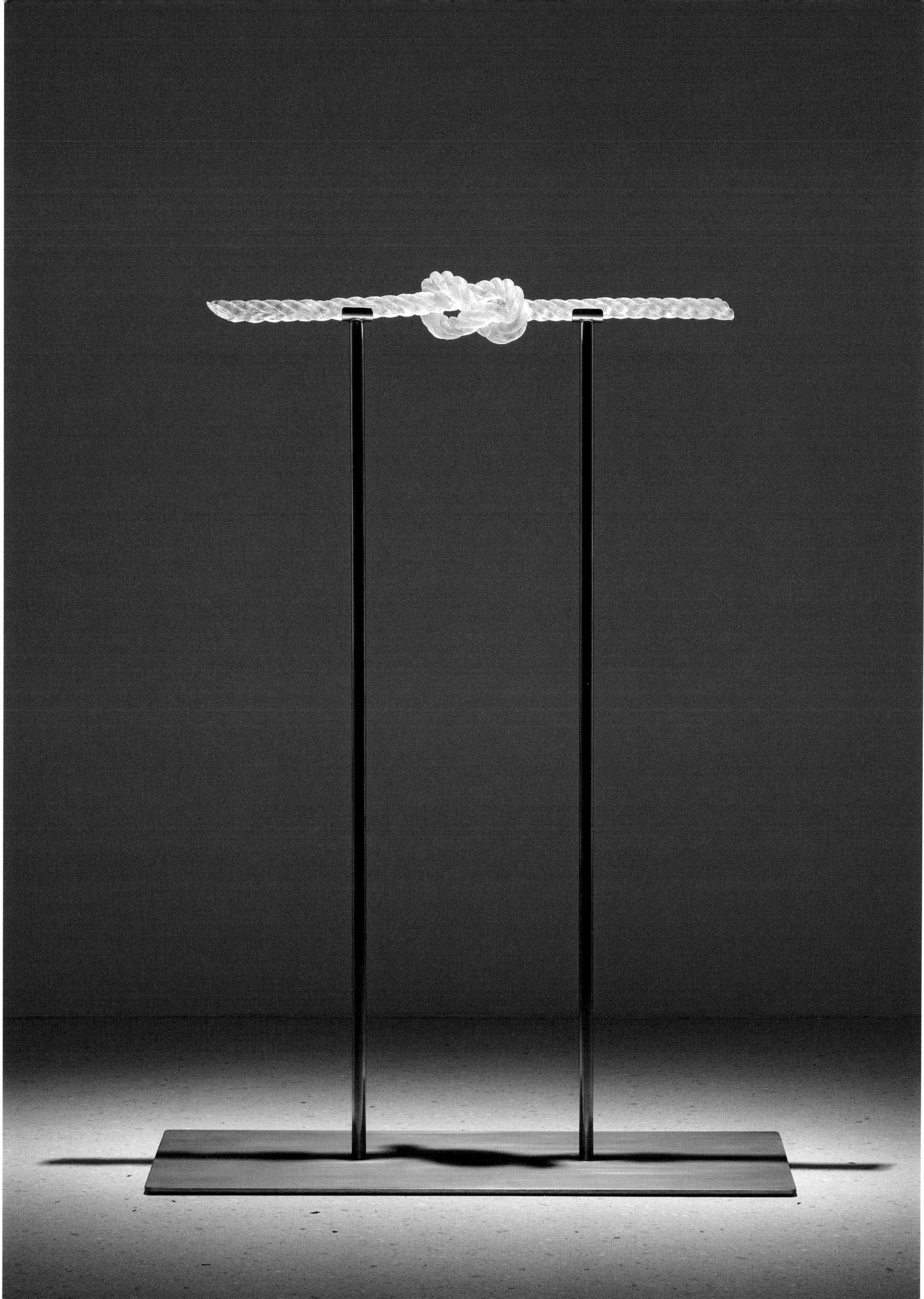

Ki-Ra Kim

born 1959 in Incheon, South Korea;
lives and works in Seoul, South Korea

Ki-Ra Kim began her studies focused on ceramics at Hongik University in Korea. While at the Rhode Island School of Design in the 1980s, she discovered glass, which has become her medium. After attending the Pilchuck Glass School, she returned to Korea in 1989. In her home country, she is regarded as a pioneer of modern studio glass—both as an artist and as a teacher. Her work has been shown in solo and group exhibitions, particularly in Korea, but also in the United States, Japan, and Australia. She teaches as part of the Glass Art and Design MFA program at Kookmin University in Seoul, Korea, and is the author of *Working with Glass* (2003). She defines her cultural identity as that of "a Korean artist who works with glass."

As an artist she works exclusively with glass, from transparent to opaque. She finds inspiration in everyday life—think of her glass houses, for example—and in nature. She is fascinated by birds, especially the crane, which is regarded as a messenger between Heaven and Earth, a symbol of the sacred and of perfection. Ki-Ra Kim has made thousands of glass feathers, lining them up horizontally, stacking them vertically, or arranging them in a circle as in the wall piece *Glass Feathers*. She sees the alternation of feathers in white and black as a representation of the perfect harmony of yin and yang. "The glass feathers represent my understanding of and reconciliation with death, freedom from restraints and a door to the closed, invisible world," says Ki-Ra Kim.[1] PGH

Glass Feather-65 III, 2015
Kiln-formed glass, steel frame
diameter 65 cm

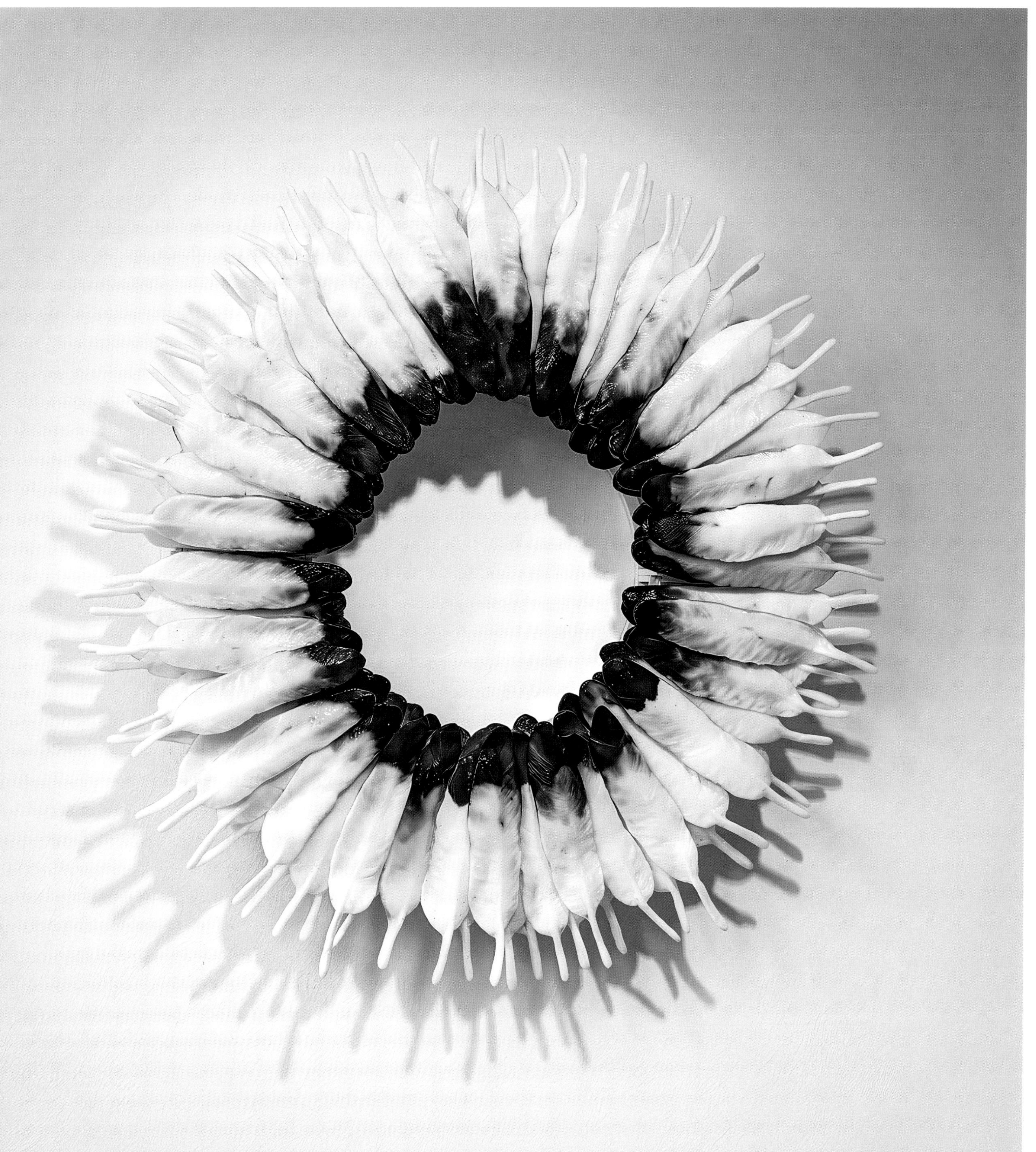

Namdoo Kim

born 1985 in South Korea;
lives and works in South Korea

The small, fascinating sculpture *Present III* (2022), made from glass and ceramic, appears like a being from another world, an alien, something between a child's toy, an object of pop culture, and a robot—as though one could "turn it on" with a key and it would begin to dance. The South Korean artist Namdoo Kim makes such whimsical figures and, through irony and humor, casts a critical glance at consumer society and its notions of success and well-being. For this purpose, glass is among his preferred media. "Glass can speak metaphorically to question and examine societal values. Other sculptural materials contribute a counterpoint and allow me more scope to reference mass-produced objects. My art is intended to stimulate awareness and consideration of the links between what we value in life and how we live in response to our values."[1]

The series of *Present* figures represents an examination of society, as Namdoo Kim has described in a statement about the work: "The crinoline dress of the *Present* series is entirely impractical, emphasizing only its flamboyancy and opulence; I used this as a motif, as it is similar in many ways to modern society. The decorative gears on the surface of the *Present*'s dress appear to intricately interlock and serve a purpose, but upon closer inspection, it becomes clear that they are different sizes and do not fit together functionally. This also symbolizes my criticism of modern society's focus on visual displays and ostentation, implying that the driving force behind society is much more complex and multidimensional than readily apparent surface-level features like folds. *Present* carries a dual, ambiguous meaning of 'current' and 'gift' and showcases both meanings in the works."[2]

Kim is an expert in working with glass. He studied medium and received a Bachelor of Fine Art in glass and ceramics at Hongik University, Seoul, South Korea (2011); a Master of Fine Art in glass from the Rochester Institute of Technology, Rochester, New York (2015); and a PhD in glass at the Australian National University, Canberra, Australia. He has had multiple residencies at international institutions, such as the Corning Museum of Glass in Corning, New York (2016) and the Pilchuck Glass School in Stanwood, Washington (2015). PGH

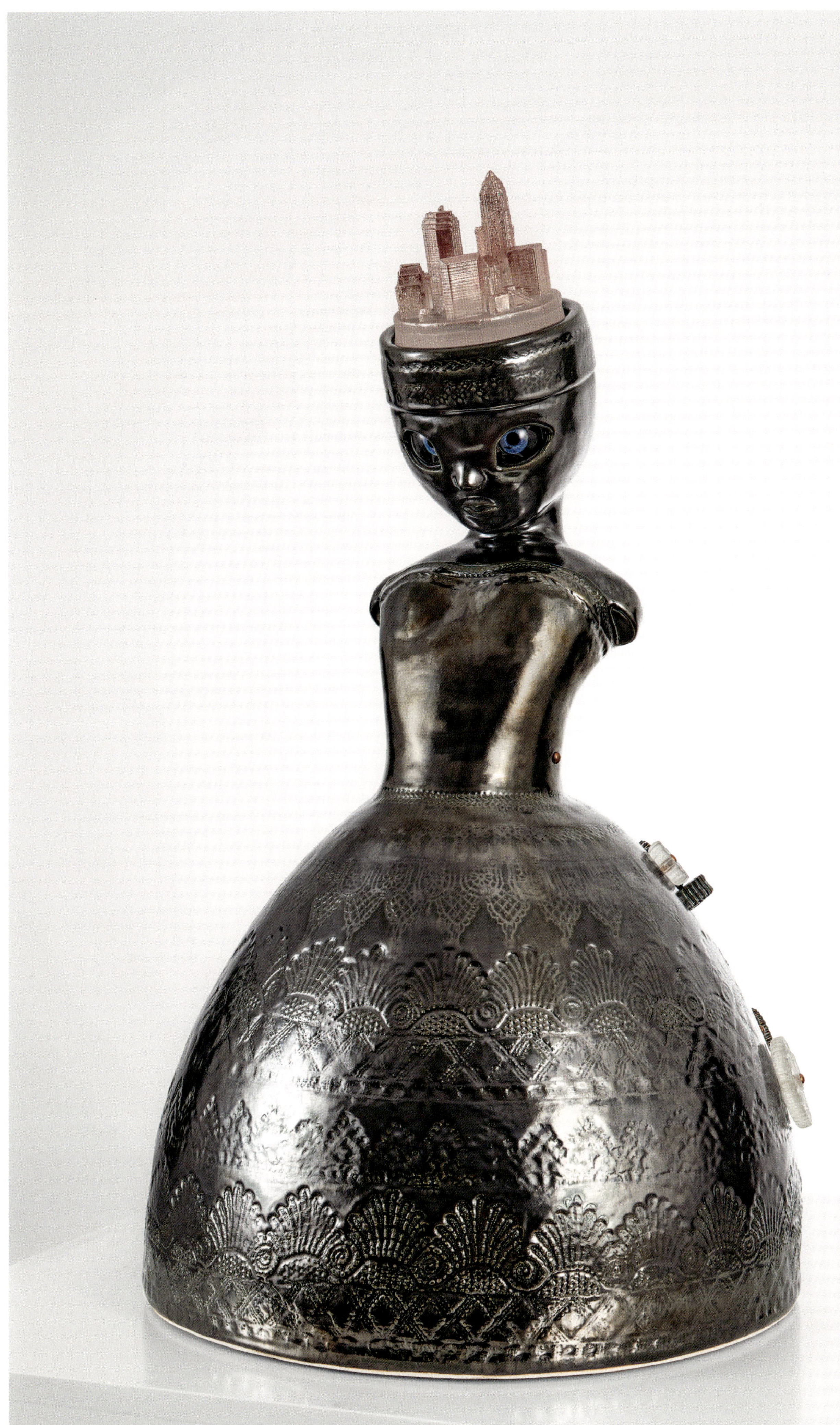

Present III, 2022
Ceramic, glass, copper, and mixed media
67 × 40 × 40 cm

Yoshiaki Kojiro

born 1968 in Japan;
lives and works in Japan

Yoshiaki Kojiro's sculpture *Hatate II* from 2012 captivates through a tension that it manages to hold momentarily, as well as an extraordinary display of glass's materiality. The white, translucent surface of the object is reminiscent of frozen, cracked ice, contrasting with the matte area below. The sculpture appears both massive and fragile at the same time and is imbued with a rather special lightness. A subtle dynamic between control and accident can be felt in the work.

Kojiro's artistic vision is deeply connected to the concept of transformation, which he understands as a kind of life cycle.[1] He regards life and nature as being in a constant state of flux: materials change under the influence of air or heat, their appearance and texture evolving at their own pace. The production of his work reflects this approach. Kojiro combines glass powder with lime powder or copper oxide powder and places this mixture in a mold.[2] Through a complex process of heating and cooling in an oven, he creates his characteristic sculptures of foamed glass in a production process that can be controlled only up to a certain point.

The properties and potential of glass as a material are masterfully revealed in this work. The form appears as if frozen in a moment of transition, just as the suspense is peaking. The artist refers to the work's title accordingly: "*Hatate* means 'at most degree'—for example, an extreme point, a climax, or an end."[3] The technical mastery, as well as the artistic intuition required to capture this moment, point to Kojiro's training. He studied architecture at the Tokyo University of Science as well as art at the Tokyo Glass Art Institute. SO

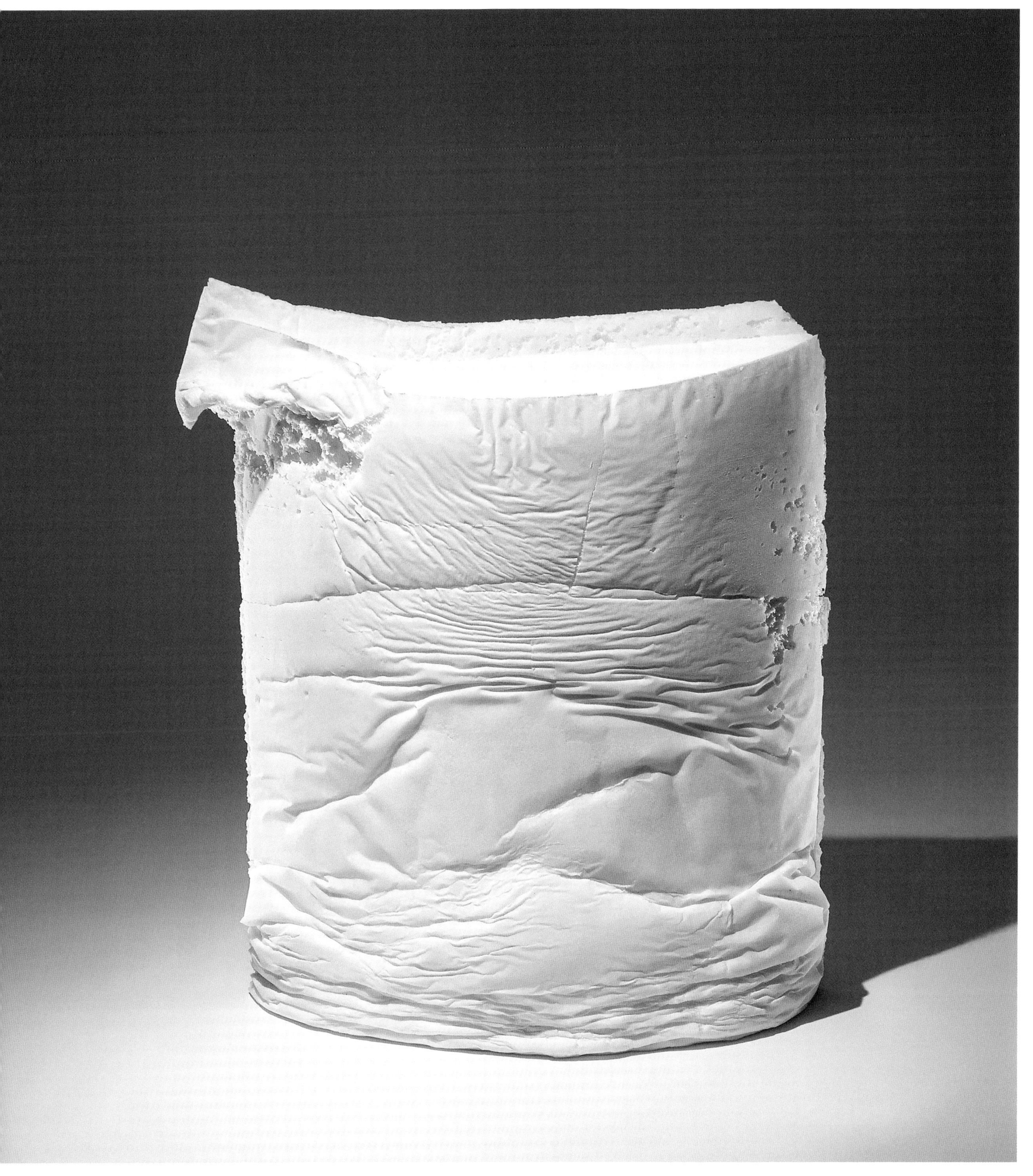

Be, 2005
Cast glass with calcium carbonate, kiln-fired
54 × 48 × 16 cm

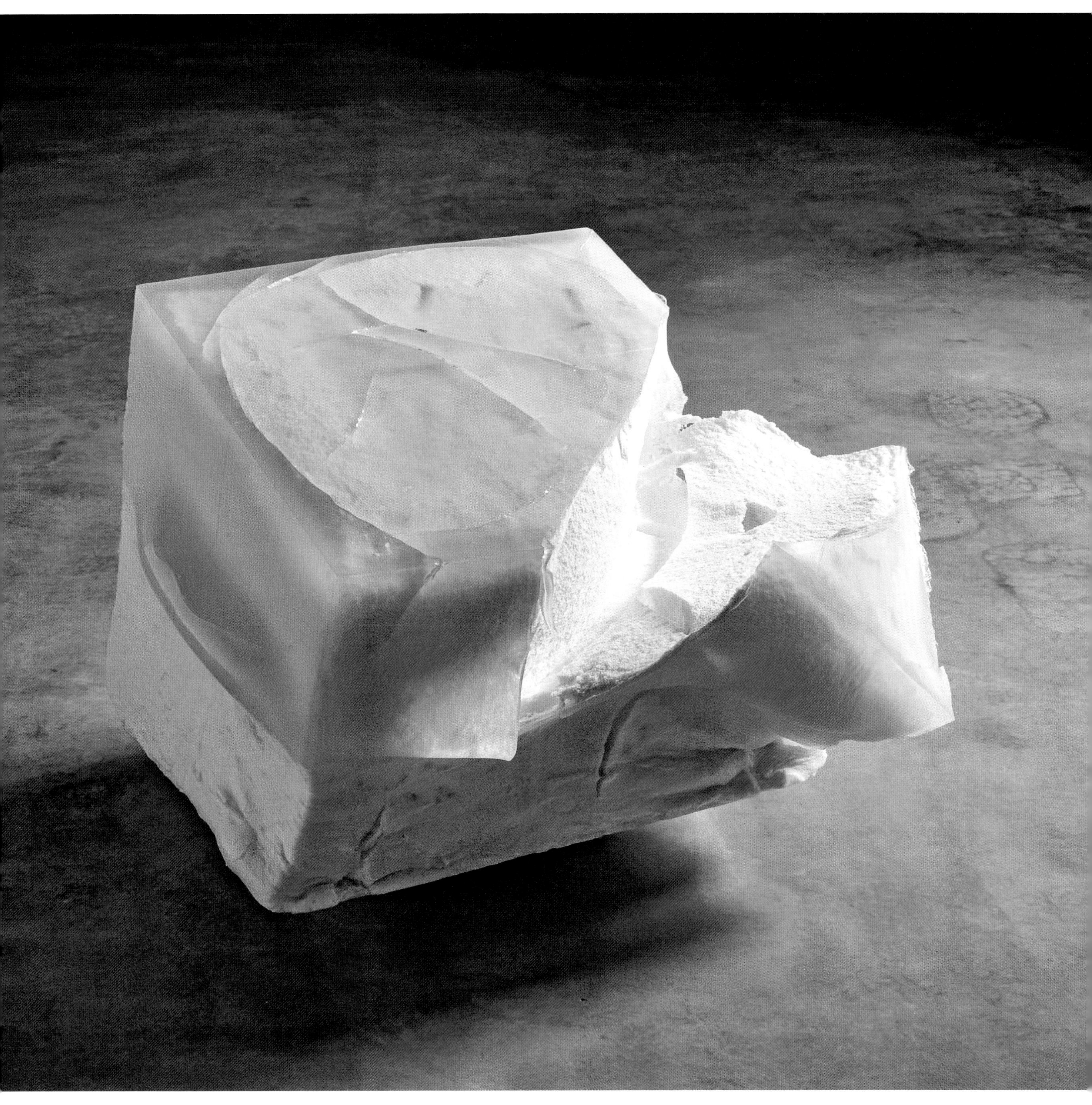

Hatate II, 2012
Cast glass with calcium-carbonate, kiln-fired
56 × 77 × 63 cm

Raimund Kummer

born 1954 in Mengeringhausen, Germany;
lives and works in Berlin, Germany

Raimund Kummer has made a name for himself with his rebellious works in public spaces. His oeuvre encompasses temporary installations, sound art, and sculpture, as well as photography and film. From the very beginning, the influence of the material on the form-finding process has been central to Kummer's artistic approach. The sentence "I am going blind," which he etched countless times into a copper plate in 1973, defines his theme: seeing. He pursues this theme by creating, revealing, and manipulating perceptive experiences that can be investigated with the human eye.

What could be more suitable to this than the medium of glass? And so, in the face of common prejudices, Kummer heightened the status of glass as a material in contemporary art by creating objects such as his floor sculptures.

The organ of sight, the eye, has fascinated the artist since 1987, when he came across a glass eye in New York, acquired it, and presented it—lying on a net in a display case—as part of an exhibition at the Brooklyn Museum. He continued by creating large glass objects such as *Mehr Licht* (More Light, 1991), in forms reminiscent of ocular prostheses, and a diagram of an ocular disease transferred and dissected into glass panes—today in the collection of the Nationalgalerie and exhibited at the Hamburger Bahnhof, Nationalgalerie der Gegenwart, Berlin: *Sublunar Interference* (2017). In his piece *Der Saal der toten Blicke* (The Hall of Dead Looks, 1987–96), eighty-four glowing, oversized eyes are on the floor, with each iris on the matte-polished eyeballs of a different color; in fact, they are the eyes of individuals, of Venetians, "translated" from Kummer's photographs and reflecting the different cultural origins and history of the city (Diözesanmuseum Freising, 2000). *Hindsight bias. Siehe! – und nicht glauben, es schon gewusst zu haben* (Hindsight Bias: See! and don't think you already knew it, 2007) is the name of the two giant glass eyes, almost two meters high, which hang from the ceiling by their own optic nerves (Stiftung DKM, Duisburg, 2007).

The two works *Sternengewölbe* (Starry Vault, 1990) and *Gespräch unter drei Augen* (Private Conversation, 1990) share this context. As a counterpart to going blind, they address seeing as a condition of knowledge. It is as if one senses the silent presence of those looking and communicating—an enlightening appeal to see the person opposite, to sit down, and to communicate. PGH

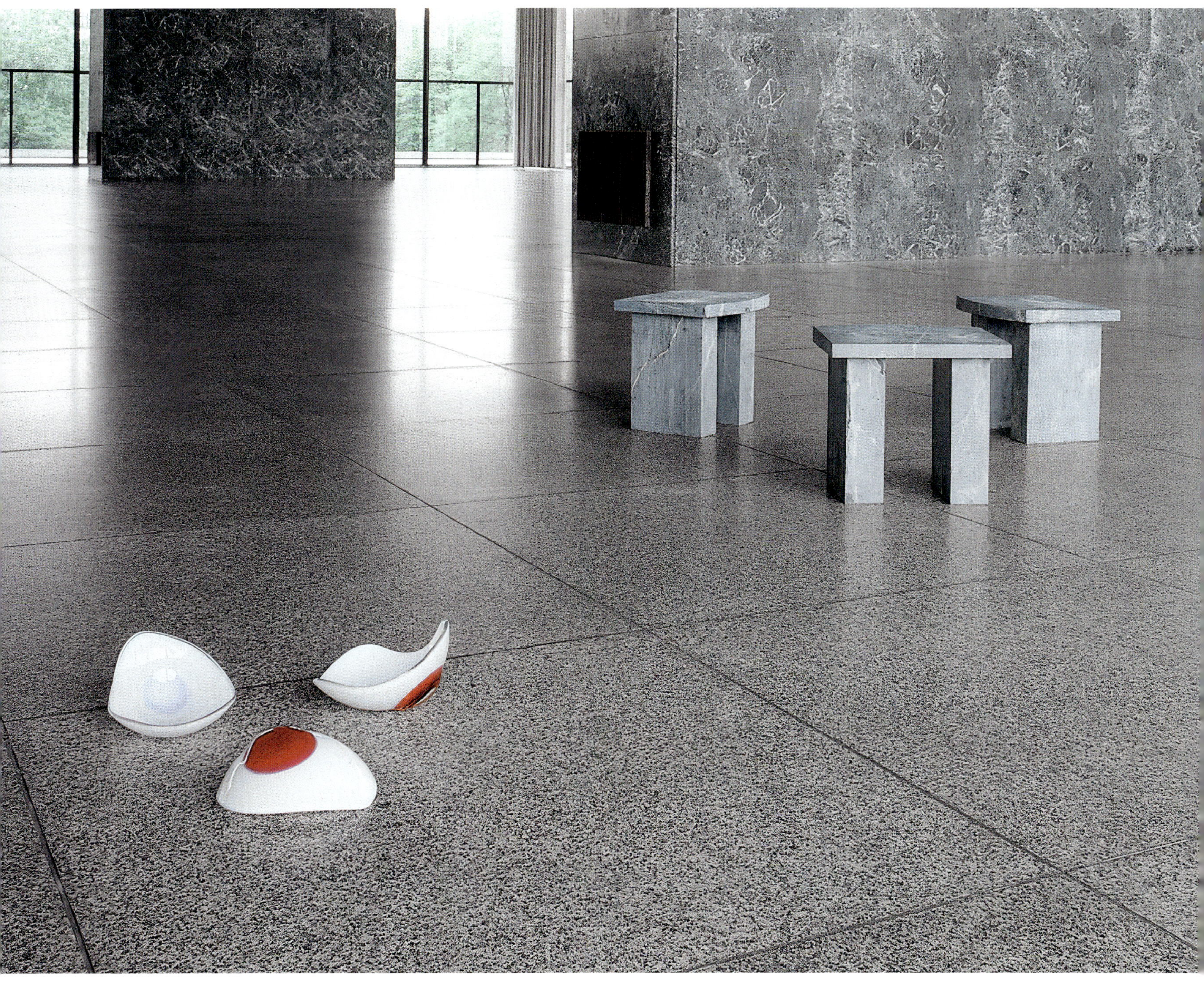

Gespräch unter drei Augen (Aus dem Albinokomplex), 1990
Eyes: 3 pieces,
Bohemian glass, each 23 cm in diameter
Stools: 3 pieces, Karacabey Black Marble,
each 44 × 48 × 40 cm

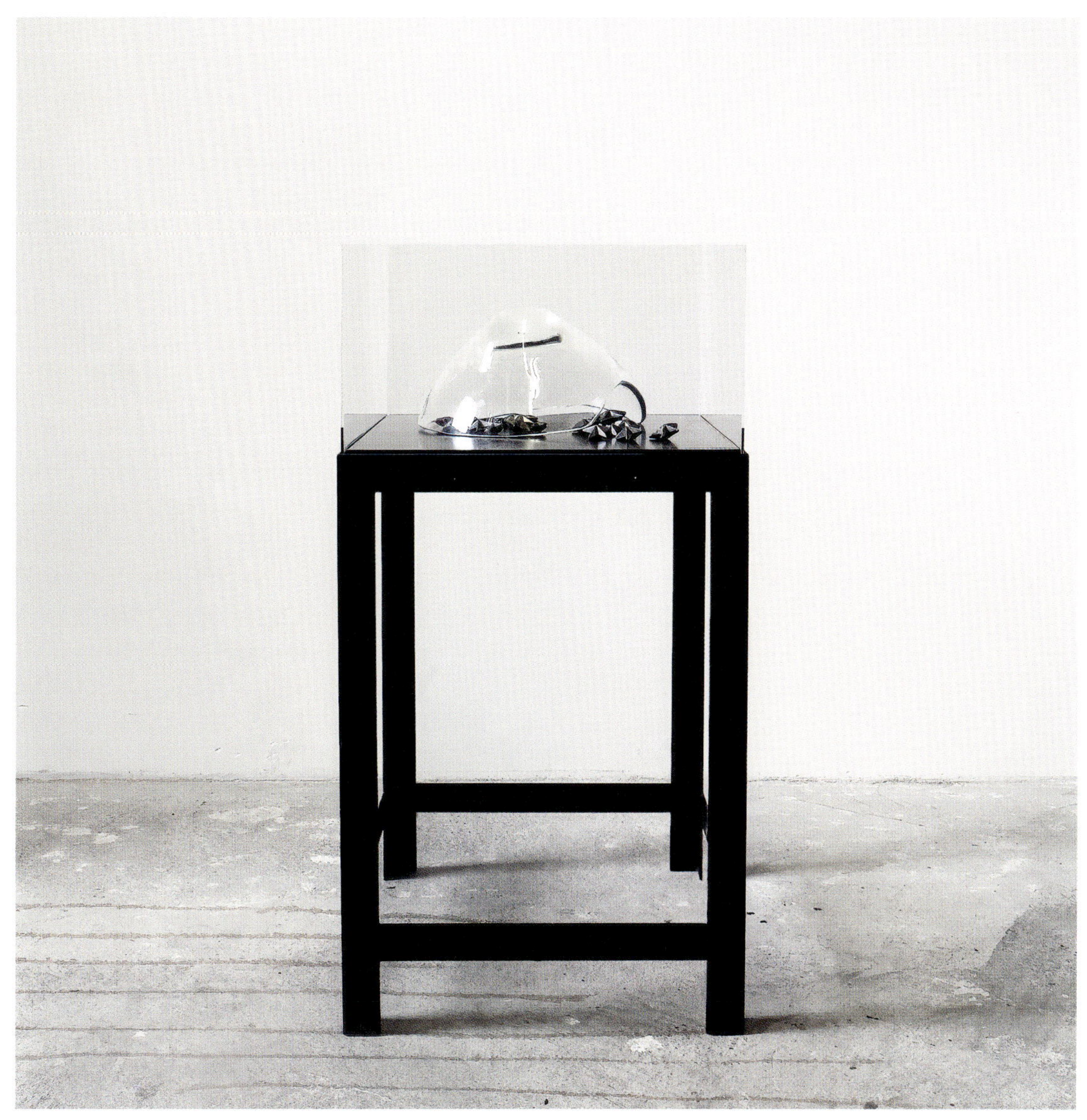

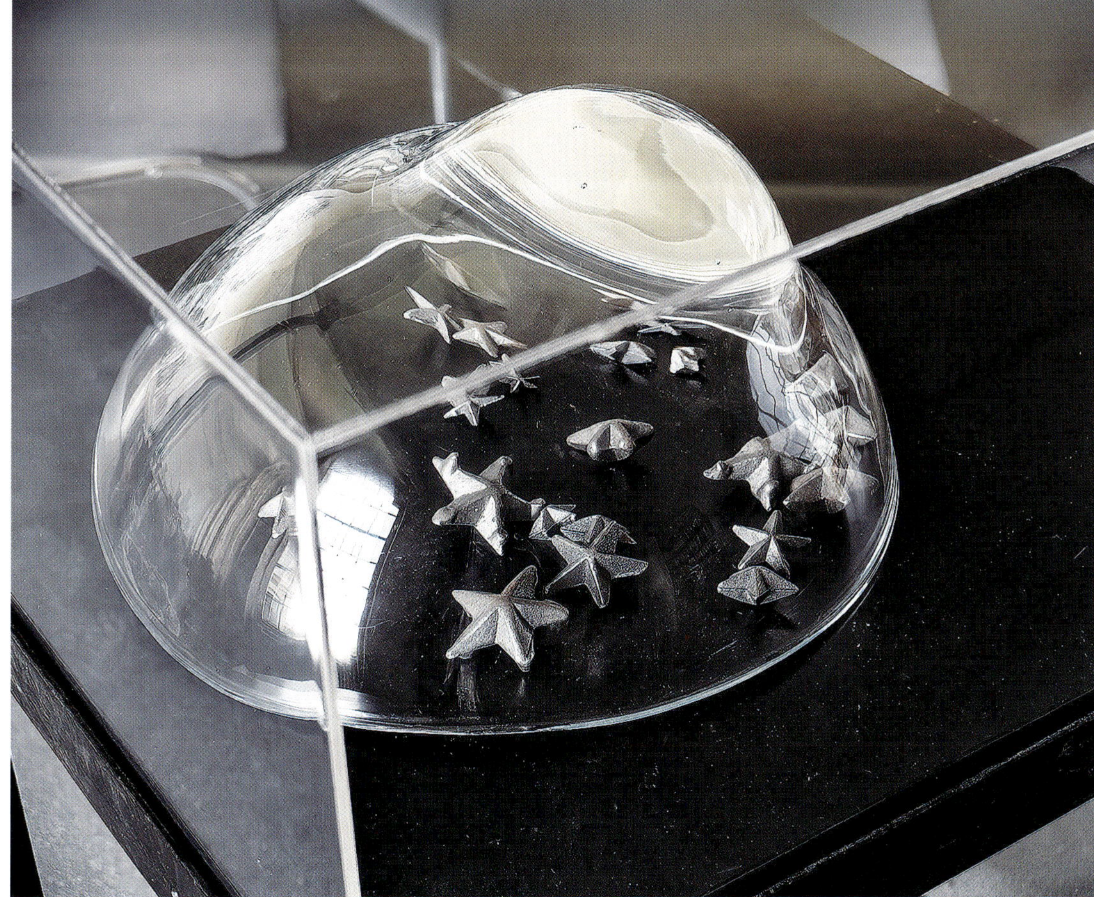

Sternengewölbe, 1990
Eye: Bohemian glass,
height approx. 18.5 cm,
diameter approx. 35 cm
Stars: cast steel, 23 pieces,
height 1.5–2.5 cm,
diameter approx. 2–5 cm
Case: steel, vulcanized
rubber and Plexiglas,
overall: 96 × 62 × 53.5 cm

Alicja Kwade

born 1979 in Katowice, Poland;
lives and works in Berlin, Germany

The work of Alicja Kwade features glass that is industrially produced, as a glass pane or mirror. Through this conceptual simplicity there emerge the qualities necessary for the artist to address her themes: challenging scientific and philosophical concepts, taking her to the limits of perception. In this, glass proves to be an ideal material, transparent and yet reflective, thus challenging the sense of sight to distinguish between illusion and reality. It is a game of light and mirroring, of glass's stability and fragility, always on the verge of smashing, collapsing, and yet—that is the astonishing result—it keeps its balance. Kwade combines glass with robust natural materials, such as massive stones, which the glass manages to support. Or does it? When she balances these oversized stones, panes of glass, and mirrors, as in the sculpture *Hemmungsloser Widerstand* (Unrestrained Resistance, 2019), she is inquiring into the order of things and nature's conformity with its own laws.

The work is part of a series, yet also one-of-a-kind, since the stones have been specifically chosen for each individual work. Thus the sculptures always appear different, even when connected by a unifying concept. Ideally the viewer moves around the piece and takes it in from varying perspectives, allowing it to open up different versions of reality and show the same object in multiple states—between the poetic and the absurd, accident and calculation, balance and instability.

Alicja Kwade is internationally recognized for her sculptures, expansive installations, films, photography, and works on paper. She has exhibited globally, including at the 57th Venice Biennale (2017), and in recent years has created increasingly large site-specific installations, such as her spectacular work on the Roof Garden of the Metropolitan Museum of Art, New York, in 2019. PGH

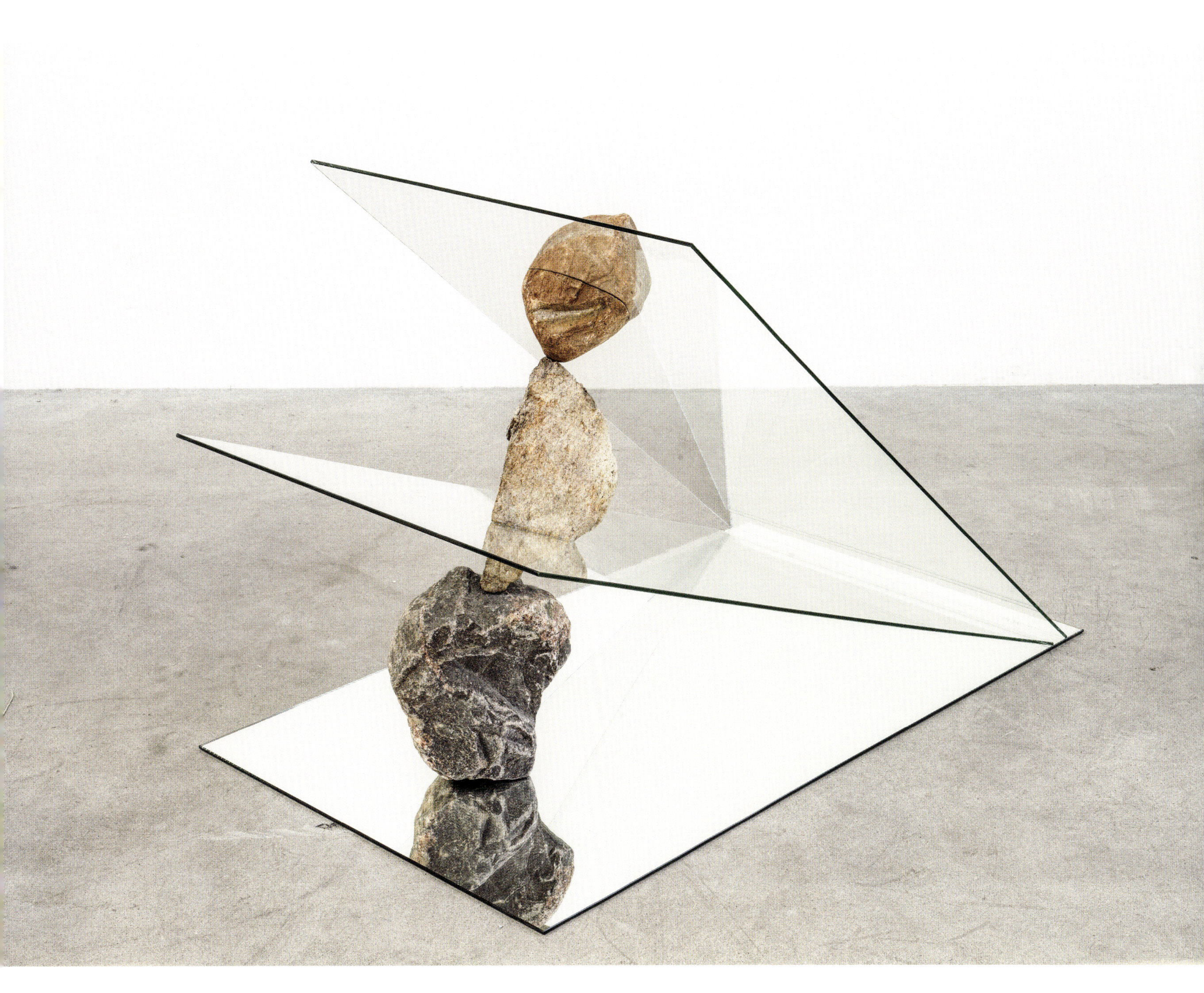

Hemmungsloser Widerstand, 2019
Mirror, found stones, safety glass
86.5 × 71 × 122 cm

Glenda León

born 1976 in Havana, Cuba;
lives and works in Madrid, Spain and Havana, Cuba

A floating sculpture made from mouth-blown glass, *Listening to the Rain* (2023) was produced by a master craftsman of the Royal Glass Factory of La Granja in Segovia, Spain. It depicts a falling raindrop, but one that has been translated into an acoustic pattern. This work by Glenda León was inspired by a conversation she had had with José Luis Brea (1957–2010), a Spanish philosopher and professor of aesthetics and contemporary theory, about the micro-sounds of nature. The work is accompanied by a recording by Alexis de la O, a Cuban composer of electronic music: thanks to the latest technological developments, the study of micro-sounds has isolated particles of sound less than a tenth of a second in duration. This poetically minimalist glass sculpture was installed in 2023–24 in the foyer of the Museo Amparo in Puebla, Mexico, and given the title *Escuchando la lluvia*.

Listening to the Rain, 2023
Blown glass, sound
270 × 43 × 43 cm

Glass, being transparent, seems to be the ideal material for symbolizing water, the element of life, in its continuous symbolic cycle. The vertical as the connection between heaven and earth, the slowing down of time: in the act of listening and pausing, of concentration and contemplation, mind, body, space, sound, and silence combine to form a whole. Such is the credo of Glenda León: in paying attention to everyday things there lies the possibility of achieving a state of expanded consciousness.

Glenda León, one of the most prominent Hispanic American artists, received a degree in art history from the University of Havana and a master's degree in new media from the Academy of Media Arts Cologne (KHM). Her early interest in dance and choreography has shaped her multidisciplinary artistic practice: she includes elements of dance, music, and literature in her drawing, video, sound, sculpture, and photography installations. León represented Cuba at the 55th Venice Biennale and has participated in the Dakar Biennale (Senegal), the Havana Biennale (Cuba), and the Aichi Triennale (Japan). *Cosmic Trace* at the OK in Linz (2024–25) is her first major exhibition in the German-speaking world. She has been awarded a Pollock-Krasner Foundation Grant, and her work is included in major public collections, including those of the Centre Pompidou (Paris, France), the Museum of Fine Arts (Houston, Texas), and the Musée des Beaux Arts (Montreal, Canada). PGH

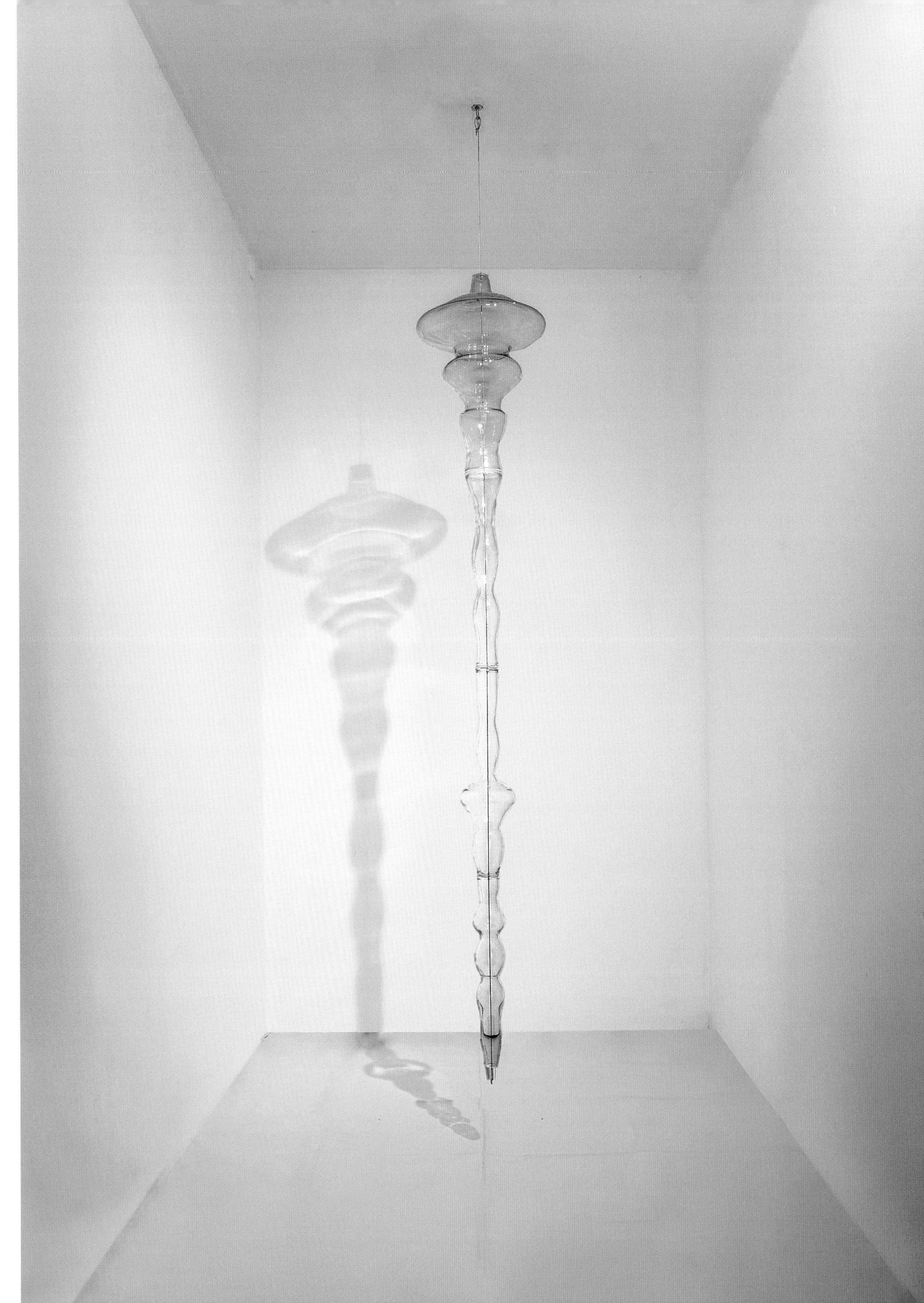

Antoine Leperlier

born 1953 in Evreux, France;
lives and works in Conches, France

Any attempt to put the work of Antoine Leperlier into words seems doomed to fail. The closer you think you are to his highly philosophical and profound works, the more they seem to slip away. The reason for this may be that the artist has dared to give bodily form to those things that cannot be grasped by the human mind, being the great themes of human and animal existence such as life, time, and transience, which he manages to capture through his preferred material, glass (pâte de verre). In this way, he explores and draws upon pictorial formulas of past eras with high recognition value. These include well-known symbols of baroque vanitas still-life paintings, such as Medusa-like snakes tangled together, eerie skulls, rotting fruit, and animal carcasses. The latter is the main motif of his work *La Chute (Vanité au Lapin VI)* from 2001: the skinned body of a rabbit, repulsive and appealing at the same time, rests vertically before the etched relief of a text fragment in contrasting tones. The excerpt from Dante's *Inferno* serves as a background to this morbid scene in more ways than one, as it recalls the inexorable passing of time, the inevitability of death, and ultimately the wasting of flesh and all other material remains. The upside-down rabbit can only scarcely be recognized as such. We look upon the now dead animal's exposed entrails, raw and unconcealed. This confrontation represents a clever allusion to the intrinsic, phenomenological details of glass as an amorphous substance. It can appear transparent, translucent, or opaque, and creates a fascinating tension between the three-dimensional medium's inner and outer dimensions, which coexist while also merging into each other. In this way, the artist opens for us a passage through the physical space to enter a spiritual plane.

Since the 1980s, Leperlier has participated in numerous international exhibitions and is now represented in more than thirty important glass collections. AB

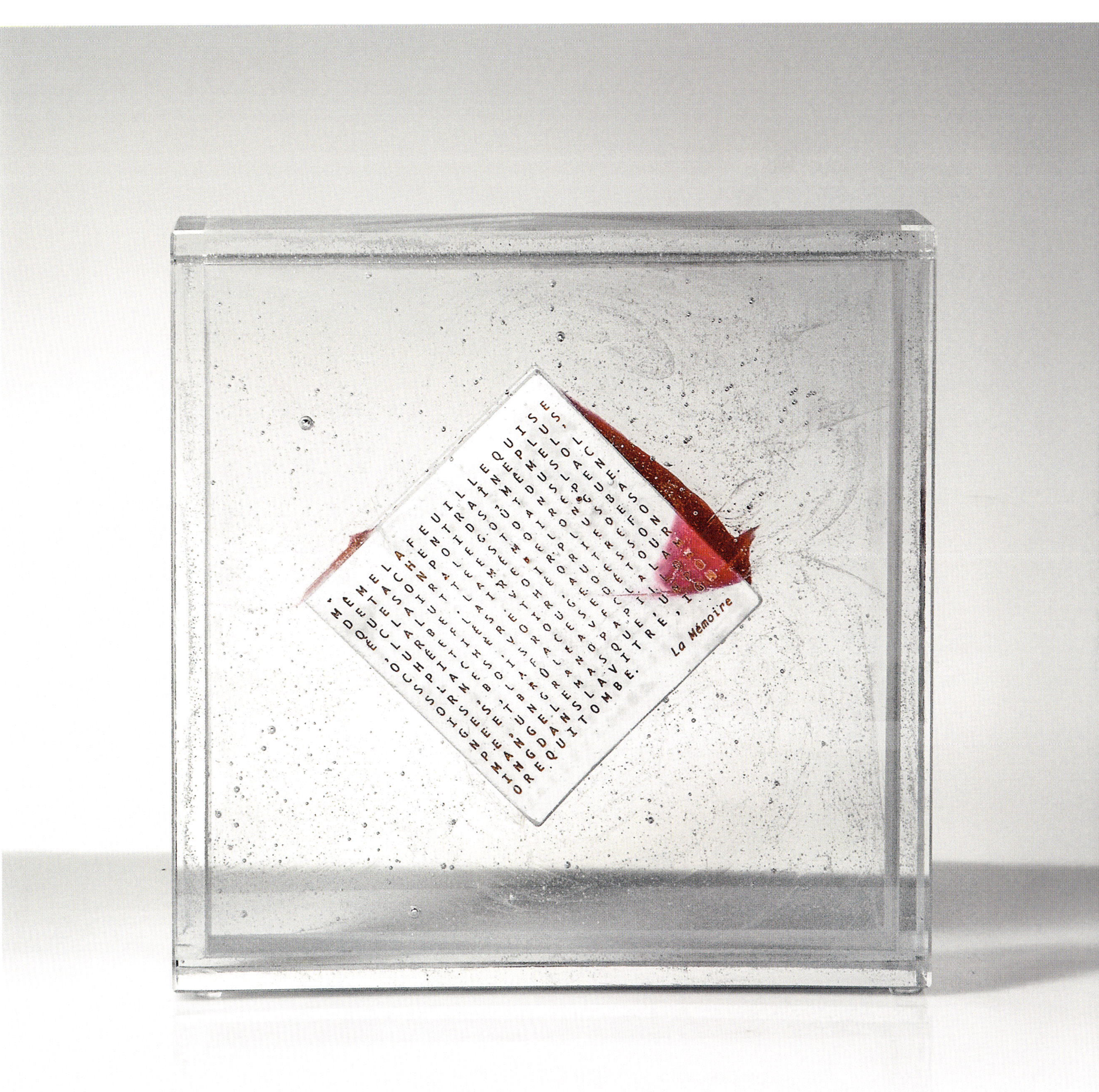

Flux et Fixe XIV, 2012
Pâte de verre
30 × 9.5 × 31 cm

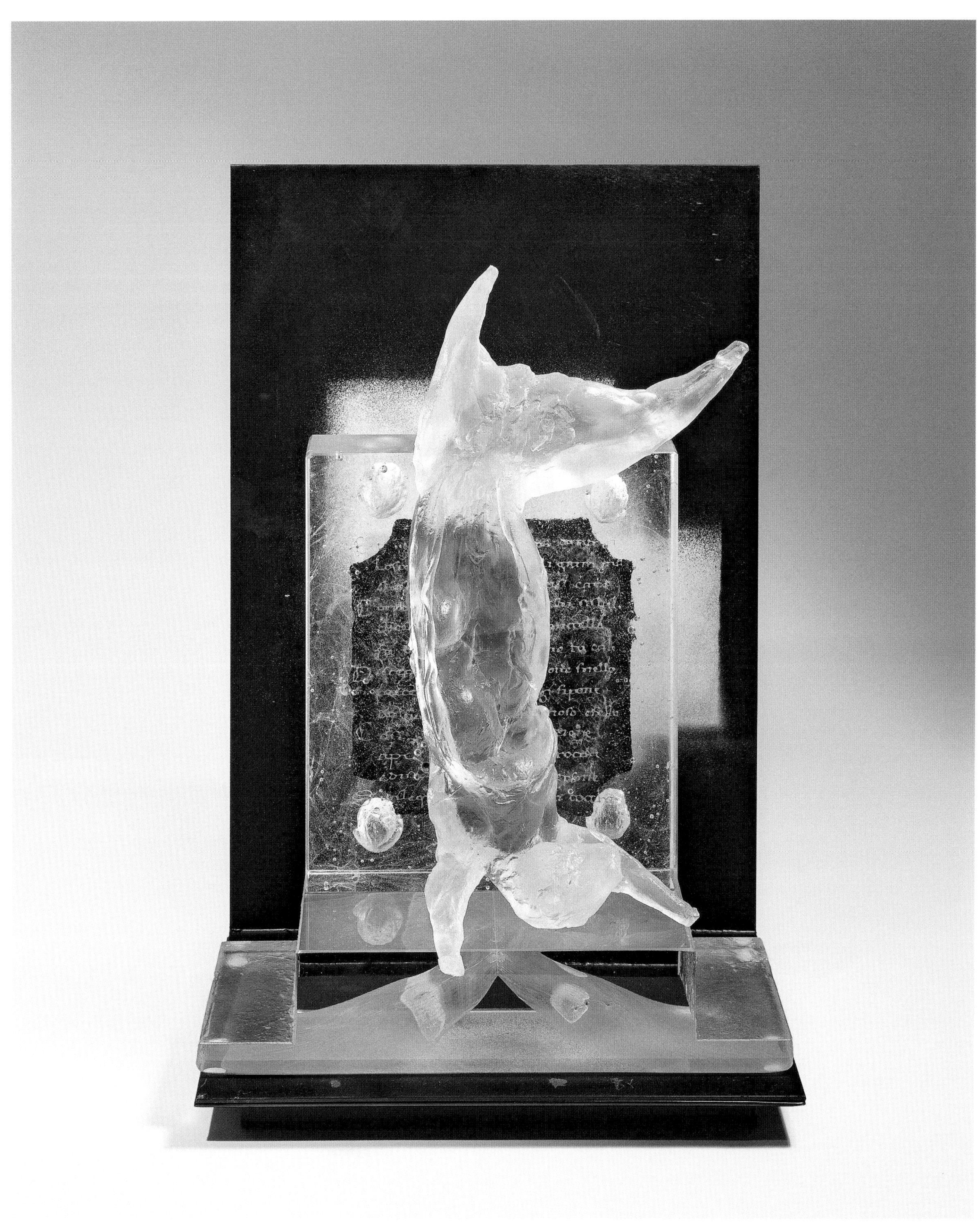

La Chute (Vanité au Lapin VI), 2001
Crystal pâte de verre, hot-sculpted
47 × 26 × 13 cm

Silvia Levenson

born 1957 in Buenos Aires, Argentina;
lives and works on Lago Maggiore, Italy,
and in Buenos Aires, Argentina

Originally focused on painting and drawing, Silvia Levenson, who along with her family fled the military dictatorship in Argentina in 1981, discovered working with glass in her new home in Italy. The new medium became a means for expressing her artistic and political concerns. "I was fascinated, not only with the beauty of glass but with the fact that glass is a material used in our daily lives. ... I don't like virtuosity in art. I love feelings, pathos, intuitions."[1] Glass is a natural material for this, a means for Levenson to capture memories of people and things. Its quality of preserving and protecting is what interests her: "For me, glass embodies the idea of resilience."[2]

Levenson tells stories of domestic violence using apparently familiar objects set in bold colors. Objects that might appear simple and innocuous, coming from the world of children or domestic life, embody for her vulnerability and the fragile nature of human existence. She is especially concerned with children and our failure to protect them, or the impossibility of doing so. Behind the decorative quality of glass, and indeed behind its pervasive presence, lies the horror. *I see you are a bit nervous* (2006) is the title of one work which shows that family is where social conflicts begin, in the isolation and the violence at home.

Falling directly in line with Levenson's sociopolitical commitment, her artistic work has helped to ensure that the injustice and unimaginable suffering of forcibly adopted children in her home country of Argentina is not forgotten. In *Identidad Desaparecida* (Missing Identity, ongoing since 2014), she recalls a trauma in Argentinian society: women who stood in opposition to the government and who had given birth in prison were murdered and their newborn children were secretly offered for adoption. At least five hundred babies were stolen in this way. Whenever one of these "children" is found—the grandmothers in particular, the "Abuelas de Plaza de Mayo," continue to campaign for this—Levenson makes a new piece of clothing. There are 132 of them to this day, cast in glass, in a continuous work that travels around the world.

Silvia Levenson received the Premio Glass in Venice award from Istituto Veneto in Venice, Italy, in 2016. Her work can be found in collections such as the Museum of Glass in Tacoma, Washington; the New Mexico Museum of Art in Santa Fe; the Museum of Fine Arts in Houston, Texas; and the National Glass Centre in Sunderland, United Kingdom. PGH

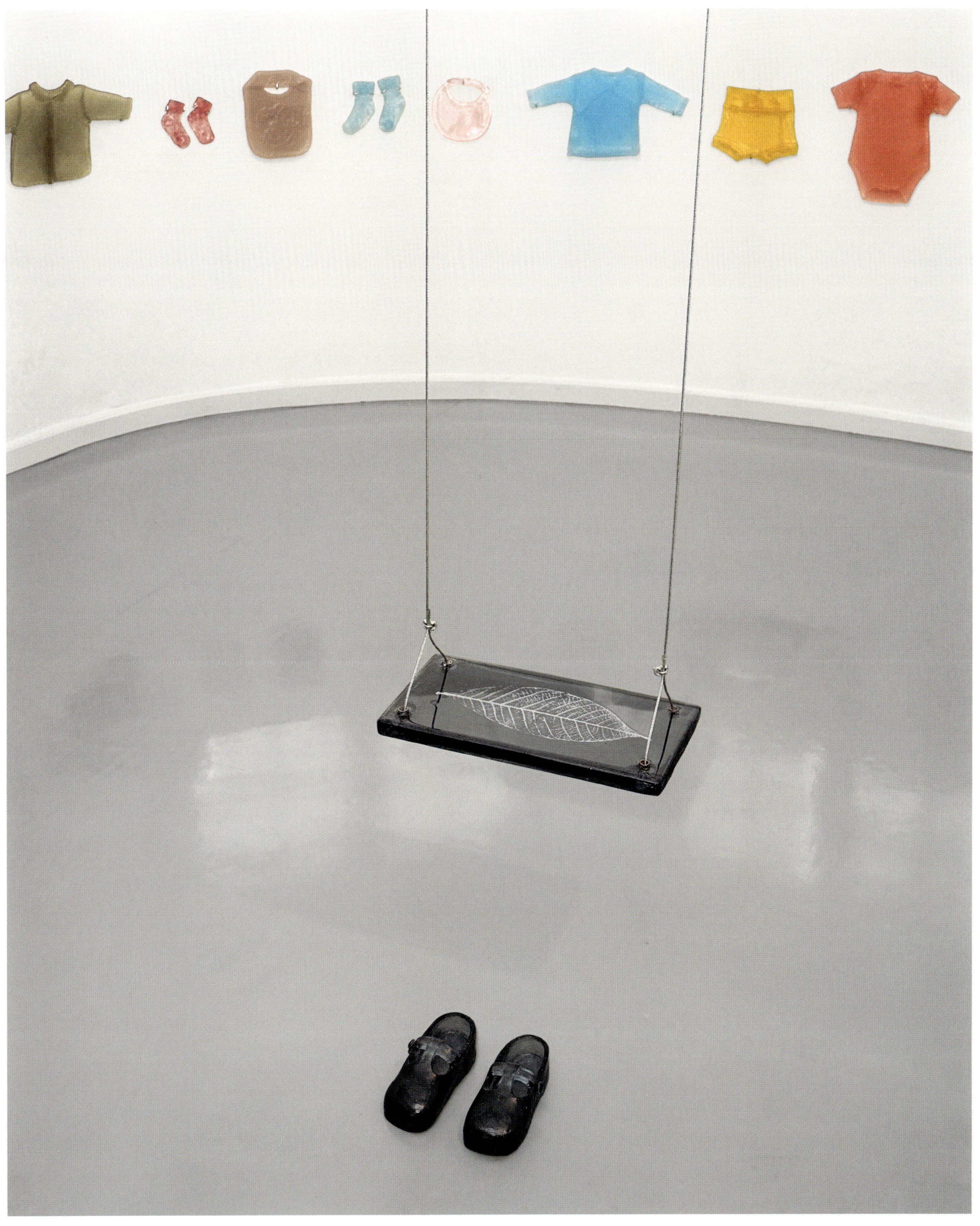

She flew away II, 2014
Kiln-cast glass
Shoes: 6 × 7 × 17 cm each, Swing: 3 × 40 × 20 cm

Recovered Identity (Detail),
2014–present
Kiln-cast glass, 133 pieces

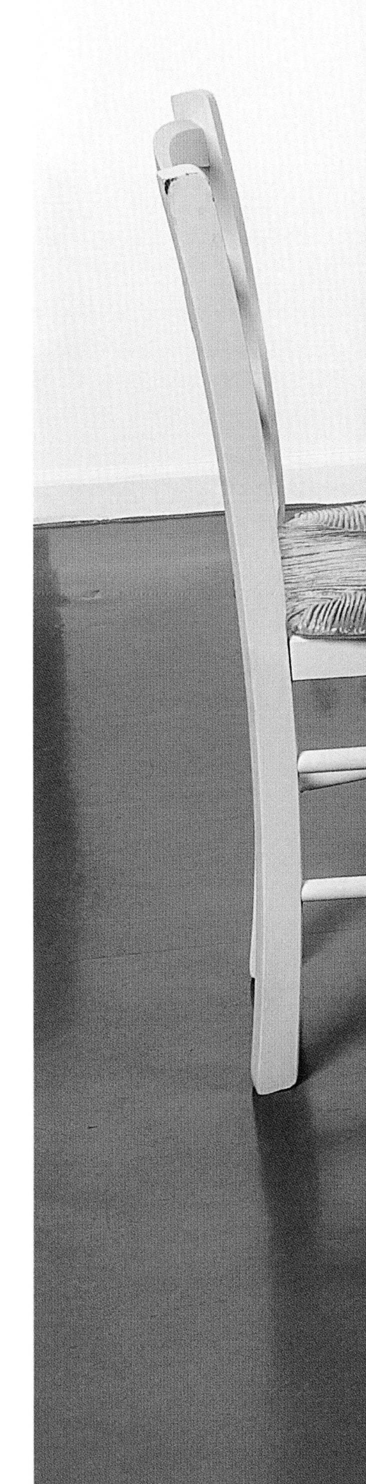

I see you are a bit nervous II, 2006
Mixed media, kiln-formed glass, wood
approx. 120 × 120 × 200 cm

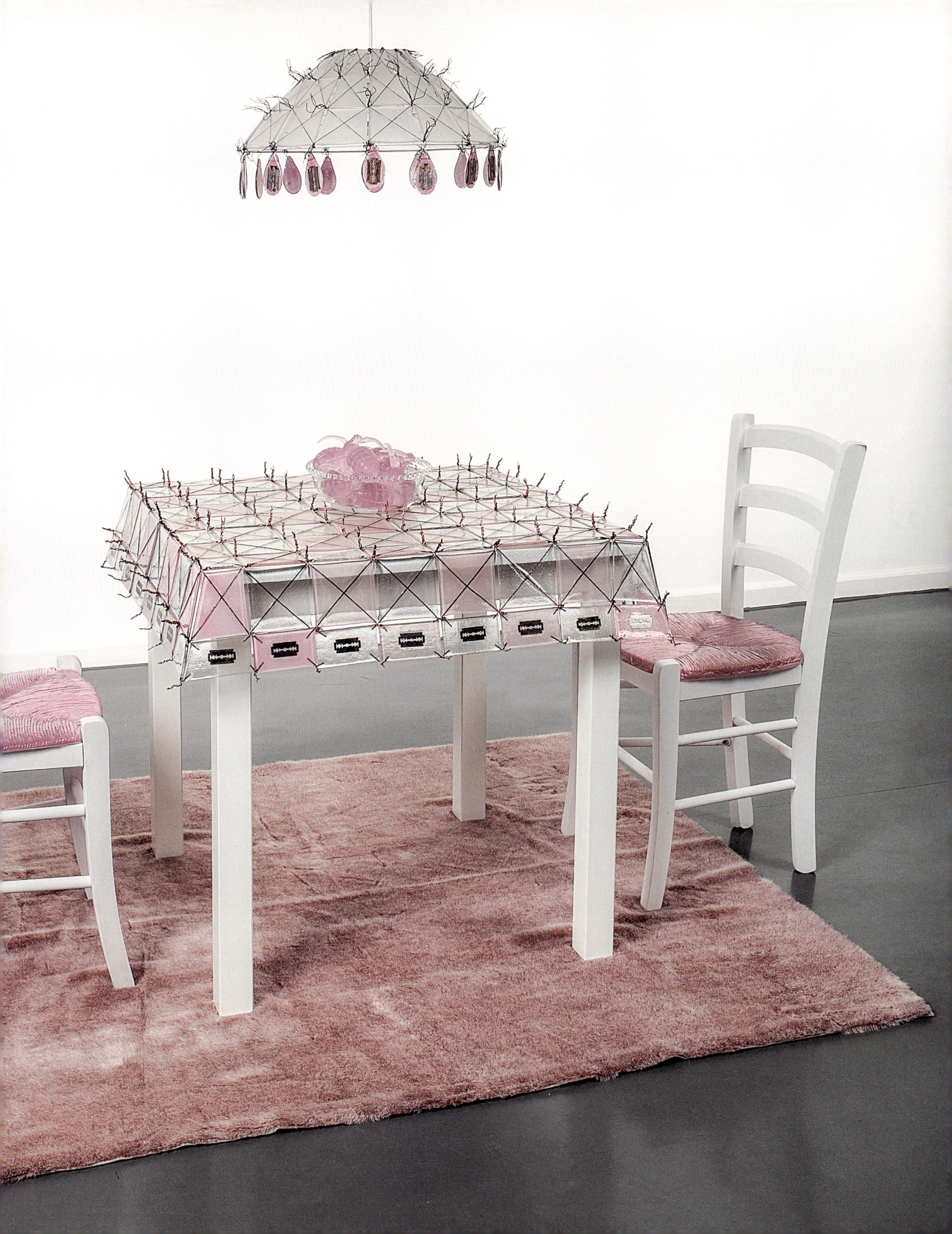

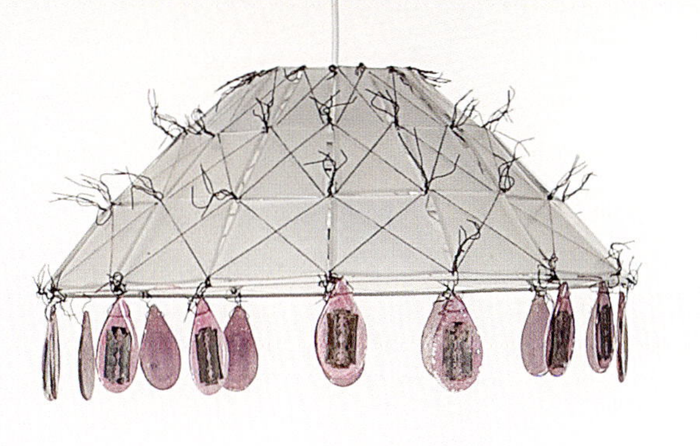

Stanislav Libenský
Jaroslava Brychtová

born 1921 in Sezemice, Czechoslovakia;
died 2002 in Železný Brod, Czech Republic
born 1924 in Železný Brod, Czechoslovakia;
died 2020 in Jablonec nad Nisou, Czech Republic

Stanislav Libenský and Jaroslava Brychtová worked together ever since meeting in Železný Brod in 1954, and in 1963 they were married.[1] Libenský and Brychtová saw glass as a sculptural material, and their works always appear solid, even when there are hollow spaces at their center. They use the technique of mold melting—never glass casting, as was once erroneously assumed. The artist couple created numerous art-in-architecture projects in the Czech Republic. In addition, Libenský directed the glass studio at the College of Applied Art in Prague from 1963 to 1987, where more than a hundred artists graduated under his supervision.[2]

The blue-gray glass sculpture *Arcus I,* dating from 1990, has an arched profile with irregular edges, in the center of which a narrow vertical opening stands out. The cast and polished glass allows light to shine through this gap, making it literally radiant.

Light is a central motif in the work of these artists, with colored light filtering through the three-dimensional bodies. Libenský came from a family of painters and Brychtová from sculptors, and those influences are readily apparent in the work of both artists. Their focus was on the immediate perception of the glass sculpture and the simultaneous perception of hollow spaces and volumes, as evoked by light.[3] *Arcus I* is a monumental abstract sculpture in which Libenský and Brychtová explore geometry and optical effects.[4] JH

Empty Throne,
1989–2004
Cast glass
90 × 70 × 26 cm

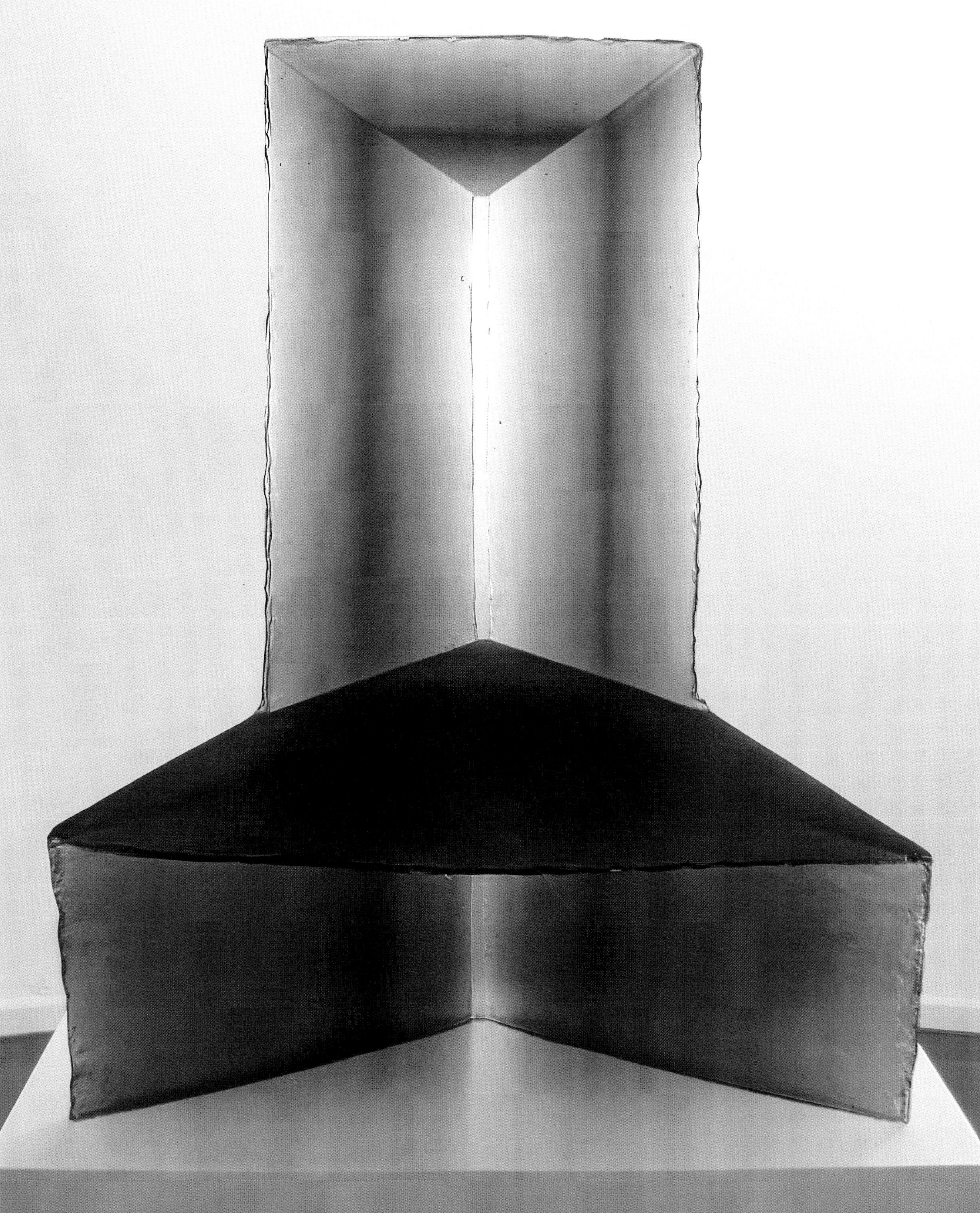

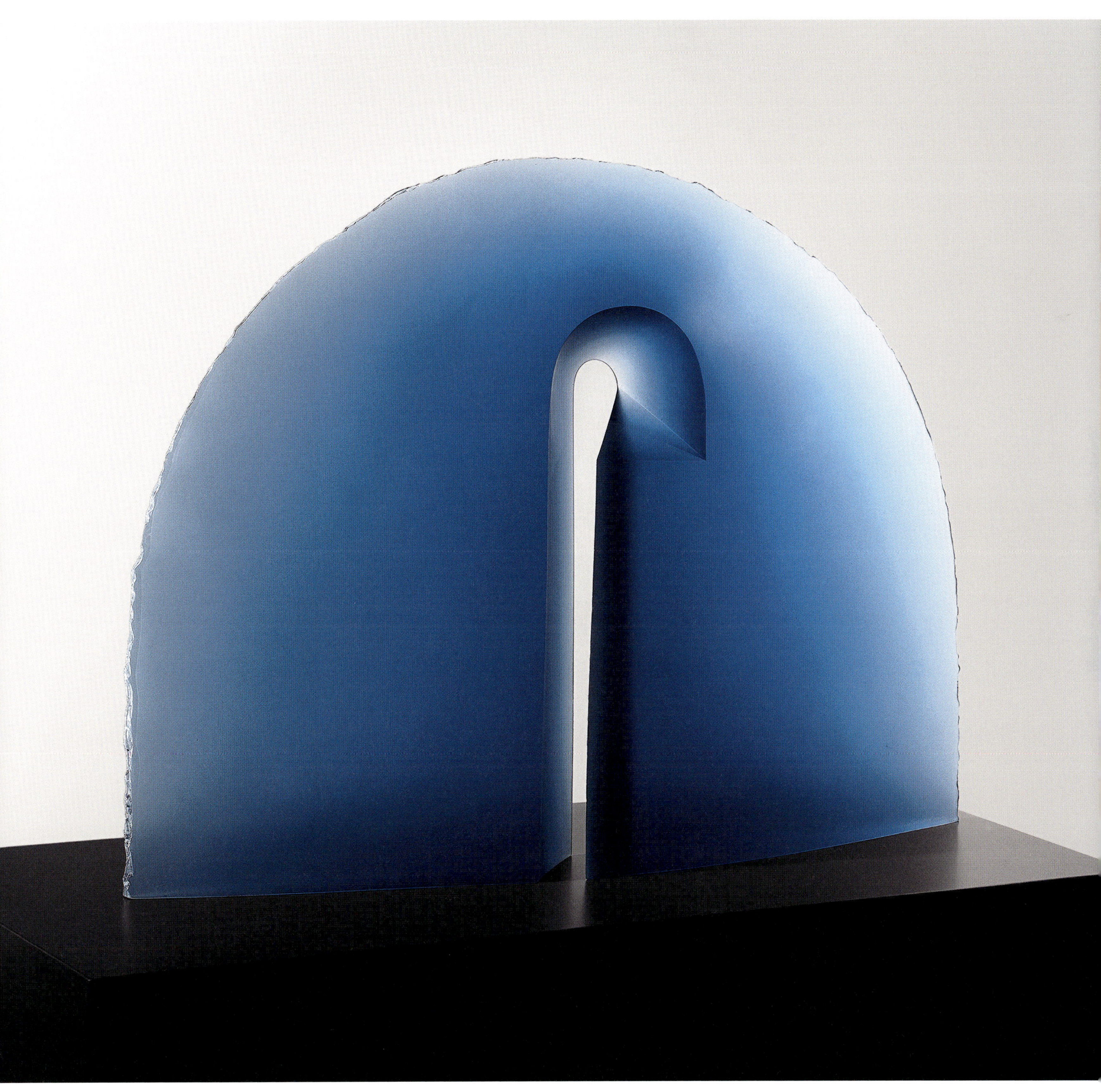

Arcus I, 1990–99
Cast glass
75 × 102 × 21 cm

Jessica Loughlin

born 1975 in Melbourne, Australia;
lives and works in Adelaide, South Australia,
Australia

Jessica Loughlin is one of Australia's most acclaimed glass artists. Alexander Tutsek spotted her extraordinary talent back at the turn of the millennium, when he acquired the arm-long punt *Between Spaces 5* as one of the earliest works for the foundation that was to bear his name. Both its boat-like shape and the handwriting place this early work firmly in a material context. Yet its striking visual effects herald Loughlin's artistic preoccupation with light and space, and show her extraordinary skill of imbuing glass with a unique sense of depth and luminosity.

Loughlin finds inspiration for her work in the vast salt plains of Lake Gairdner in South Australia, a monumental landscape that she transforms into astonishingly simple and compact visual analogies. On rare occasions, heavy rainfall floods the parched flatlands of Lake Gairdner. The punt shape of *Between Spaces 5* alludes to this natural phenomenon and reflects the deep understanding of place throughout Loughlin's work. She divided her glass barge lengthwise with a thin blue line like a flat keel. Next to it hovers a layer of handwriting: no readable words, but an overlapping rhythmic writing structure of hand-drawn characters running forward and back. This multilayered visual poetry is but one example of Loughlin's extraordinary technical dexterity. She engraved and enameled the intelligible characters on two pieces of glass, then fused them facing each other. She then added dark gray glass—itself fused onto white—and slumped the ground piece into a mold to give the work its punt-like shape.

If you lift the punt up and hold it against the light, the opaque surface turns translucent and the rockered hull expands into a wide nocturnal panorama that gently wraps around your field of vision: above a pitch-black landscape, a gray sky looms. In it, a most delicately crosshatched cloud hovers above a stretch of clear blue water far in the distance. The scribbles have turned into a cloud of mindful murmur, a flow of thought that speaks of a human presence in this empty space, of a cultural sensitivity within dull twilight. "The further we are out there, the further we go into ourselves," Loughlin quotes her fellow artist Brian Blanchflower in an early artist statement.

While the asemic writing in *Between Spaces 5* speaks eloquently of Loughlin's training in Japanese calligraphy, *Open Space* builds upon her education in Suibokuga, the art of Japanese monochrome ink painting. Completely devoid of any human traces, this work in just two hues of warm opaline is a masterful rendering of the feeling of landscape. There is a sense of above and below, of proximity and distance, of an overcast sky in heavily diffuse sunlight. The white line in the lower half of the work is not an open cut in the style of Lucio Fontana, but an inlay of opaque white glass. While this imaginary landscape has a feel of Marc Rothko's timelessness to it, Loughlin gives the balmy gray luminosity a powerful hard edge and specificity: Is the white line a stretch of glaring salt crust from Lake Gairdner? Or a last pool of rain reflecting a gleaming ray of sunlight?

A close-up view further reveals a myriad of tiny bubbles spread evenly within the glass. Loughlin masterfully created these "raindrops," dust particles, or snowflakes during fusing by spraying water onto the surface. Loughlin further enhances the sense of atmosphere and space by mounting the work about half an inch away from the wall. The semitransparency of the monochrome glass and its shadows and reflections on the wall give a real sense of the shifting light—an artistic halo around the work that the home cinema industry created artificially with LEDs as "bias lighting." JG

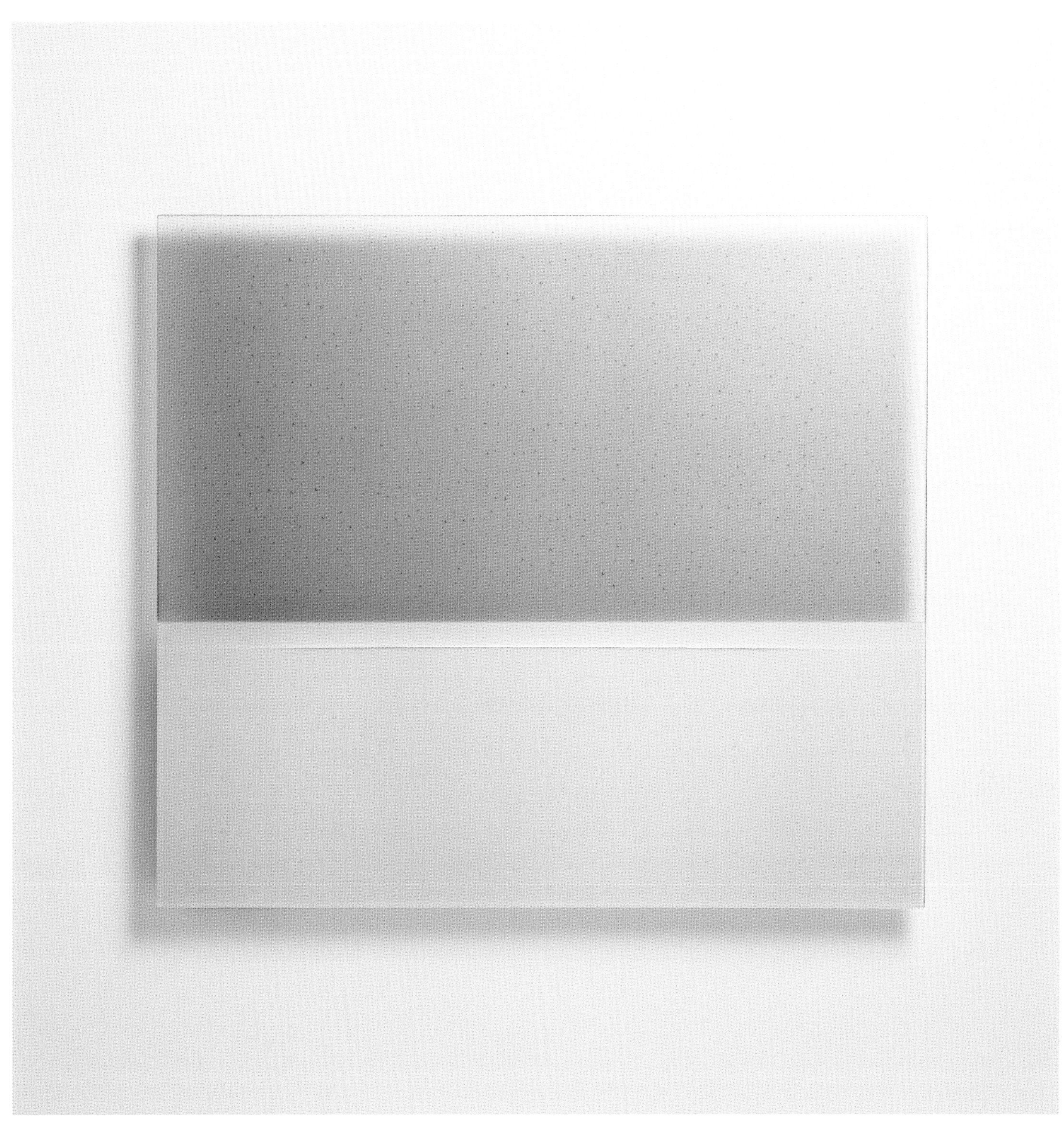

Open Space 19, 2005
Kiln-formed and wheel-cut glass
67.3 × 74 × 3.8 cm

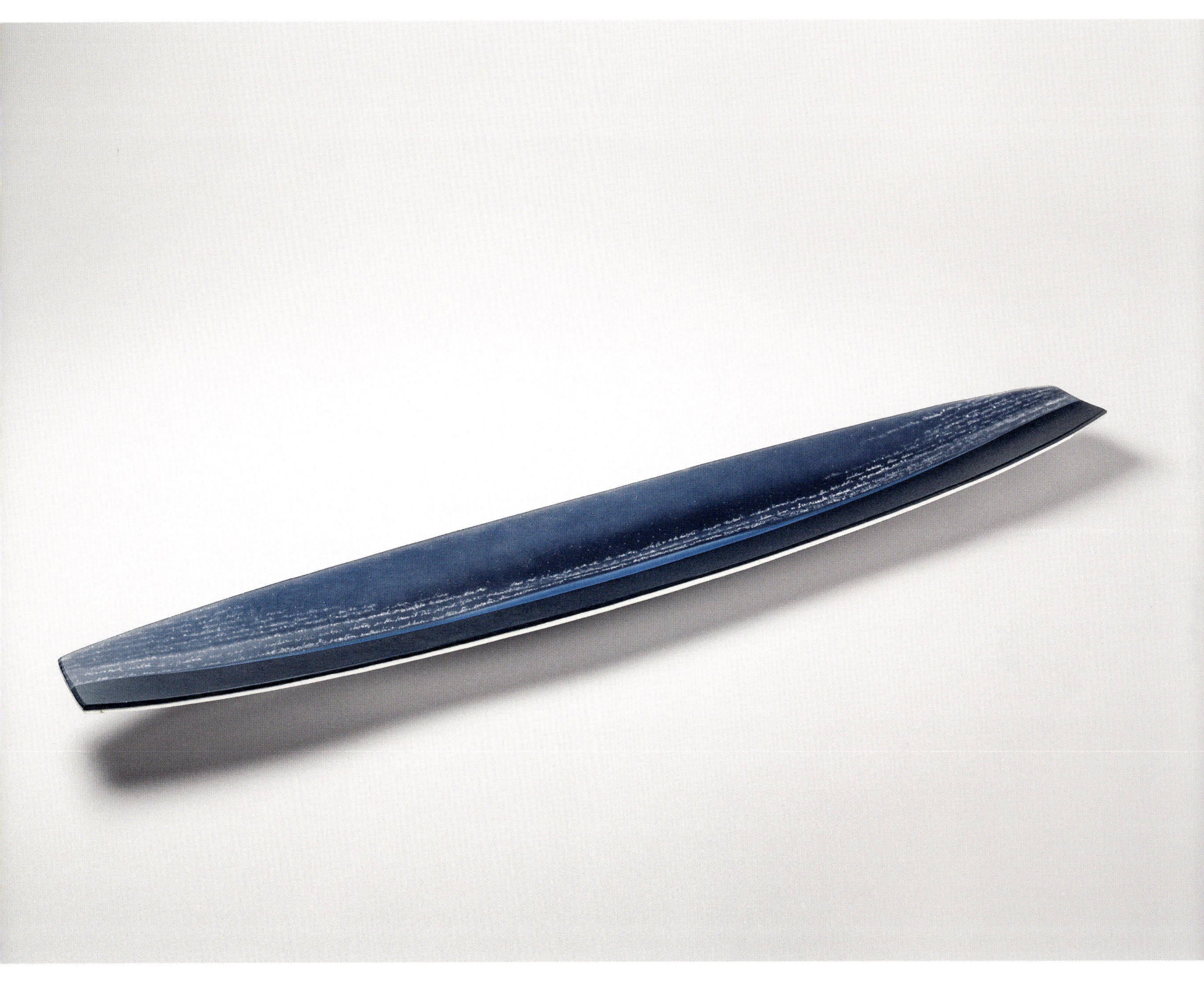

Between Spaces 5, 1999
Glass, fused, engraved, wheel-cut, slumped
81.9 × 15.9 × 4.1 cm

Haroon Mirza

born 1977 in London, UK;
lives and works in London, UK

The Pakistani British artist Haroon Mirza is internationally recognized for installations in which he orchestrates a complex interplay of light and electricity into a multilayered sensory experience. He often adds an interactive element by using pulses of electricity or light, or sometimes the motion of the viewer, to change the work. Mirza also sees himself as a composer: using sound, video, electric circuits, and everyday objects, he creates complex, multifaceted works in which the function of their components changes, as does the meaning of their cultural and social codes.

In the series titled *Solar Powered LED Circuit Compositions,* Mirza combines industrially produced solar panels, electric circuits, light, and pigment into painterly wall pieces that change with the incidence of light. As in the work *Aurora B* (2021) from this series, glass is also used in the form of solar panels, forging a connection between painting and contemporary technology, and thus referring to environmental issues as well.

"In the footsteps of Isa Genzken's aesthetic sensibility and Gerhard Richter's process-related approach, Mirza creates in his own sensitive vocabulary: compositions of technoid components paired with symbolic elements, evoking images of the aurora borealis and interstellar landscapes; similar to the serial candle paintings and canvas smudgings. The intensity of the LEDs is directly dependent upon the light incidence of the solar panel, allowing the external influences to become part of the *Solar Powered LED Circuit Composition*—the candles of the LED matrix only flicker when the light is very bright. Mirza interrogates the merging of energy and electricity of heterogeneous components, creating a closed circuit that can be understood on a conceptual and metaphorical level as an analogy of human social systems."[1]

Haroon Mirza received the Silver Lion at the 54th Venice Biennale in 2011 and the Nam June Paik Center Prize in 2014. The artist has had solo exhibitions at the New Museum, New York (2012), the Museum Tinguely, Basel (2015), and the Australian Centre for Contemporary Art, Melbourne (2019). Most recently, his works were presented at the Islamic Arts Biennale, Jeddah (2023), the Lille3000 Triennale (2022), and the Liverpool Biennale (2021). PGH

Illuminated Amanita Harvest (Solar Cell Circuit Composition 22), 2023
Solar cells, polyurethane resin, copper tape, electrical wire, magnetic wire, LED tape, miniature painting by Brishna Amin Khan, cables on glass, and anodized aluminum
146.8 × 146.8 × 7.6 cm

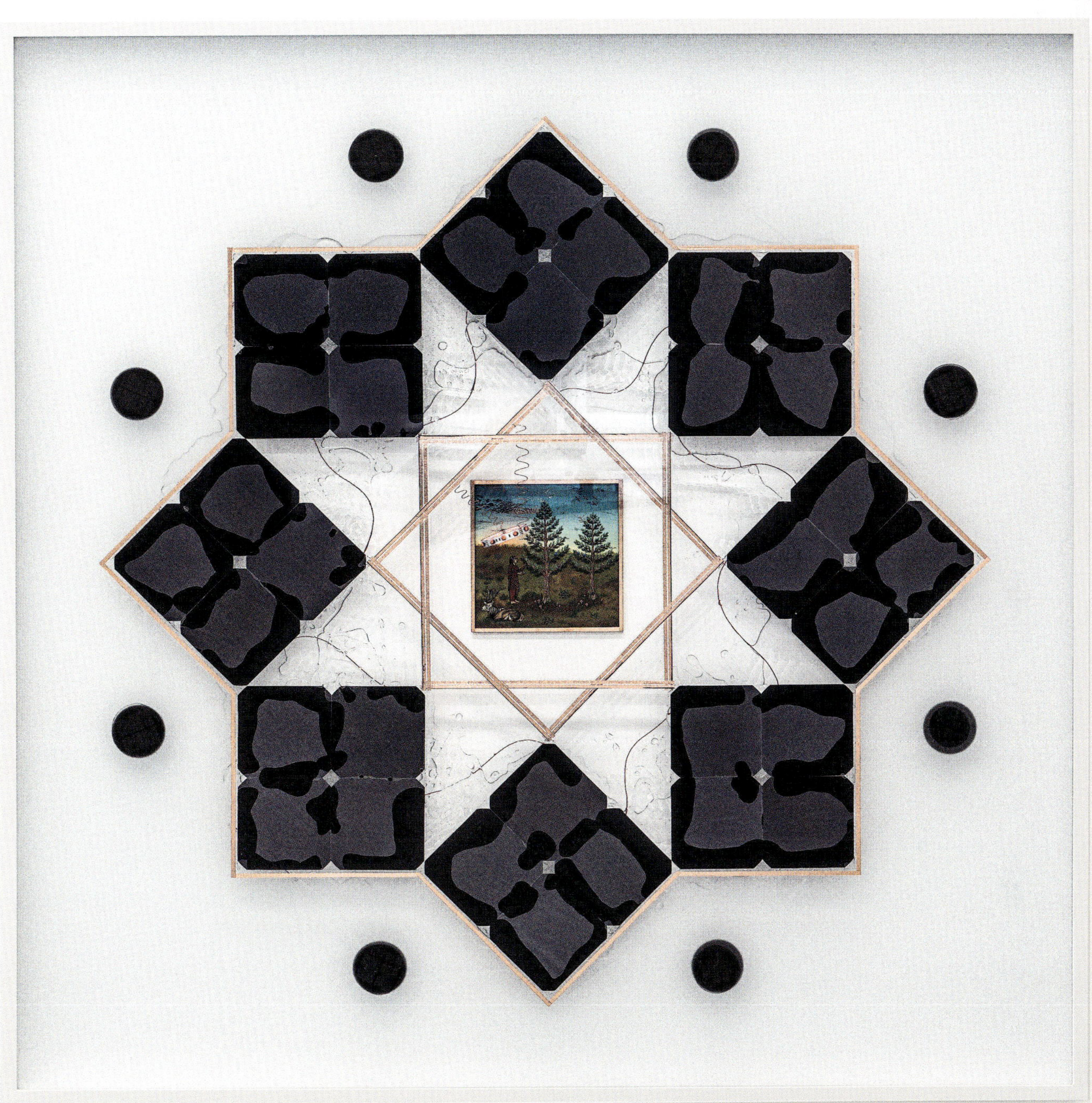

Aurora B (Solar Powered LED Circuit Composition 43), 2021
Addressable LEDs,
electrical wire, copper tape,
magnetic wire, LED matrix,
polyurethane resin,
metal pigments, acetate,
oil on canvas, and QT Py
on photovoltaic panel
164 × 100 × 8 cm

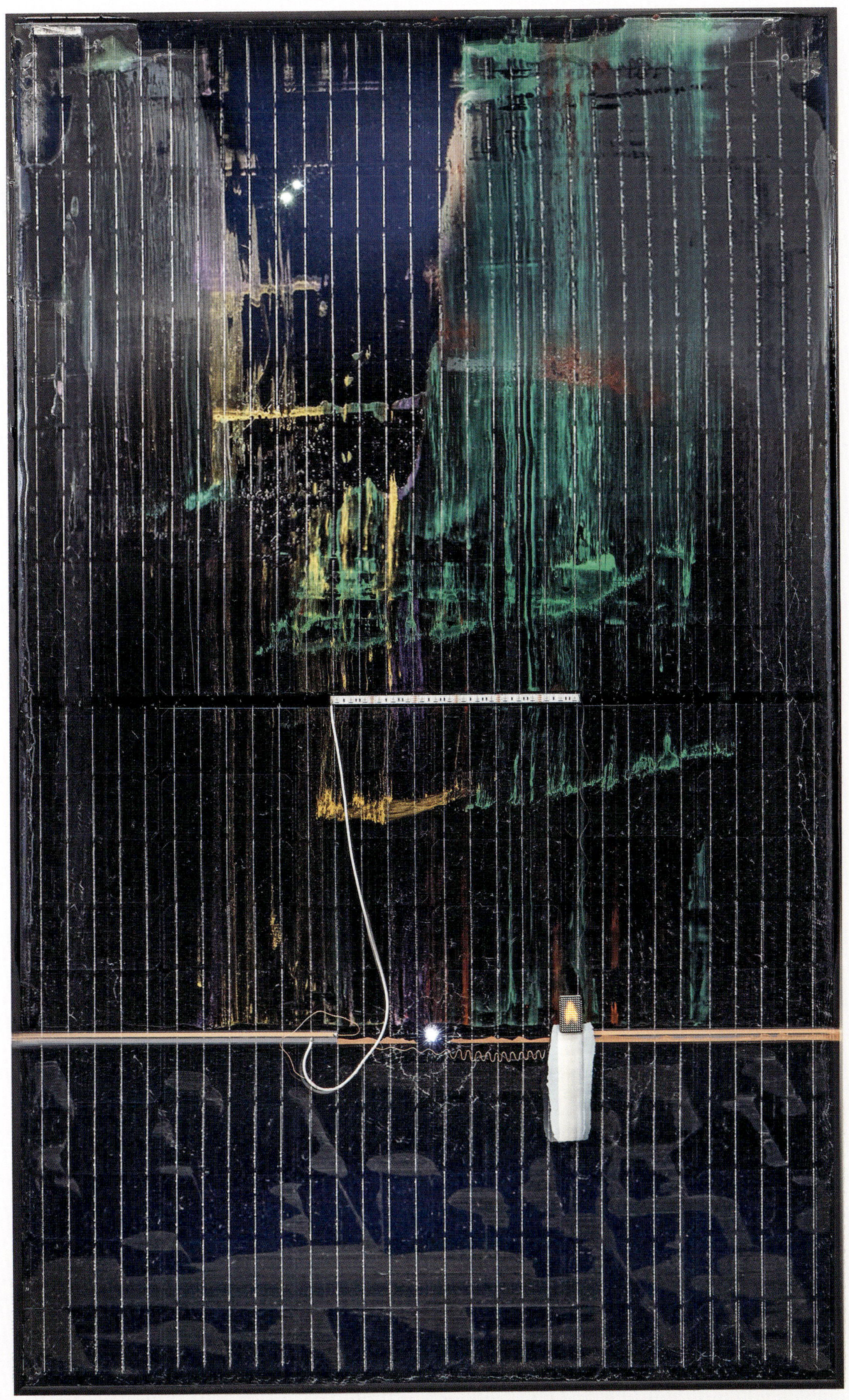

Masayo Odahashi

born 1975 in Mie, Japan;
lives and works in Japan

A young woman sits on a pedestal, her legs dangling over the edge. Her petite body is wrapped in a transparent lilac-colored dress. Turning in on herself, she keeps her gaze lowered; with a soft gesture, she holds her hands in the shape of a bowl. The tiny puddle of water that she holds like a treasure appears, however, only to those who come within a few centimeters of the small sculpture and look very carefully. Whether the woman sees her own reflection in the water or is keeping her eyes closed—perhaps in concentration so as not to lose a single drop, perhaps in a state of deep contemplation—this we cannot know.

Calm of Water V, 2004
Cast and enameled glass
50 × 17 × 18 cm

Just as soft and fragile as the glass forming this figure is the magical moment the artist has captured: the liquid seems about to run out of the woman's hands at any moment. And yet—nothing happens! Her inner calm and alert composure are transferred to her counterpart.

In this work, *Calm of Water V* (2004), the Japanese artist Masayo Odahashi has created a masterful dialogue between sensory perception and the materiality of glass—that medium which, out of the melting of sand, becomes fluid before hardening into its final form. In this case, however, the process seems to have been reversed: the gaze of the viewers transforms the glass before their eyes back into clear, flowing water. While the figure does not see but only feels, we see but do not feel.

To Odahashi, sculpting is a means of seeking self-knowledge and a way of communicating with the world that transcends language. The human body serves her as a figurative "vessel"[1]—accessible, universal, and easy to read. AB

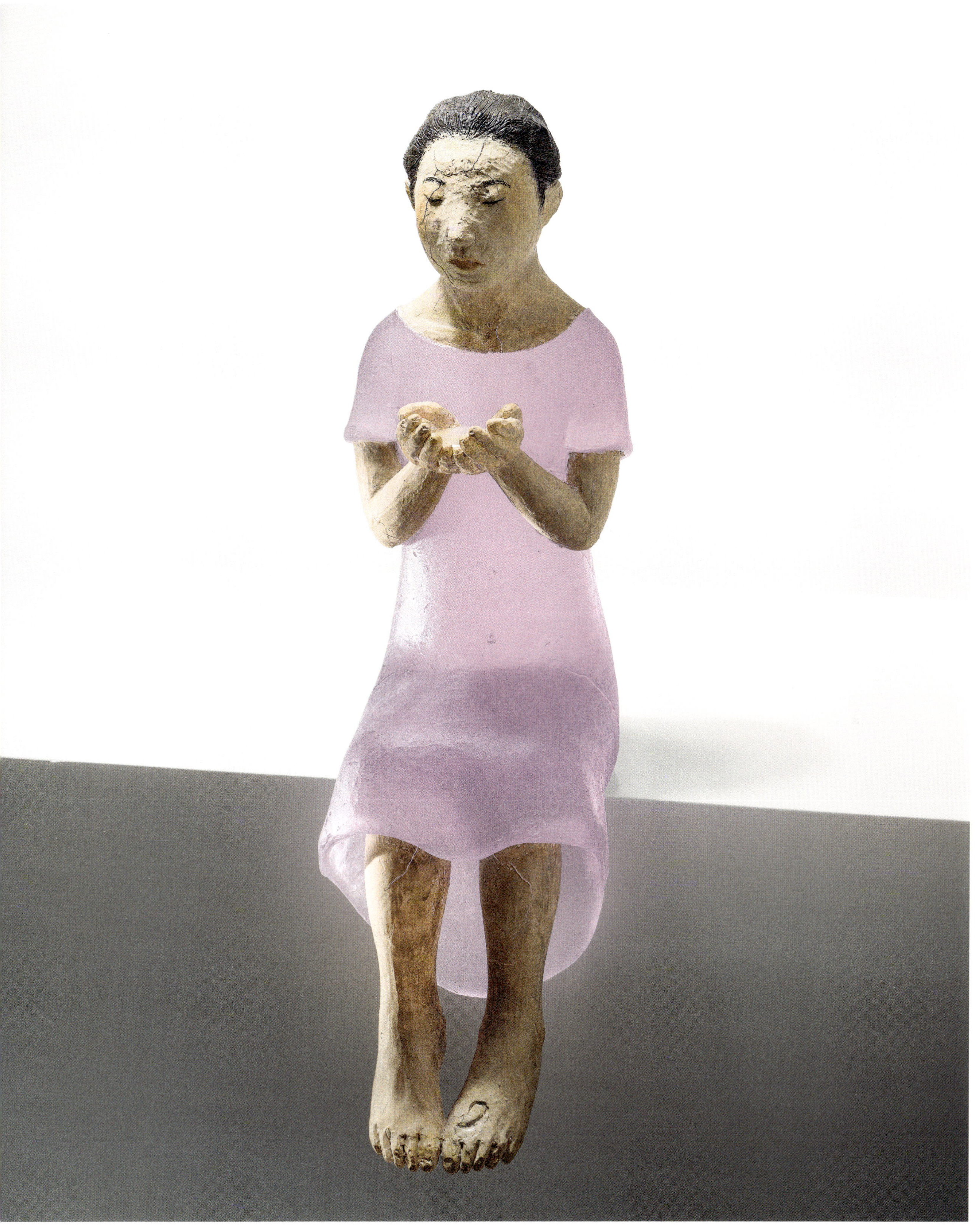

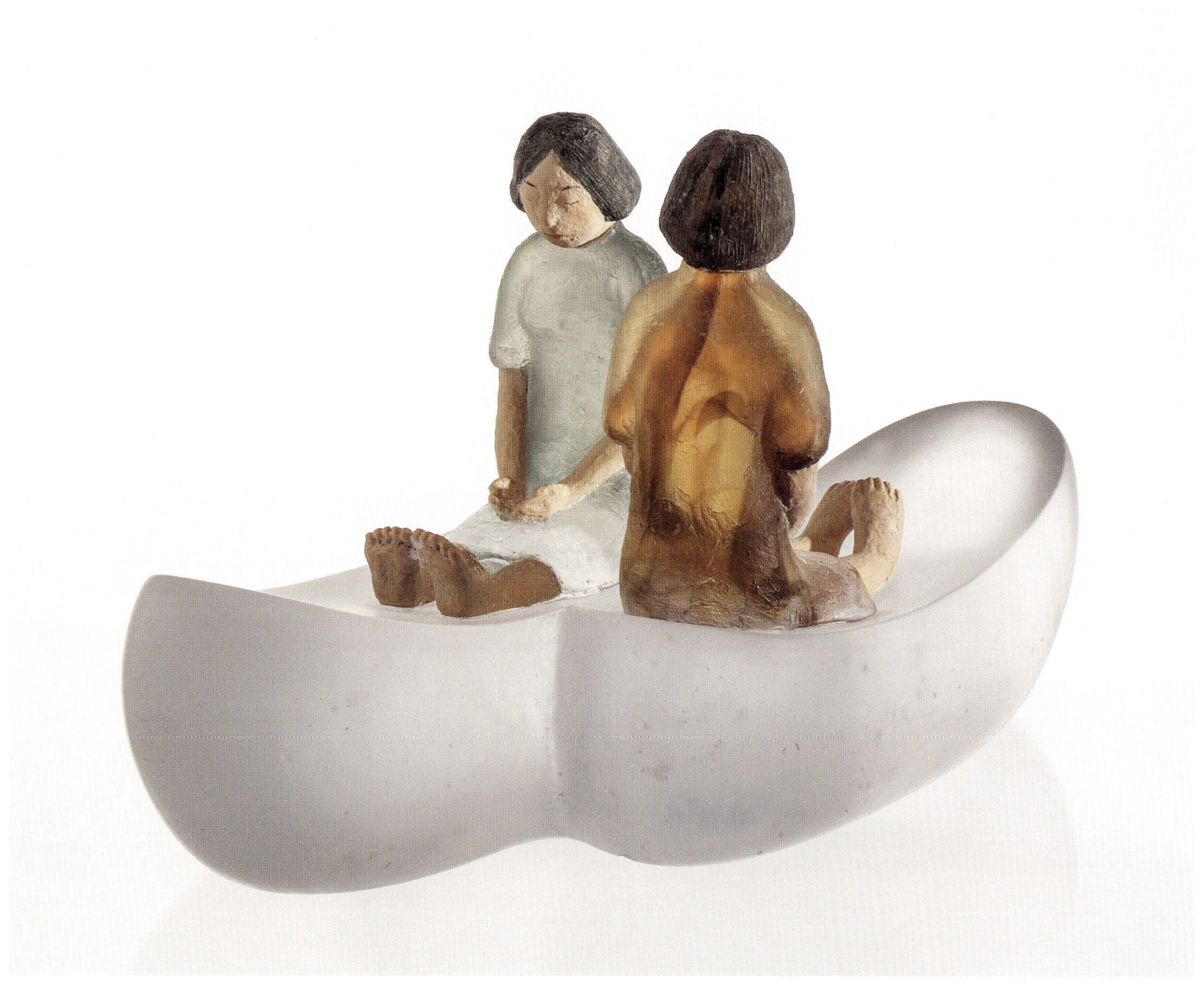

Two Directions, 2009
Cast and enameled glass
26 × 45 × 18 cm

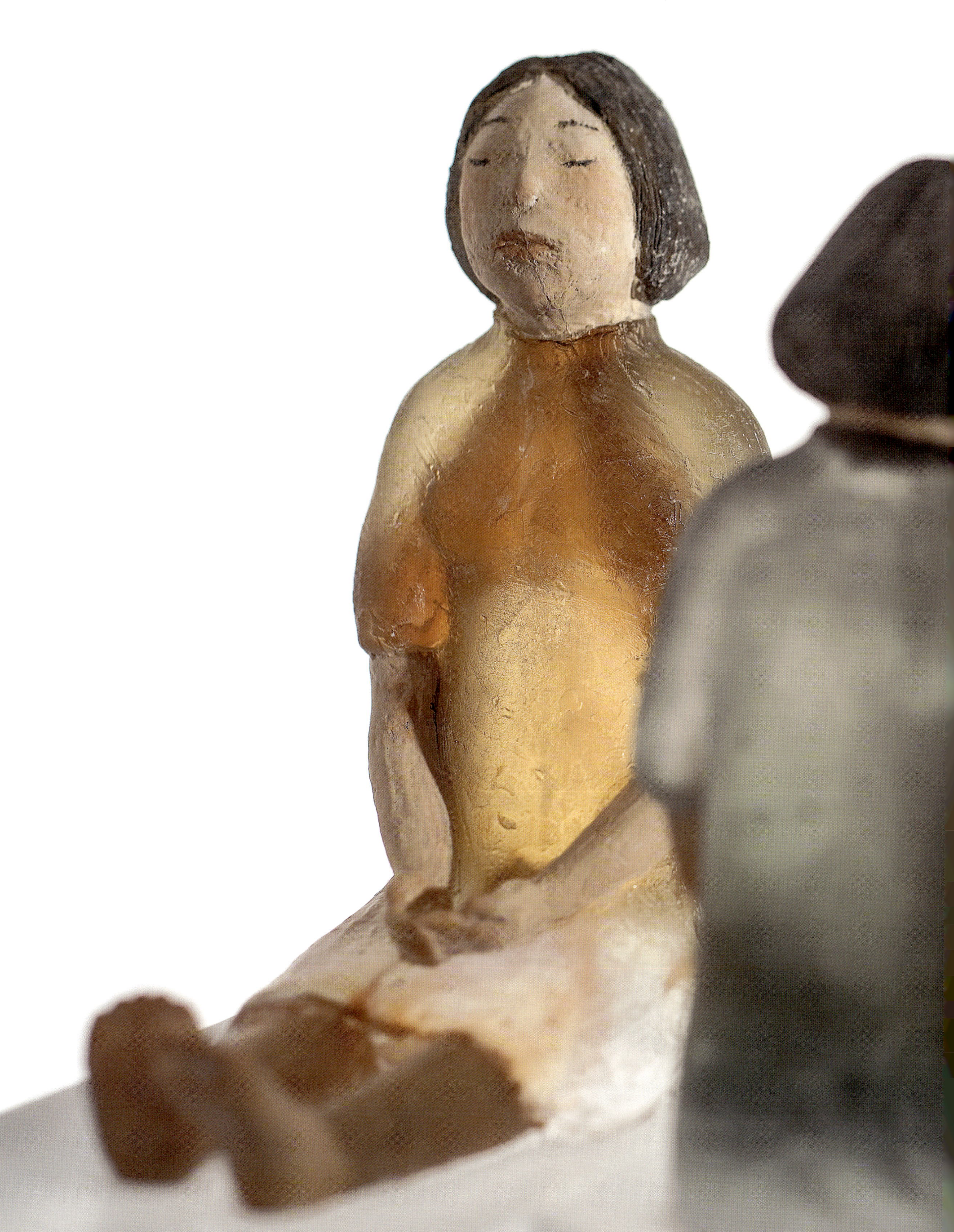

Sibylle Peretti

born 1964 in Mulheim-Ruhr, Germany;
lives and works in Germany
and in New Orleans, USA

A soft, dreamlike haze surrounds the sculpture *Twins*, made from white glass. Two life-size busts of children gently lean together with their eyes closed. The facial expressions are striking, conveying a mysterious depth and childlike innocence. An aura of communion between the two children, completely intimate and moving, almost otherworldly, surrounds the work. The matte tone of the untreated white glass is reminiscent of marble and contrasts with the transparent glass beads applied afterward that seem to emerge out of the sculpture like tears. The beads enhance the poetic and dreamy character of the work, lending it a quiet sadness as well.

Sibylle Peretti, known for her sculptures and wall installations, created *Twins* in 2002 from white glass cast in a kiln. Children are a recurring theme in her work. She writes: "I use images of children to open our eyes to a mysterious sensibility we may have lost. My children-protagonists are immaculate in their innocence, transmitting a savage view of our own isolation."[1] It is the combination of that special sensibility—and thus strength—and vulnerability that runs through Peretti's artistic exploration of the subject of children. This exploration began during her student days in Cologne, when she accidentally came across medical photographs of sick children from the 1930s and became interested in their peculiar facial expressions.[2] Although *Twins* is not directly based on those photographs, it nonetheless shows Peretti's intention of giving her child subject both vulnerability and a new, almost mystical power of resistance, achieved through the transformative process of art. Peretti's use of glass can also be understood in this sense: as a material, glass is both fragile and extremely durable. *Twins* thus becomes a symbol of all interpersonal relationships, which may be characterized both by loneliness and connectedness; at the same time, the sculpture tells of human vulnerability and resilience, inherent qualities of life. SO

Twins, 2002
Pâte de verre, glass droplets
27 × 23 × 13 cm

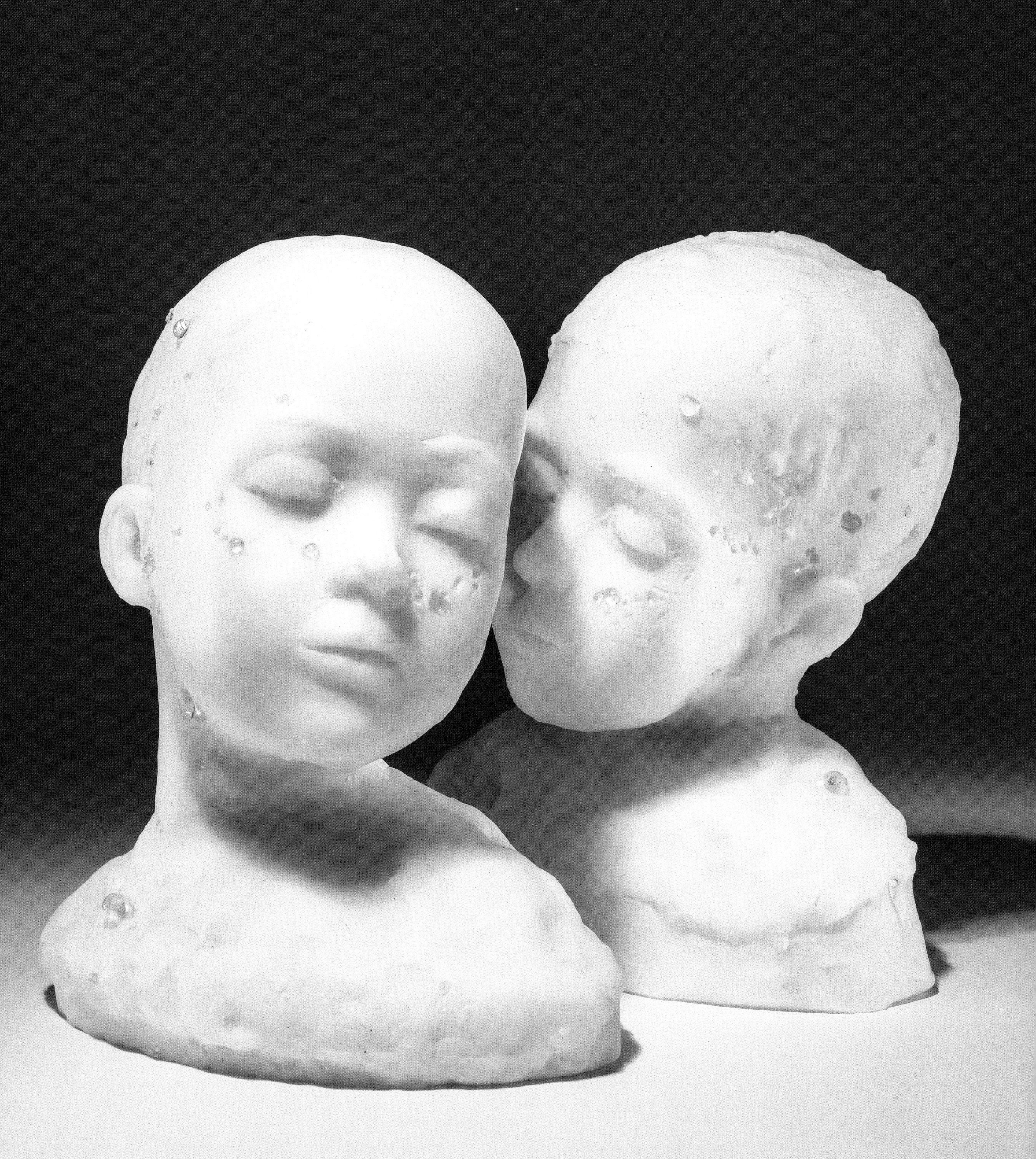

Laure Prouvost

born 1978 in Lille, France;
lives and works in Brussels, Belgium

The artist and filmmaker Laure Prouvost, known for her large-scale mixed-media installations, received the Turner Prize in 2013, represented France at the 58th Venice Biennale in 2019, and has had solo exhibitions at the New Museum, New York (2014), Haus der Kunst, Munich (2015), Palais de Tokyo, Paris (2018), Kraftwerk, Berlin (2025), and many other venues. She creates entire environments, imaginary worlds that are often bizarre and include complex narrative structures that blur the boundaries between reality and fiction.

In Prouvost's sculptures of bright colored glass, utopia and surrealism meet in ingenious ways—and with a very specific sense of humor. Her works include a series of hand-blown Murano glass creatures, which the National Museum in Oslo presented as part of a solo exhibition in 2022. Human, bird-like, and aquatic beings are intertwined, symbolizing the interconnectedness and interdependence of species in our age of climate change and global migration. Prouvost's ecological awareness is expressed in a series of works titled *We Will Keep Cool (Las Pozas)* (2024). The glass sculpture *Cooling System 3 (For Global Warming)* (2018) evokes a shower, if one views the corresponding watercolor as an instruction: a tongue-in-cheek proposal for solving global warming. In other works, Prouvost mounts female breasts made of glass on a fountain, as a kind of "water dispenser" *(GDM Drinking Fountain (For Grandad to Come Back), 2017)* or as a shower in *Cooling System 2 (For Global Warming)* (2017).

Cooling System 3 (For Global Warming), 2018
Glass, wooden stick, framed drawing
Fountain: 224 × 127 × 126 cm

"Art is mostly drawing on memories that are aroused through emotion and smell. So the narrator's voice wants to create a moment of comfort, coziness, or heat. At the same time, it raises questions about the work: how does that make us feel sweaty, how do we trick our brain?"[1] PGH

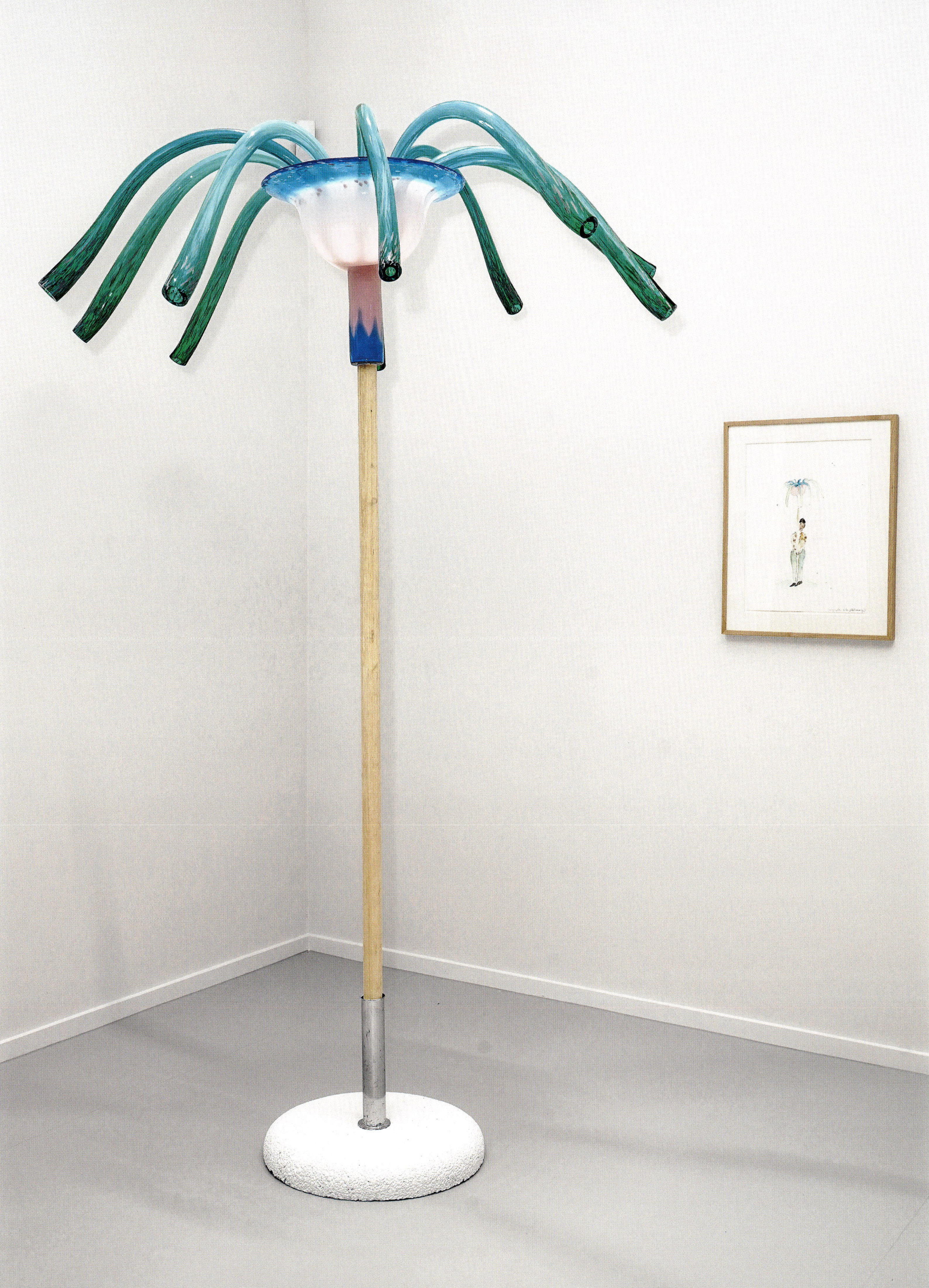

Colin Reid

born 1953 in Cheshire, UK;
lives and works in Gloucestershire, UK

Colin Reid's *Ring of Fire R1739* (2013) demonstrates his mastery in the area of kiln-cast glass, reinforcing his reputation, even beyond England, as one of the leading artists working in cast glass. His large-format sculptures made from optical glass captivate the viewer through their brilliant purity, radiant color palette, and simple yet significant forms. The best example of this may be *Ring of Fire R1739*, for which he received the prestigious Alexander Tutsek-Stiftung Prize for Senior Artists (aged forty-five and older) at the Coburg Glass Awards. This monumental flat ring has a staggering diameter and is formed from blazing red, wafer-thin leaves encased in optical glass. Through their varying curvatures, they possess a dynamic and almost organic quality of movement, entrancing the viewer.

Colin Reid is a patient perfectionist who has refined the process of producing his artworks down to the last detail, optimizing it through innovation. Due to the size of his works, he uses an extended firing process that generally takes about three weeks—yet even then, the work is not complete. The pieces continue to develop through multiple stages of cold-state work such as grinding, polishing, and sandblasting until they achieve a certain level of quality that speaks to him. Chance also plays a role in this process: "The tension between what is planned and controlled and what is unexpected can be both creative and disastrous."[1] He draws inspiration from everything around him that touches him spiritually, above all the natural environment: "If I were to identify a single thread that runs through my work it would be the influence of nature. That is the source to which I return for inspiration and fresh material for my work."[2]

After training at St. Martin's School of Art in London, Reid initially found employment as a "scientific glassblower" until he returned to his artistic path and completed a degree in glass at Stourbridge College of Art in Stourbridge, UK. He has exhibited internationally at renowned institutions and art fairs, and his works are now represented in more than fifty museum collections worldwide. KW

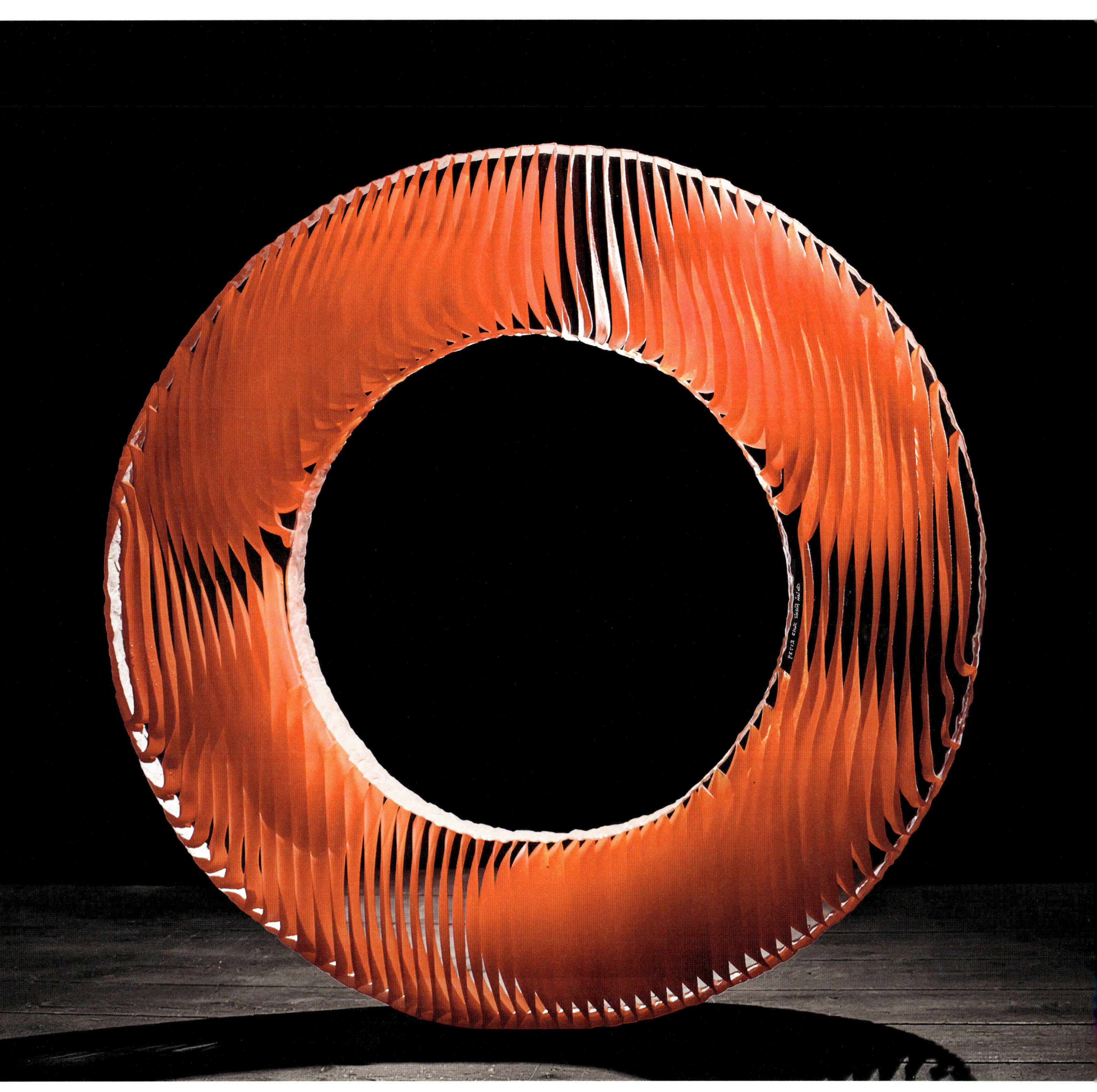

Ring of Fire R1739, 2013
Kiln-cast glass, ground, polished
91 × 92 × 10 cm

Gizela Šabóková

born 1952 in Nové Zámky, Czechoslovakia;
lives and works in Prague, Czech Republic

In stark contrast to her often massive, seemingly rigid sculptures, the renowned Czech artist Gizela Šabóková herself appears to be in constant motion: restless and tireless, filled with a drive for action and boundless curiosity. She uses various materials, such as glass, metal, and cast iron, while testing the boundary between sculpture and architecture and constantly exploring the possibilities offered by public spaces.[1]

She began her career in the 1980s as a painter, using not only canvas but also plate glass as a surface for her art. Soon enough, however, she felt an increased desire to release painting from its two-dimensionality and bring it into harmony with three-dimensional forms. This led her to sculpture. Šabóková began to fire glass, to cast and cut it, thus creating new forms of images that play with apparent contradictions such as surface and depth, light and shadow, and technical simplicity versus formal details. The search for a harmonious combination of stained glass and glass sculpture remains an essential part of her work today. And yet Šabóková firmly rejects stylization without content, mere formalism—she always strives for authenticity and content.

The Slim One, 1998
Cast glass
70 × 12 × 12 cm

Despite achieving international success, Šabóková still works without the support of a large team. Sharing her creative energy and standing at her side, both professionally and personally, is her husband, Karel Bartoníček. Over weeks, months, or even years, the two will return to a work and continue to refine it until it finally embodies the precise meaning that Šabóková intends.

Numerous works by Šabóková are now in major collections, including the Musée des Arts Décoratifs in the Louvre. For her artistic achievements, she has been decorated by institutions across the globe, including being given the main prize at the Vessels museum awards in Koganezaki, Japan, in 2000. In her decades-long role as a teacher, she has been passing on her extensive knowledge to the next generation of glass artists. AB

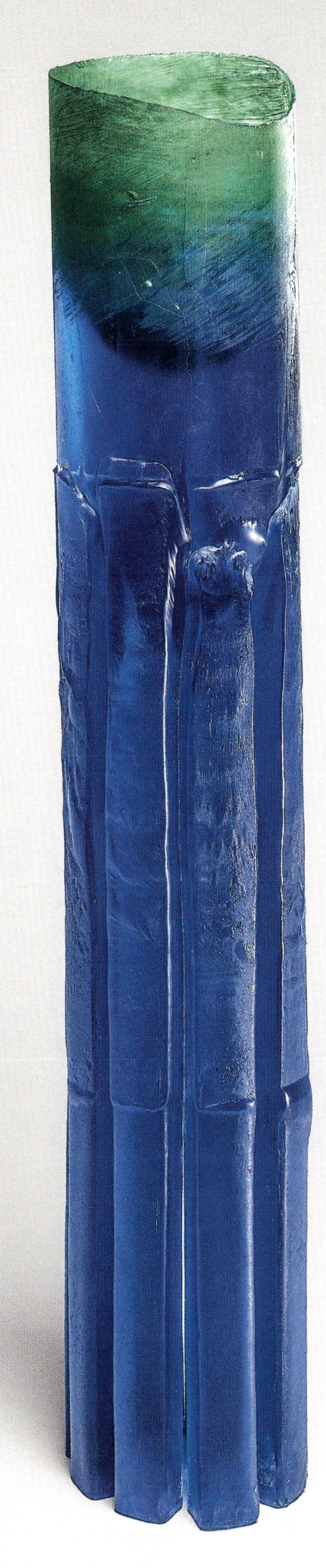

Anri Sala

born 1974 in Tirana, Albania;
lives and works in Berlin, Germany

Anri Sala works across a range of media, including video, photography, and installations. In his exploration of sound in all its dimensions, he intertwines image, sound, and architecture, merging the faculties of seeing and hearing. This approach led to his series of works titled *No Window No Cry,* which began with a small music box fixed onto glass; when activated, it plays a rendition of the song "Should I Stay or Should I Go?" by The Clash. First designed for the Centre Pompidou in Paris, the work was installed directly onto one of the windows facing outside, so that, being at ground level, it would attract the eyes and ears of pedestrians *(No Window No Cry (Richard Rogers and Renzo Piano, Centre Pompidou, Paris),* 2012). Sala later reconstructed this window for the exhibition *Architecture into Art: A Dialogue* at the Fundación Botín Art Centre building in Santander, Spain, thus forging a connection between the windows of the first famous museum, designed by Renzo Piano, and that of the newer one, the Centro Botín.[1] It was in this context that *No Window No Cry (Luigi Cosenza, la fabbrica Olivetti, Pozzuoli)* (2015) was created, as a vertical glass sheet in a metal frame, positioned like a large, freestanding window within the space, transforming the glass from an architectural element into sculpture. It also supports a small music box that, when manually operated, plays the song by The Clash. "What I am interested in is the way in which sound can be infused with reality. ... The visitor must be able to approach the works without necessarily knowing everything, allowing themselves to be carried away, open and willing to experience moments of loss of daily gravity. It is a form of release. They must give experience time to build."[2]

Through his multichannel sound and video installations, Sala, who was honored with the Young Artists Prize at the Venice Biennale in 2001, explores how to create musical compositions within the architectural conditions of exhibition spaces. This is exemplified by such works as *Ravel Ravel* and *Unravel* for the French Pavilion at the Venice Biennale (2013) and *The Present Moment* at the Haus der Kunst in Munich (2014–15). PGH

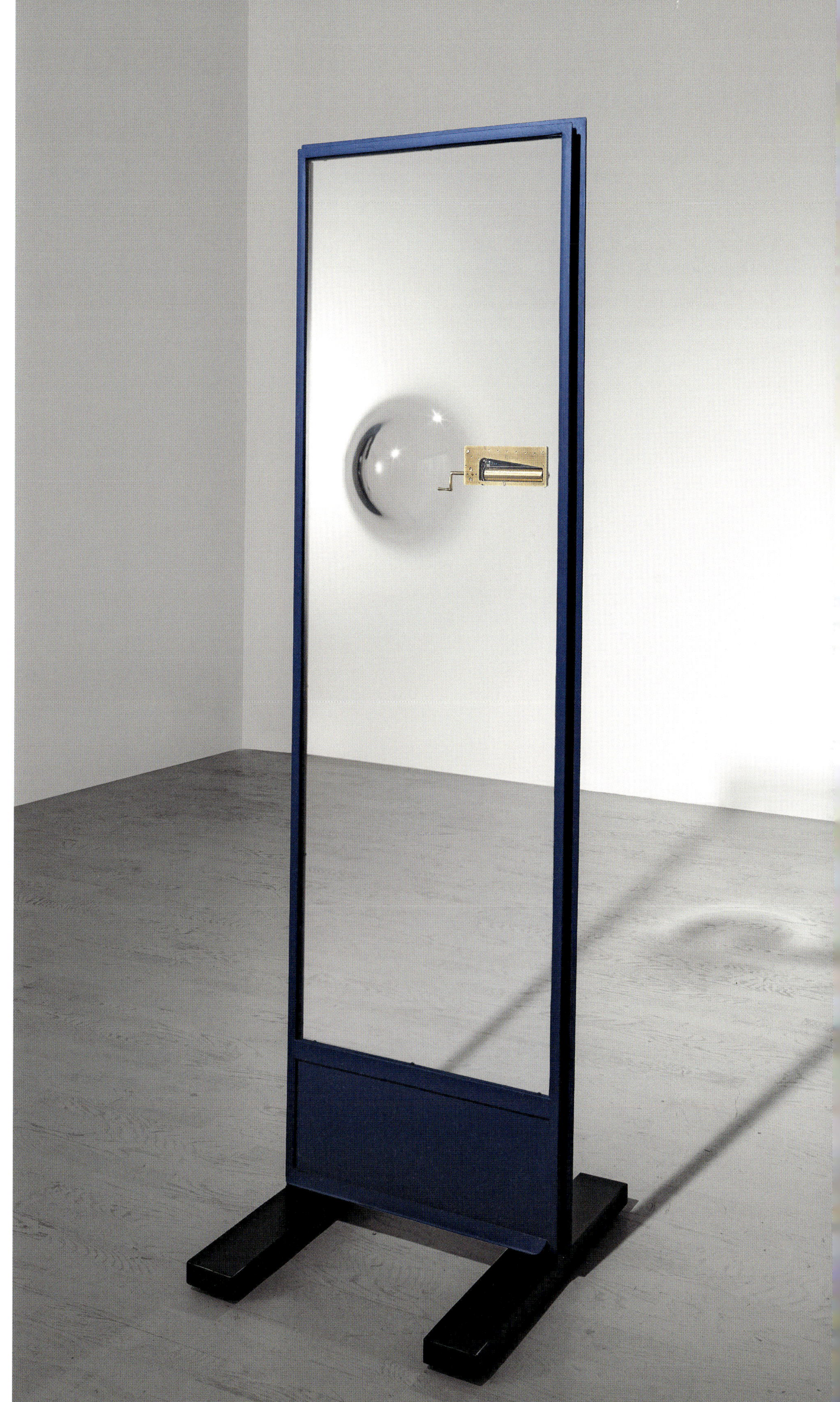

No Window No Cry
(Luigi Cosenza, La Fabbrica
Olivetti, Pozzuoli), 2015
Music box, glass, metal,
window frame
202.5 × 60 × 3.5 cm

Masahiro Sasaki

born 1969 in Nagoya, Japan;
lives and works in Nagoya, Japan

Bone-like, twisted into helices, visually captivating—forms reminiscent of paleontological relics. Perhaps the fossilized spine or the hardened skin of a prehistoric animal? Yet Masahiro Sasaki's works are just as likely to resemble dynamic, far-reaching climbing plants, captured in a fleeting moment between movement and stillness. The volumes of these works alternate between open and closed, as though concealing or revealing an invisible inner core.

Sasaki studied glass art at the Aichi University of Education and the Toyama Institute of Glass Art. However, since Japan does not have a distinct glass tradition of its own, colleges there since the 1970s mainly taught and practiced the Western studio glass movement. This one-sided education led Sasaki to question his own identity: What does it mean to be a Japanese glass artist? While his training was heavily focused on conceptual approaches, he discovered a new perspective through the philosophy of Japanese *kogei* (handcrafts), in which the creative process begins with the realization that each material has its own character, even its own spirit.[1]

Tensei 0911, 2009
Blown glass, sandblast
30 × 31 × 73 cm

Inspired by this idea, Sasaki developed a way of working that does not aim to create a predetermined form. Instead, he is led by an understanding of the material and his own intuition. Without a clear motif in view, his works develop gradually through a process of blown glass vessels that he works on intuitively through feeling and experience. This involves another principle of his method: the *tensei* that gives the finished objects their names.[2] This term means something like "metamorphosis" and is often used to allude to reincarnation. Under extreme heat, sand is transformed into glass, and a part of it becomes sand again under the impact of the sandblaster. According to Sasaki, he, too, is part of this cycle—of this ongoing transformation through fire and wind.[3] AB

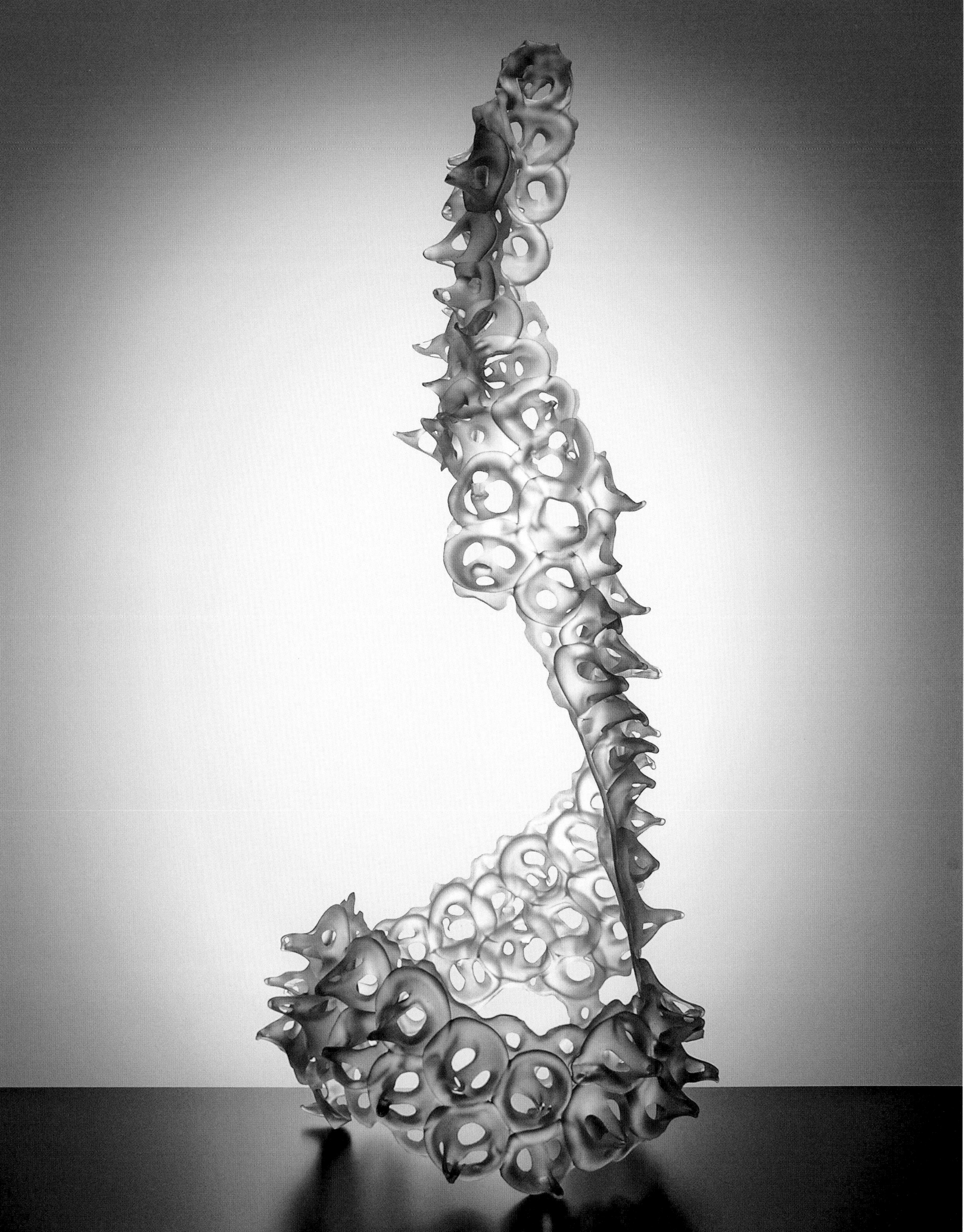

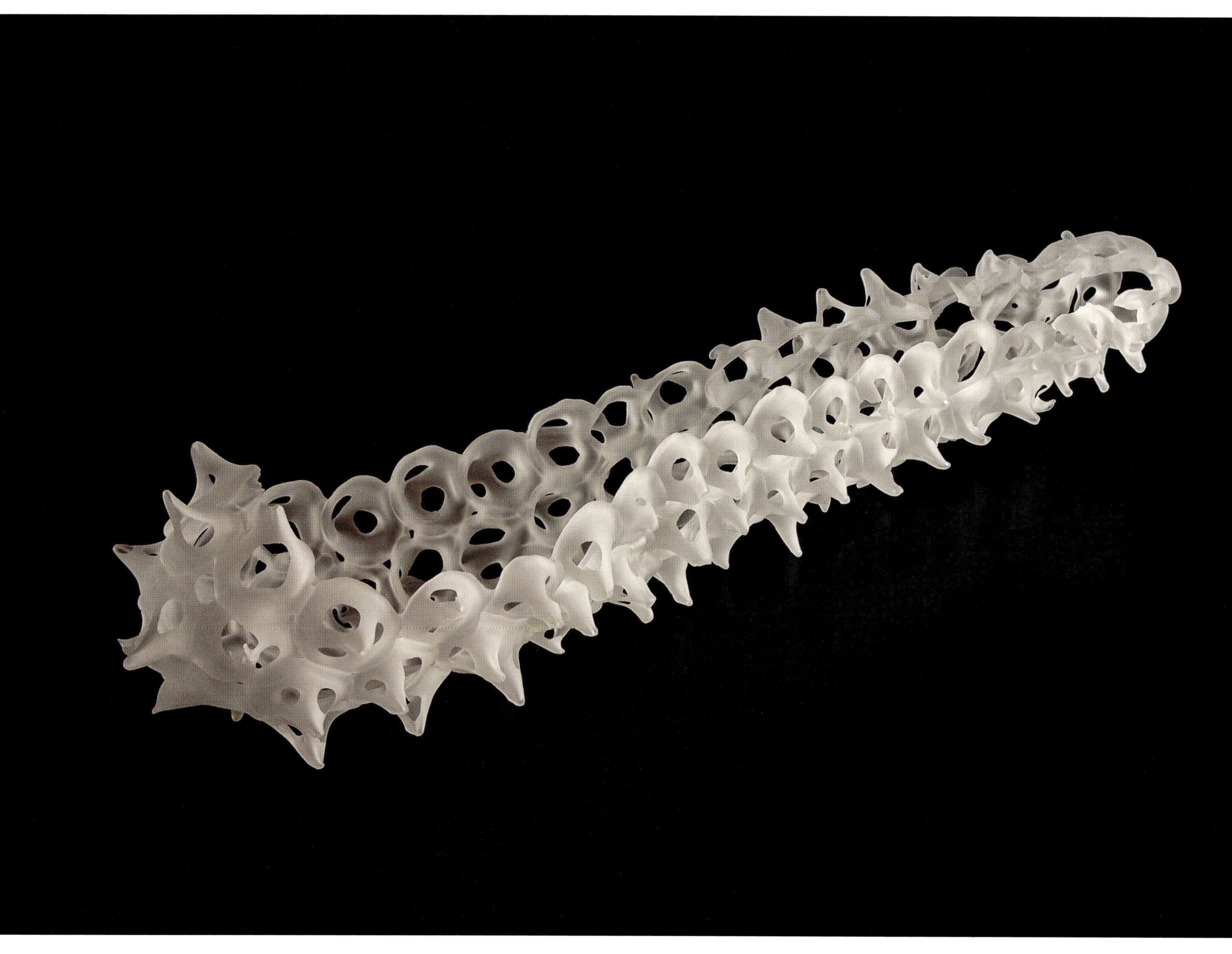

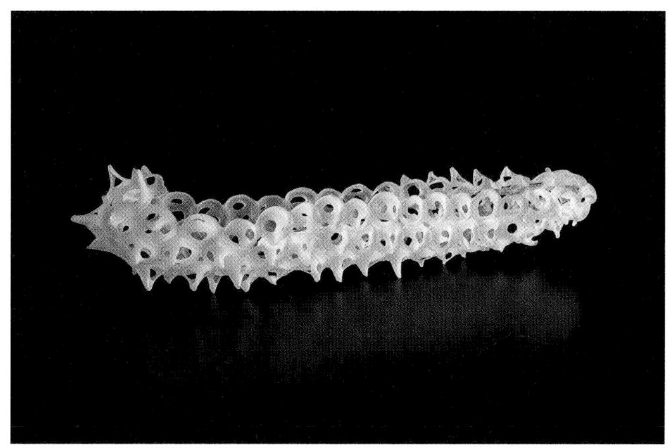

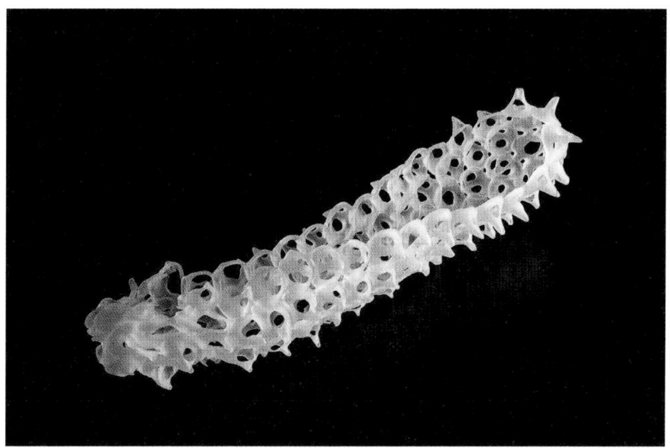

Tensei 1108, 2011
Blown glass, sandblast
71 × 19 × 19 cm

Alejandra Seeber

born 1968 in Buenos Aires, Argentina;
lives and works in New York, USA and
Buenos Aires, Argentina

The Argentinian artist Alejandra Seeber has first and foremost been a painter. The close attention she pays to everyday subjects represents a central theme in her multifaceted paintings: employing a rich palette, she places these subjects on canvas as if through spontaneous movements. Her work mixes abstract and expressive forms with figurative elements, often creating architectural spaces. In 2009, she translated this theme of observing the world into a new medium for the first time. She created glass sculptures, "speech bubbles," transparent and empty, hanging from the ceiling, as if to be filled by the viewer with words and thoughts, memory and history. The installation, which was shown at the Fundación PROA in Buenos Aires, was titled *Dialogville* (2009).

Suspended in space, the three sculptures, which the artist created in the workshops of Murano, have an almost painterly surface. It seems as though they are inviting us to replace the absence of speech with dialogue, be it political, philosophical, or personal. Coming from the world of comics, it is only natural that these *Speech Bubbles* communicate with our thoughts in a playful way. PGH

Speech Bubble (iride), 2014
Murano glass and steel cable
39 × 48 × 20 cm

Speech Bubble (verde iride), 2014
Murano glass and steel cable
46 × 33 × 18 cm

Speech Bubble (opalina), 2014
Murano glass and steel cable
45 × 62 × 20 cm

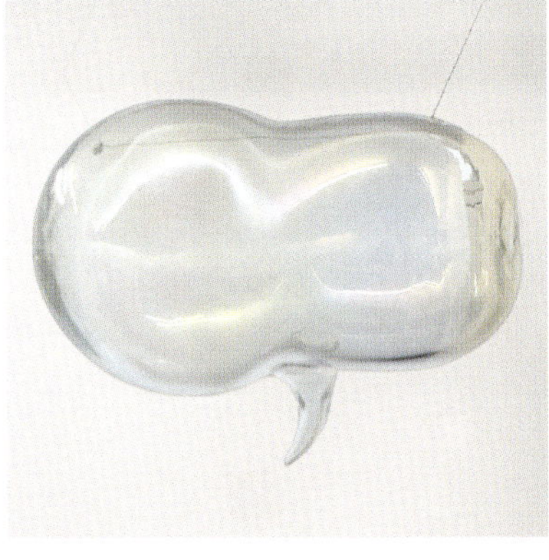

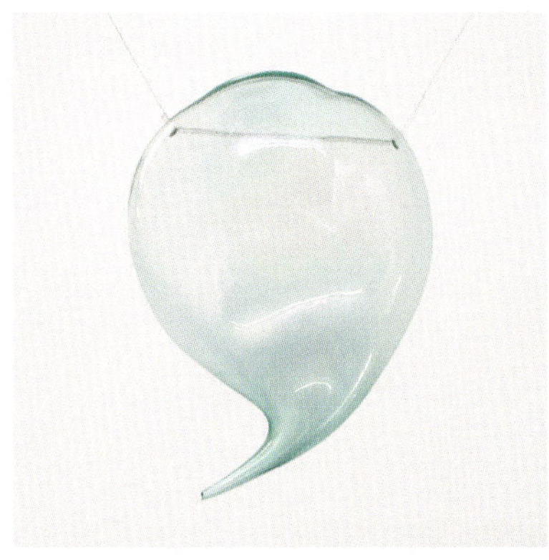

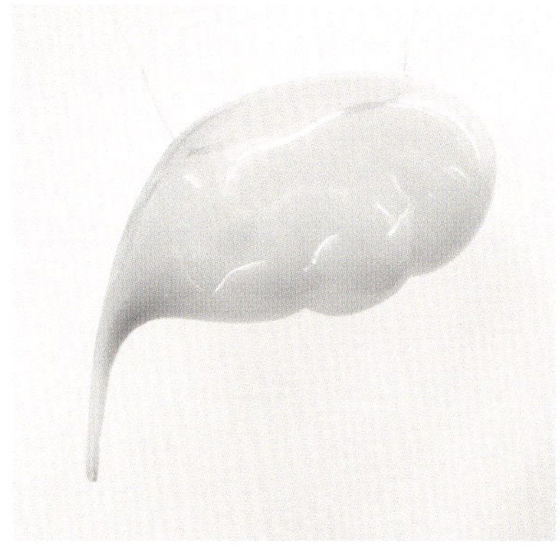

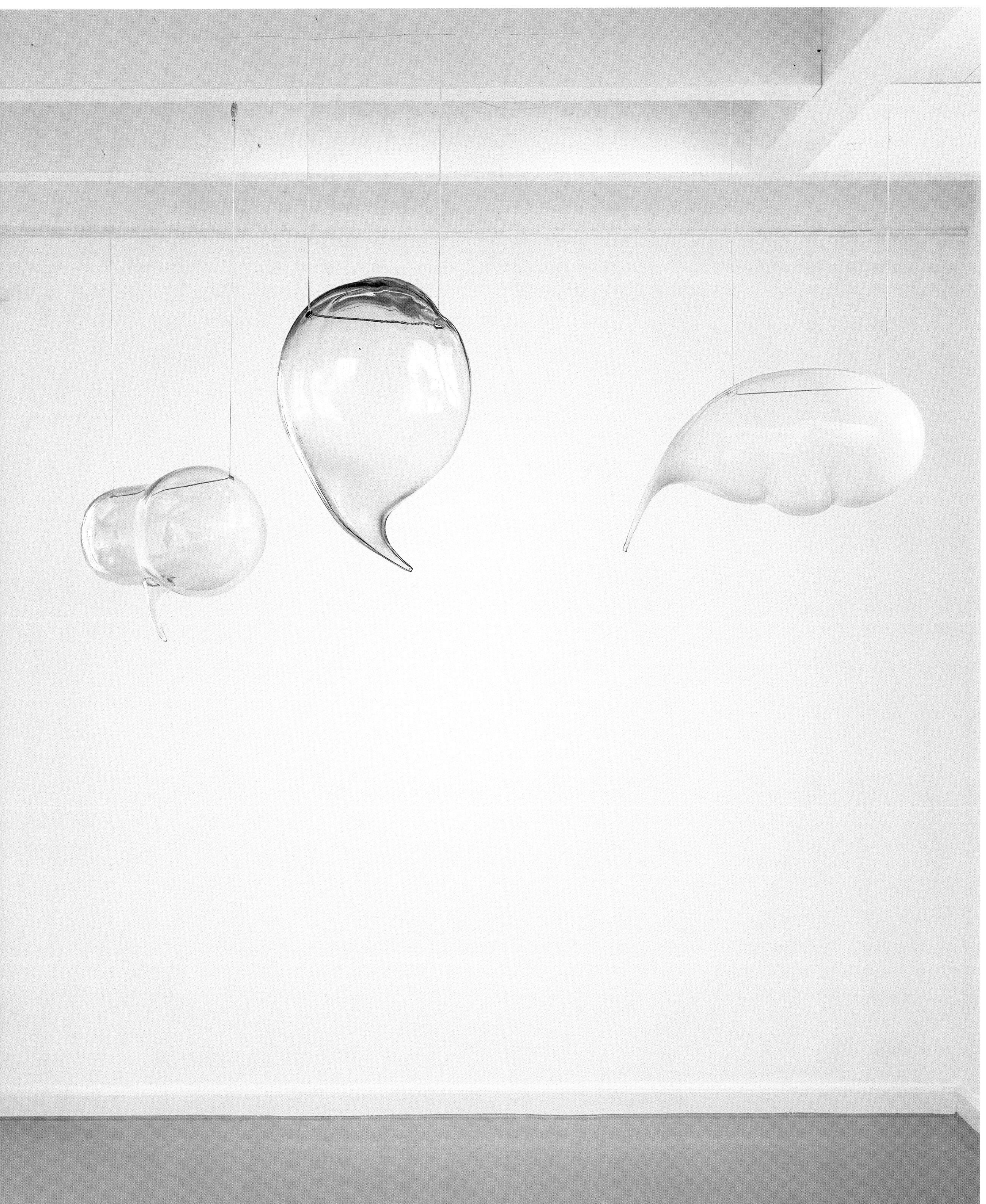

Eric Sidner

born 1985 in Houston, Texa, USA;
lives and works in Berlin, Germany

The hanging sculpture of blown glass, brass, and cast bronze is a vision of the imagination, playful and happy in its colors and forms, even to the point of being grotesque. Eric Sidner, working together with craftspeople, created this work in the Czech Republic using centuries-old methods of Bohemian glass manufacturing. *Drops* (2022), which weighs close to 80 kilograms, is a work that belongs to a series of glass sculptures that comprise both figurative and abstract elements and are held together by bronze suspensions. Inspired by a variety of sources and a wide range of imagery, they often feature anatomical forms referring to the human organism, including arteries, blood, the heart, and life energy. "The thematization of air and a logic of circulation unite these works, with their interconnected blown-glass vessels, representing human, vegetal, and animal forms."[1]

The piece includes recognizable forms, such as white gloves hanging down and its resemblance to a chandelier, as well as the vibrant colors recalling the designs of the Memphis Group from the 1980s. A multimedia artist who attended De Ateliers in Amsterdam, the Städelschule in Frankfurt am Main, and the California College of the Arts in San Francisco and Oakland, Sidner experiments with materials and subject matter. His glass sculptures, at times outrageously bizarre, appeal to the viewer's imagination. PGH

Drops, 2022
Glass, bronze, brass
145 × 85 × 32 cm

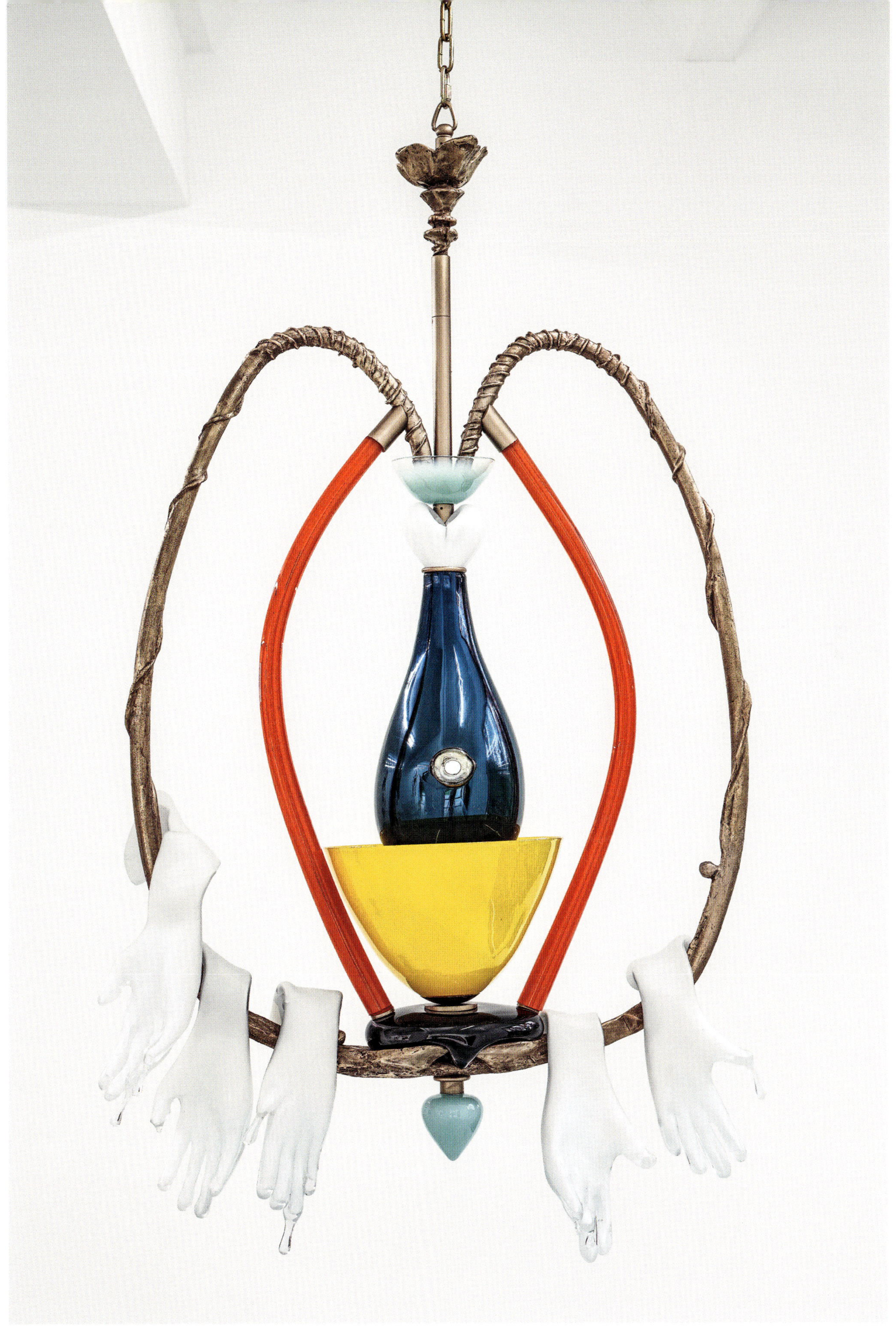

Kiki Smith

born 1954 in Nuremberg, Germany;
lives and works in New York City
and upstate New York, USA

Kiki Smith, one of the outstanding artists of our time, addresses political, social, philosophical, and spiritual aspects of human nature in her work. Ranging from sculpture, drawing, and painting to photography, film, video, prints, multiples, and books, her oeuvre is expansive. She has explored a wealth of materials such as bronze, plaster, and aluminum, porcelain, paper, fabrics, and precious stones. In the mid-1980s, Kiki Smith discovered the medium of glass—its transparency making it ideal for her investigations of human anatomy. She continues to work with glass today, whether in a painterly way, as in *Saint Geneviève and the Deer* (1999), or a sculptural way, as in *Ashen* (2010) and *Mine* (1999).

In the 1980s, Kiki Smith worked at the New York Experimental Glass Workshop (1983) and later learned glass painting. In collaboration with various glass workshops, she created numerous works ranging from small sculptures to large installations, such as the spectacular 80-foot-long glass mosaic in Grand Central Madison Station in New York (2022), in collaboration with the Mayer'sche Hofkunstanstalt, Munich. The oval stained-glass window for her *Chapel of Mary's Mantle* (2023) on the Domberg in Freising was also created there in a multifaceted process of painting and etching, grinding, washing, and firing. Kiki Smith had previously created a monumental rose window in mystical blue, hand-blown glass for the Eldridge Street Synagogue in New York.

Her glass flowers, which grow out of an open wooden coffin (*Ashen,* 2010), visualize the mystery of the radical cycle of dying, death, and new life, the dandelions serving as a metaphor for transience and renewal. Kiki Smith also paints flowers in oil paint on clear antique glass with white and yellow gold leaf (*Untitled (Oil Color Flowers*), 2008). The red three-dimensional glass stars scattered on the floor, *Mine* (1999), join the many other stars in Kiki Smith's work, connecting man to the universe, but here they have an explosive power embedded in the title's ambiguity. *Saint Geneviève and the Deer* (1999), two glass tableaux with drawings so typical of Kiki Smith, address the bond between humans and animals. Animals are companions in Kiki Smith's work—companions like the wolf, the bird, the cat. It is about friendship, survival and protection, as in the story of Saint Geneviève of Brabant, who fled from false accusation and lived in a cave with her newborn son for six years and was cared for by a doe with the help of the Mother of God. PGH

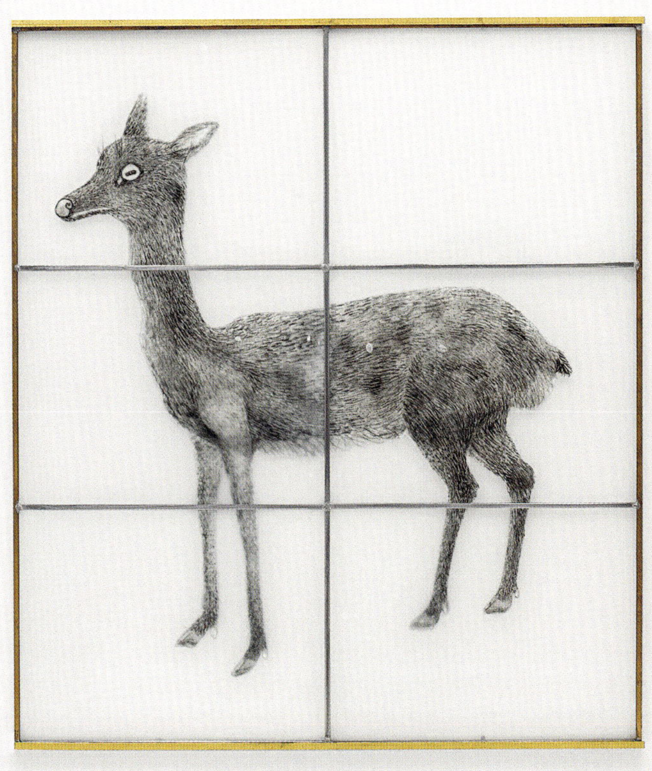

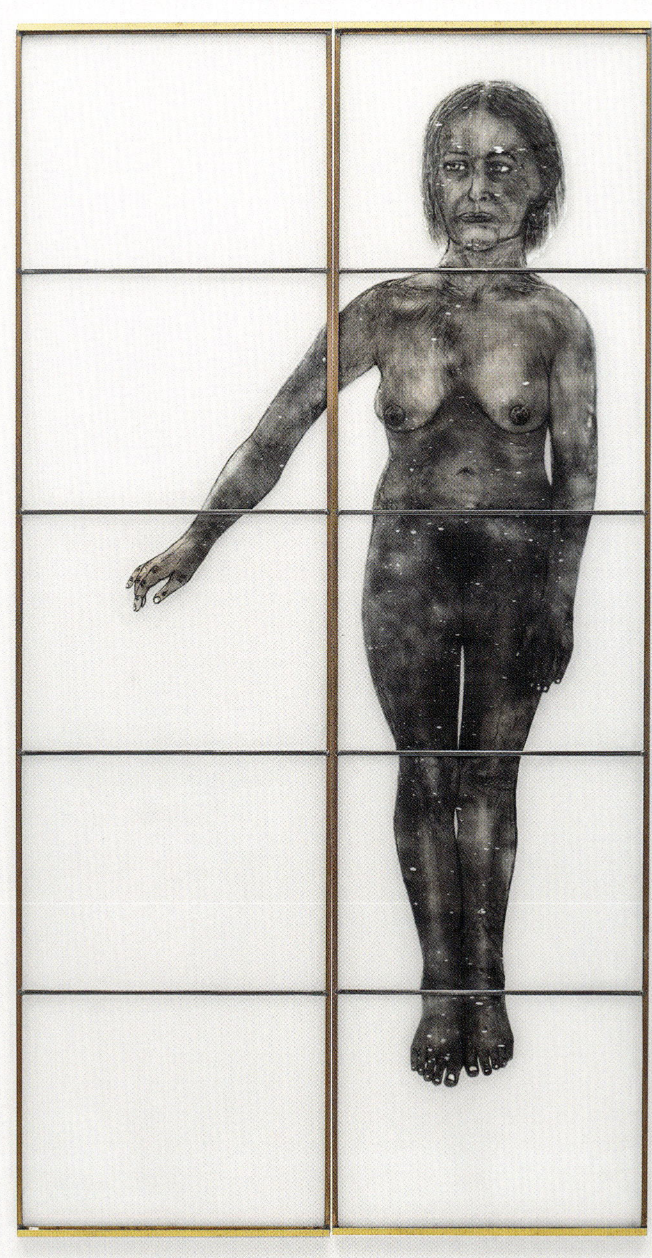

Sainte Geneviève and the Deer, 1999
Fired paint on glass panels
2 panels ranging from 137.8 × 122.9 cm
to 226.1 × 118.7 cm

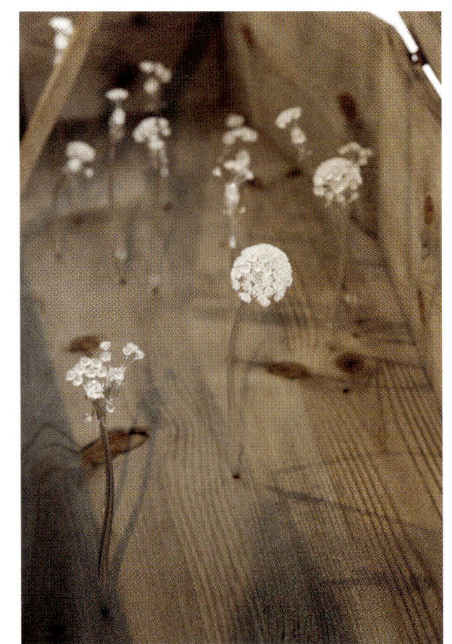

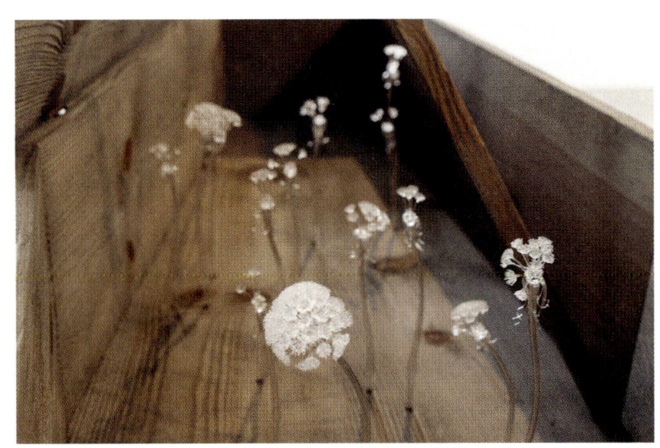

Ashen, 2010
Wood and lamp glass
Overall installation dimensions variable
Coffin open: 83.8 × 156.2 × 56.5 cm
Coffin closed: 30.5 × 158.1 × 56.5 cm,
Drop-leaf table: 75.56 × 101.6 × 48.26 cm,
15 dandelion puffs: 21.9 × 2.5 × 2.5 cm
to 26 × 7.9 × 7.9 cm

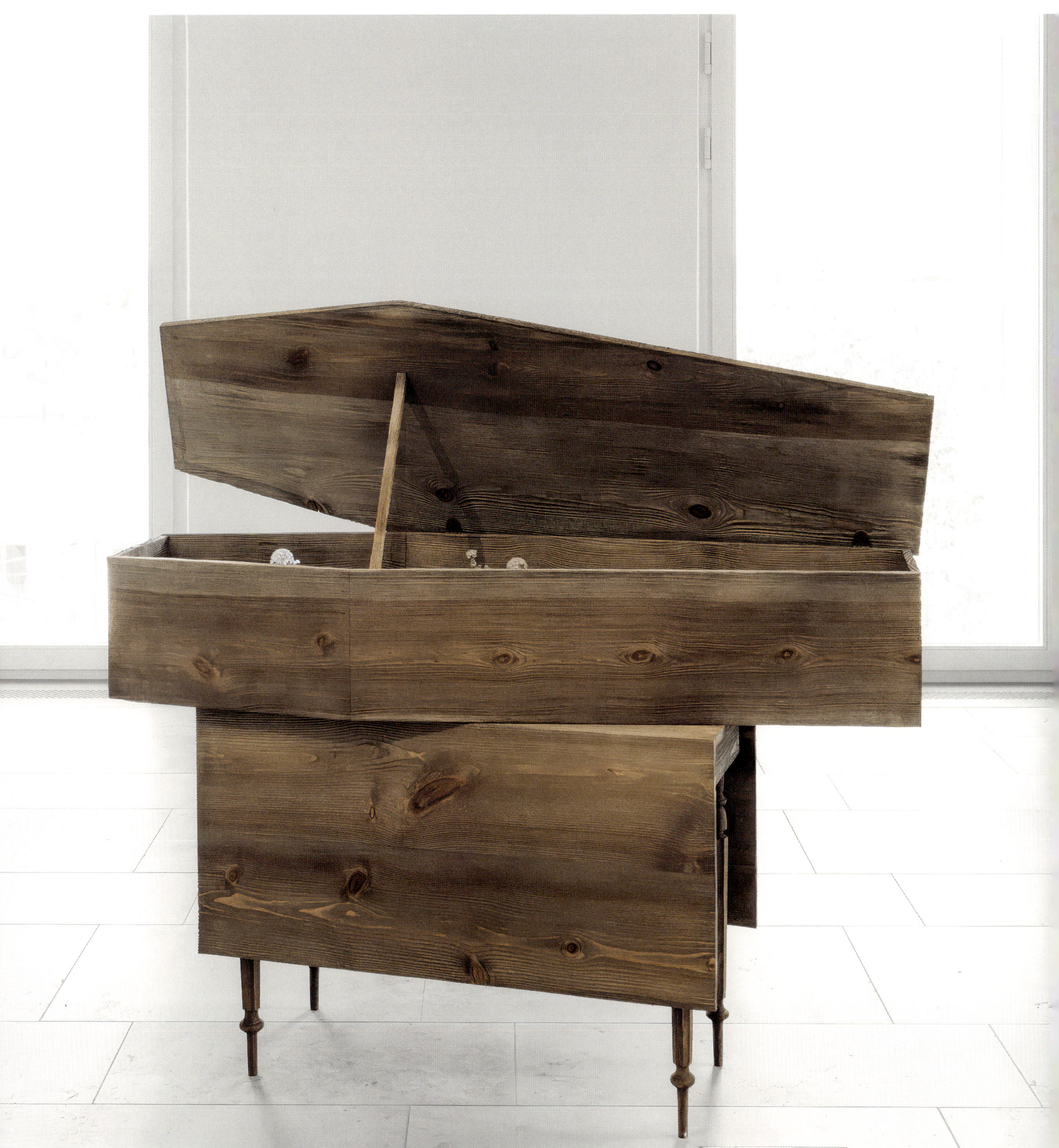

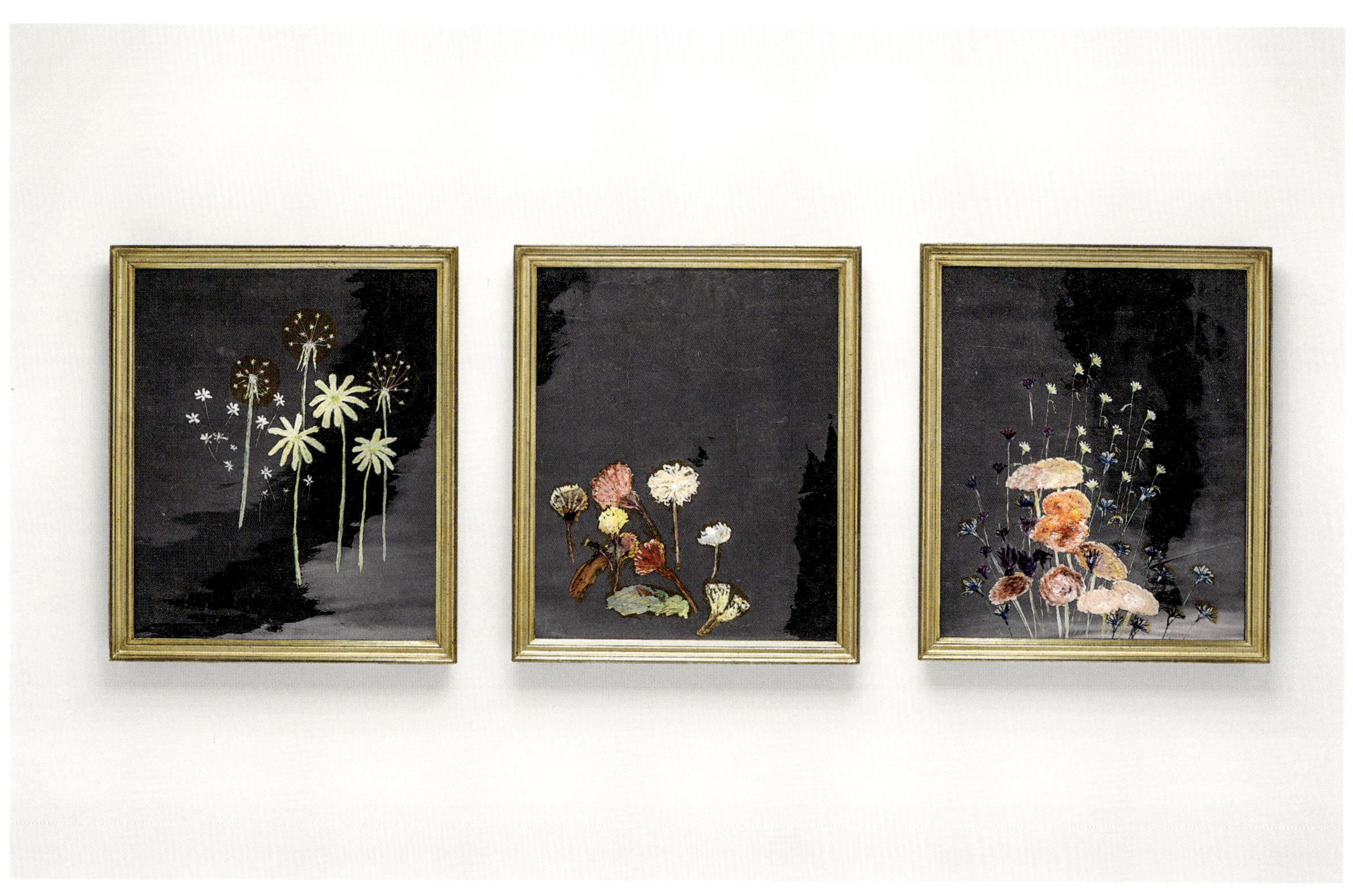

Untitled (Oil Color Flowers),
2008
Oil paint on mouth-blown
clear antique glass with white
and yellow gold leaf
3 framed glass panels, each
60.3 × 50.2 × 4.4 cm

Mine (Detail), 1999
Glass
9.5 × 11.4 × 12.1 cm
to 17.8 × 18.4 × 9.5 cm,
38 units

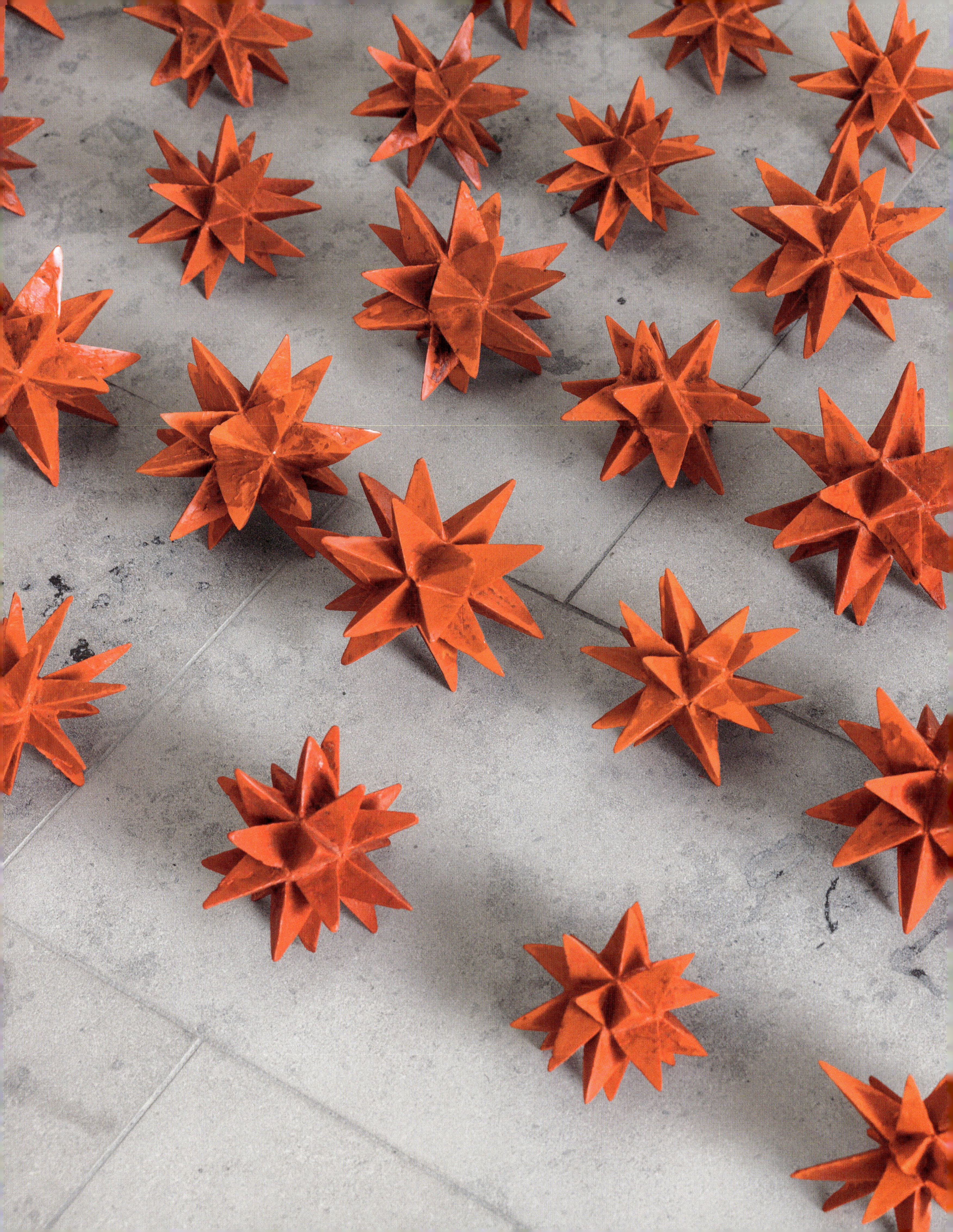

Jana Sterbak

born 1955 in Prague, Czechoslovakia;
lives and works in Montreal, Canada

Jana Sterbak, who emigrated to Canada with her parents in 1968 in the wake of the Prague Spring, explores themes such as body and identity, power and control, physical and psychological processes, and cultural and social conditions in multimedia works that encompass sculpture, performance, film, and photography. Representing Canada at the 2002 Venice Biennale, she caused a sensation with her feminist work Vanitas: *Flesh Dress for an Albino Anorexic* (1987), a dress made of meat.

Jana Sterbak began working with glass in 1998 when she first came to CIRVA (Centre International de Recherche sur le Verre et les Arts Plastiques), a famous glass workshop in France. She began with *Vase for a Solitary Flower,* which was followed by numerous other projects, such as the installation of thirty large hand-blown spheres (2000–2) alluding to medieval cosmologies. To Sterbak, glass is a substance that derives its magic from its transformation of the semi-liquid into the solid, from its transparency, weight, and raw mineral materials.

Vase, sphere, vessel—Sterbak translates mundane objects into works of art made of glass, such as the *Hard Entry* bowls (2003), a unique piece consisting of nine parts, hand-molded and mouth-blown, solid and of great weight. This is a set of nested containers that are difficult to separate. When the viewer's eye follows the line from above, they have a concentric effect and conjure up the shape of a spiral. The constriction and lack of space can give rise to many interpretations; for example, the ensemble of containers has been seen as a metaphor for the difficulty of human integration into our complex social system, or as a fear of confinement and imprisonment. The title of the work, however, is a reference to Zen philosophy. As the artist has said, the ōryōki bowls that Zen monks use to receive food, are stacked inside each other in a similar way, and refer to the rigor, discipline, and concentration of Zen.

Jana Sterbak: "Working with glass is a sort of dance executed by the glass blower to the tune of the work envisioned by the artist. It requires a good deal of physical intelligence and hand–eye coordination, along with an acute sensitivity to temperature and to the mass of material at the end of the glass-blowing pipe. To obtain outstanding results amid asymmetrical forms, a clear line of communication must be established between the glass blower and the artist, both of whom must adopt what I would call a Zen attitude."[1] PGH

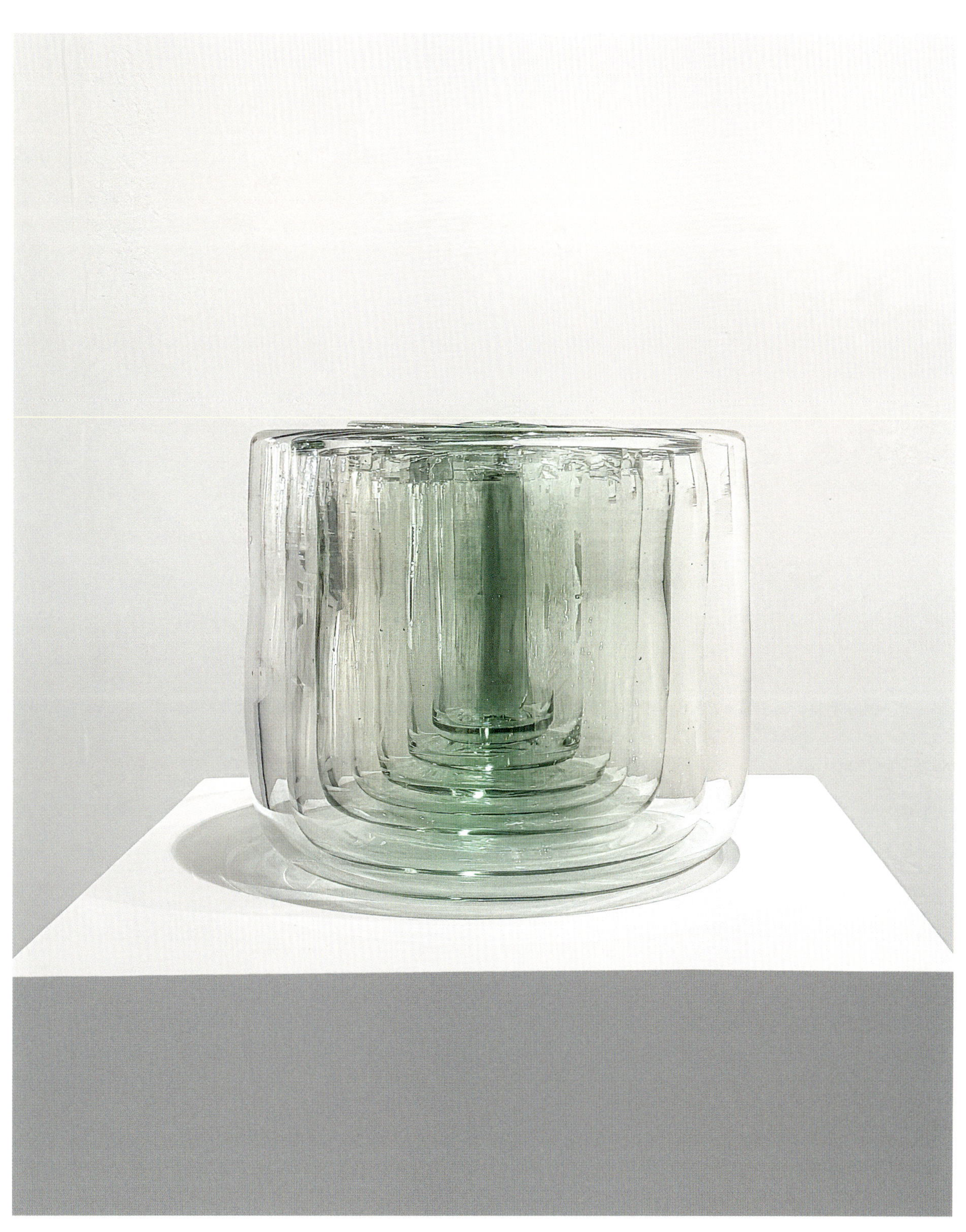

Hard Entry, 2003
Glass, hand-blown,
hand-shaped, 8 pieces
height 28.5 cm,
diameter 32 cm

Jenna Sutela

born 1983 in Turku, Finland;
lives and works in Berlin, Germany

Jenna Sutela's three-part glass work *Indigo, Orange and Plum Matter* from the *I Magma* cycle consists of a series of lava lamps made of cast glass in the shape of the artist's head. Illuminated by spotlights, the glass heads rotate slowly and incorporate the surrounding space through wall projections. Glass, a heat-resistant vessel, here becomes a sculpture in which hot colored wax ascends and descends in bubbling forms. Sutela, who was a visiting artist in 2019 and 2021 at the MIT Center for Art, Science & Technology (CAST) in Massachusetts, chose the lava lamp as a source of mathematical unpredictability. The unique shapes are melted in unpredictable ways, making them ideal for use as random number generators—as they were in Silicon Valley in the 1990s—as well as for modeling encryption codes today.[1]

For *I Magma,* which was exhibited for the first time at the Liverpool Biennial, Sutela also developed an "oracle" in the form of an app, in collaboration with the American poet and programmer Allison Parrish and the Turkish artist Memo Akten. To create daily divinations for its users, the app used machine learning to recognize patterns in the random movements of the heated wax together with an artificial intelligence trained on texts from the Internet Sacred Text Archive and from Erowid, an educational organization focused on psychoactive substances. The resulting work has many surprising facets, interpretative levels, and "potential applications."

In a photogram, the contours of the glass head appear directly on light-intensive paper without an interposed negative. "The light reflected by the wax and glass expands and distorts the image of the head and so, according to Sutela, visualizes the expansion of the mind."[2]

Jenna Sutela's work has been shown in solo exhibitions at the Serpentine Gallery in London (2019), Haus der Kunst in Munich (2022), the Shanghai Biennale (2021), the Kiasma Museum of Contemporary Art in Helsinki (2022), the ZKM in Karlsruhe (2020), the Moderna Museet in Stockholm (2019), and the Guggenheim Museum in Bilbao (2018).Jenna Sutela has been selected to exhibit in the Pavilion of Finland at the 61st International Venice Biennale in 2026. PGH

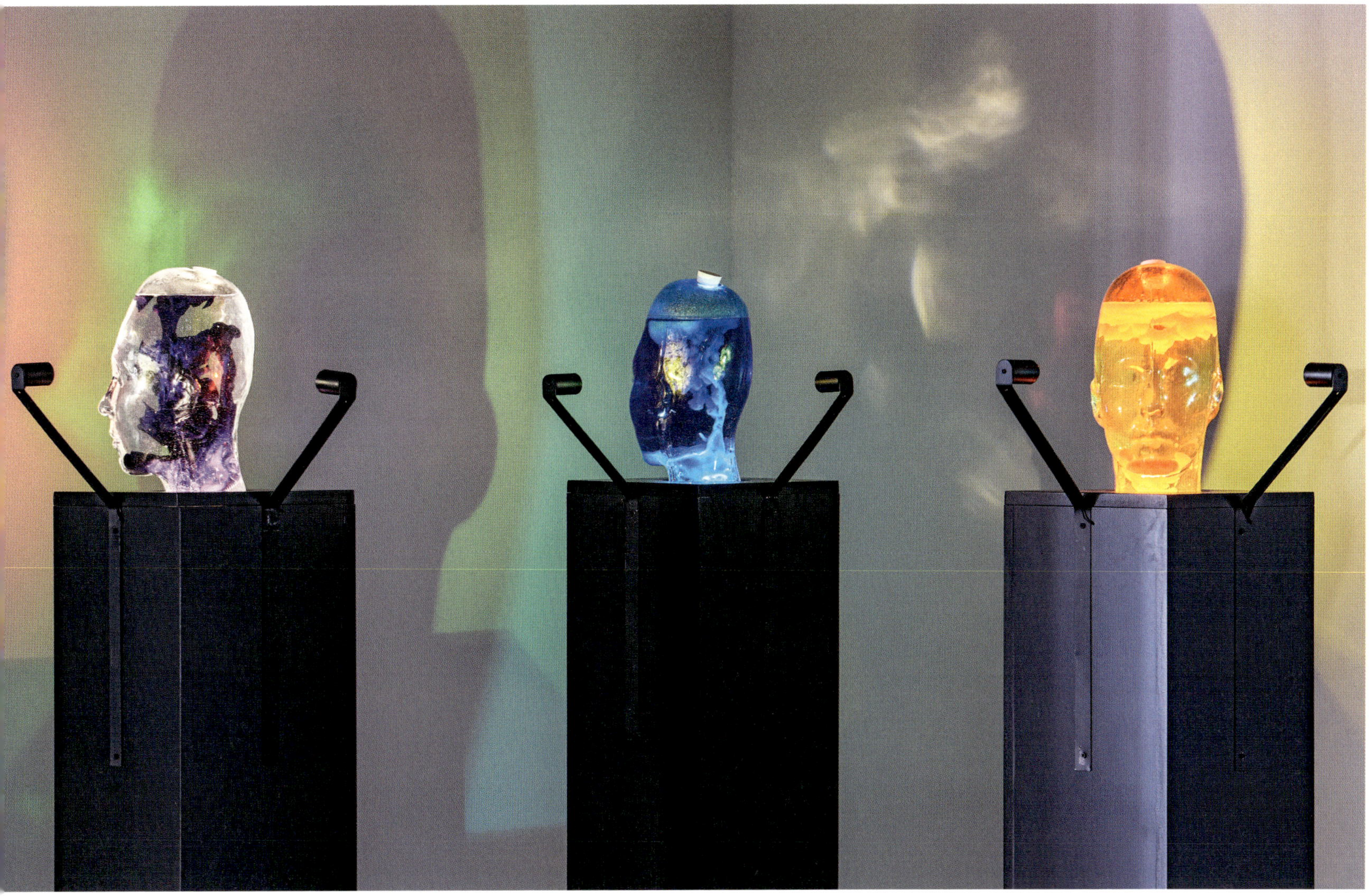

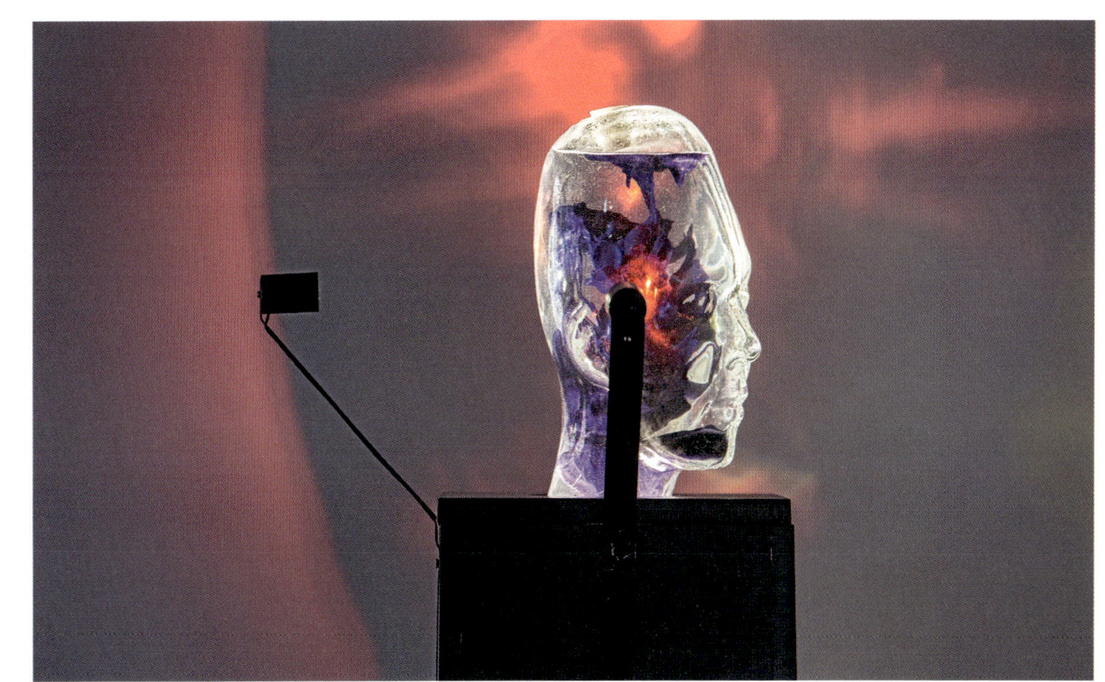

Indigo, Orange and Plum Matter (I Magma cycle), 2021
3 pieces, blown glass, goo, heating and lighting equipment, custom plinths with motors and LED lights with projectile lenses
Each head approx. 35 × 23 × 18 cm

Hui Tao

born 1987 in Yunyang, Chongqing, China;
lives and works in Beijing, China

Cast in colored glass, lifelike chains of chicken feet hang on threads from the ceiling to the floor. Alluring in their bright colors, while at the same time eerie, they divide the room and mark the threshold to the exhibition Hui Tao: In the Land Beyond Living at Tai Kwun Contemporary in Hong Kong (2024–25). As if through a curtain of traditional motifs, you enter a world of large video screens, film stills, and avant-garde architecture by this young Chinese artist. Chicken feet are commonplace in China, and not just delicately prepared as a dish. In some regions, they are used for fortune-telling: cut from live chickens, the lines on the feet are examined to divine the fate of the coming year.

"Money-grabbing": chicken feet are a symbol of wealth and therefore good luck and are considered a talisman. Through their transformation into the medium of glass, the everyday "object" is made surreal, drawing the astonished viewer into reflection. The glass chicken feet become a vehicle of history and cultural values, of habits and ways of life, and a manifestation of social identity.

Hui Tao's work is characterized by subversive thinking and explorations of social inequality and alienation.[1] He creates haunting, often provocative, works situated between fantasy and reality, opening up new perspectives on contemporary Chinese society and the human condition in general. He received his BFA from the Sichuan Fine Arts Institute and was honored with the Hugo Boss Asia Art Award for Emerging Asian Artists in 2017. His work is represented in collections such as those of the Kadist Foundation, San Francisco; Fondation Louis Vuitton, Paris; K11 Foundation, Hong Kong; M+ Museum, Hong Kong; New Century Art Foundation, Beijing; The National Museum of Modern and Contemporary Art – MMCA, Seoul; and the Ullens Center for Contemporary Art – UCCA, Beijing. PGH

Money Grab Hand
(Detail), 2024
Cast glass
380 pieces, each approx.
14 × 4 × 4 cm

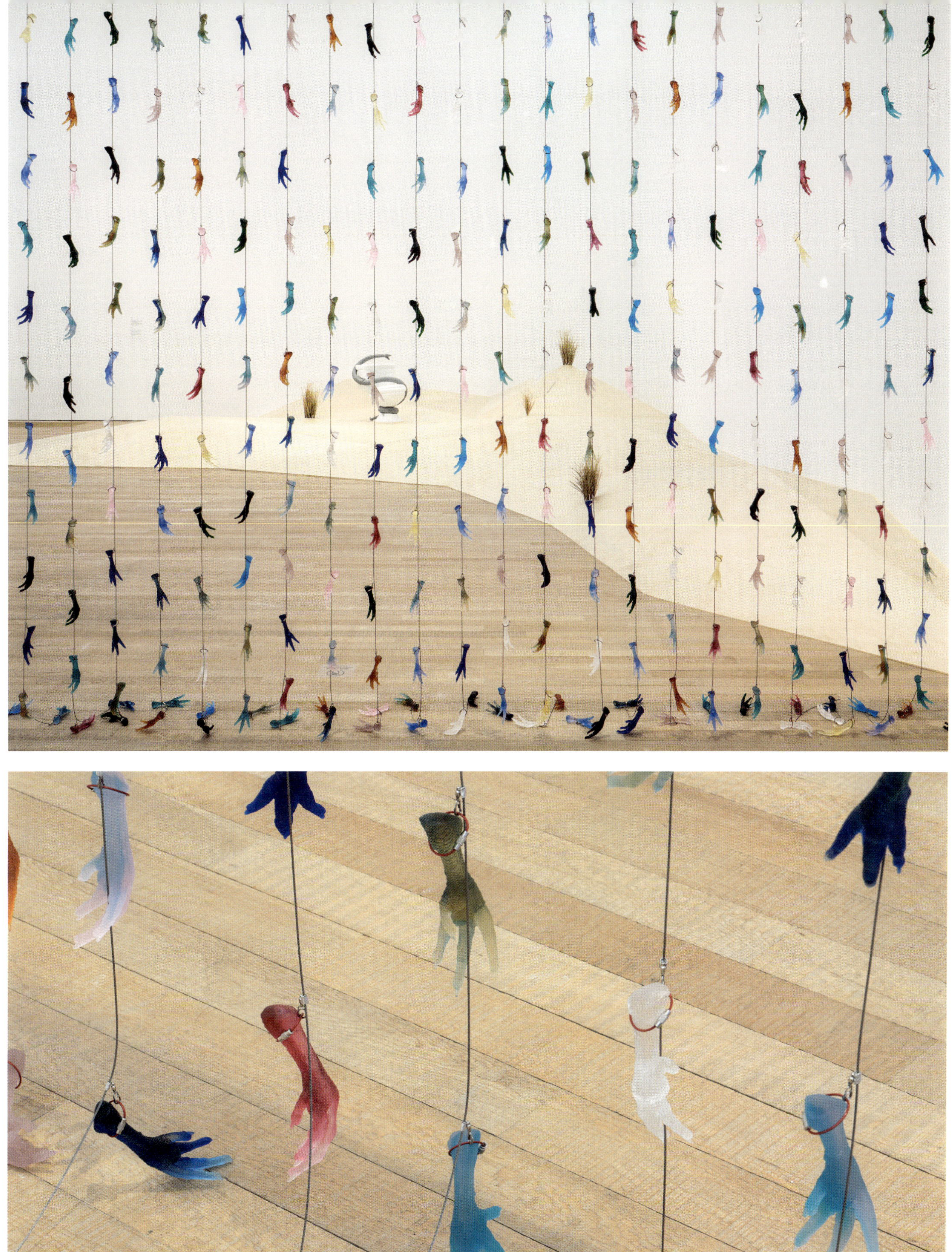

Neringa Vasiliauskaitė

born 1984 in Lithuania;
lives and works in Munich,
Germany

Neringa Vasiliauskaitė's works *400–700/1 and 400–700/2* from 2016 come from her series of mirror works. In these, the artist explores the qualities of light in a room and the role of the viewer. The numbers 400 to 700 refer to the part of the electromagnetic spectrum discernible by humans—that is, visible light—measured in nanometers. Not only do we fail to perceive the full electromagnetic spectrum; the nature of light is also dependent on our viewing angle and the quality of our perception. Her preoccupation with light began with her interest in Andrei Tarkovsky's 1972 science-fiction film *Solaris,* which confronts the protagonists with the limits of perception while also showing how differently we experience the new and unknown. To the artist, light is a tool with which to create a mood in the room. The highly reflective and transparent glass that Vasiliauskaitė uses, also known as dichroic glass, is coated with a fine layer of metal oxides so that it reflects light in a complementary way. The colored areas are created solely by refracted light and change depending on the viewing angle and position.[1]

Vasiliauskaitė was born in Lithuania in 1984 and studied glass painting at the Vilnius Academy of Fine Arts, graduating with a master's degree in 2008. From 2011 to 2018, she studied glass at the Academy of Fine Arts in Munich. She received the Art Karlsruhe Prize in 2017. AC

400–700 / 1, 2015
Curved coated glass,
Optiweiss glass,
multiplex board
diameter
117 × 3.8 × 4 cm

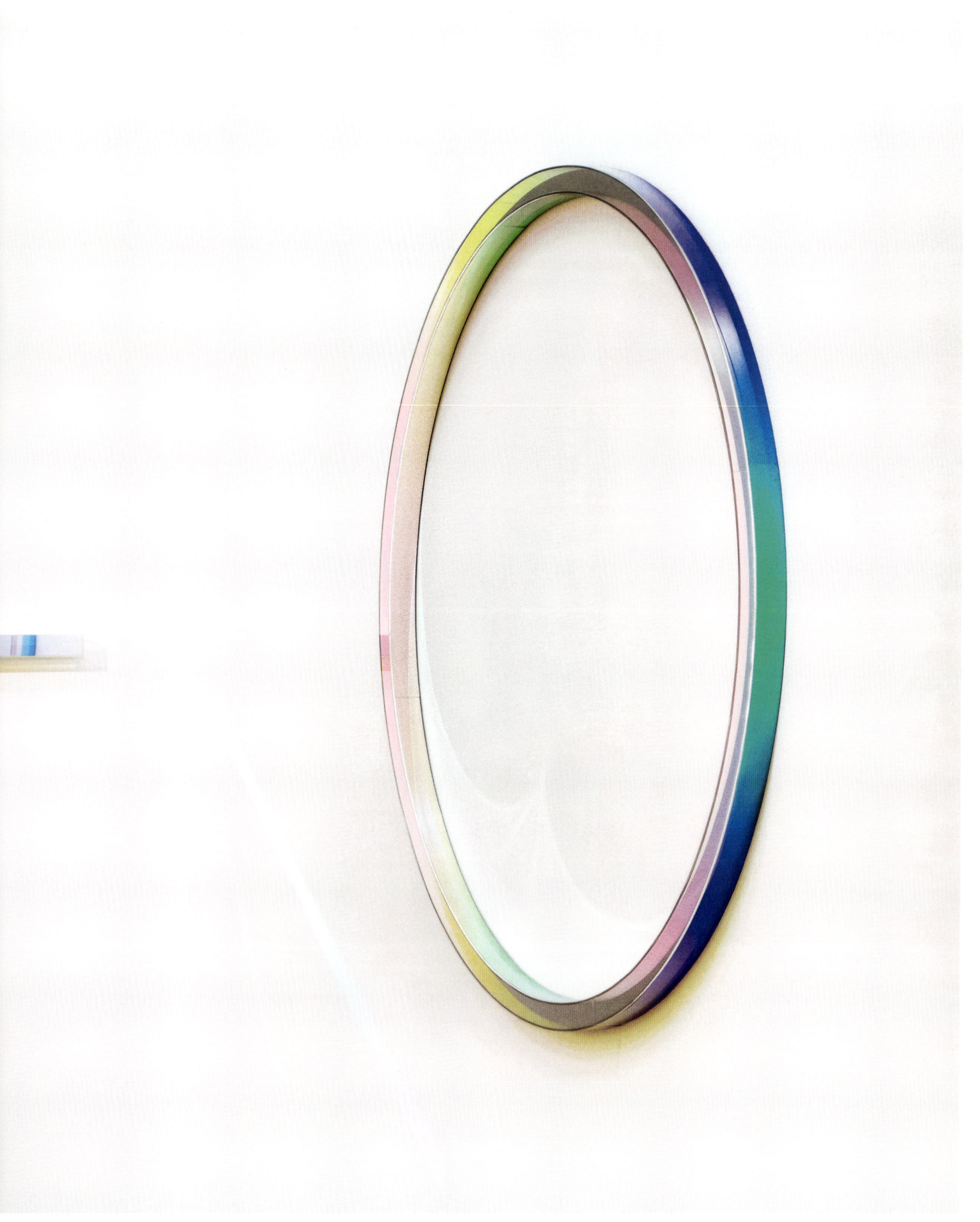

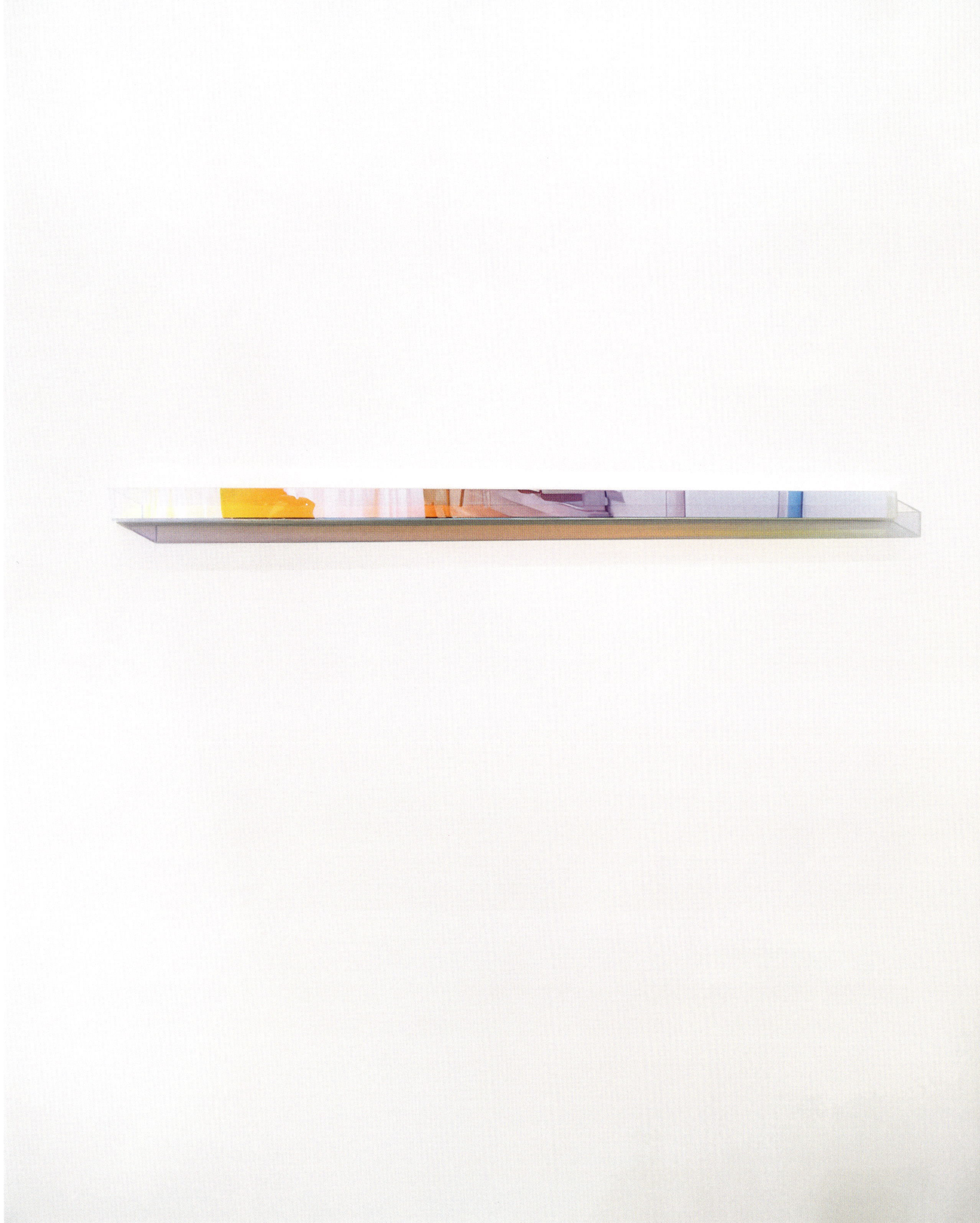

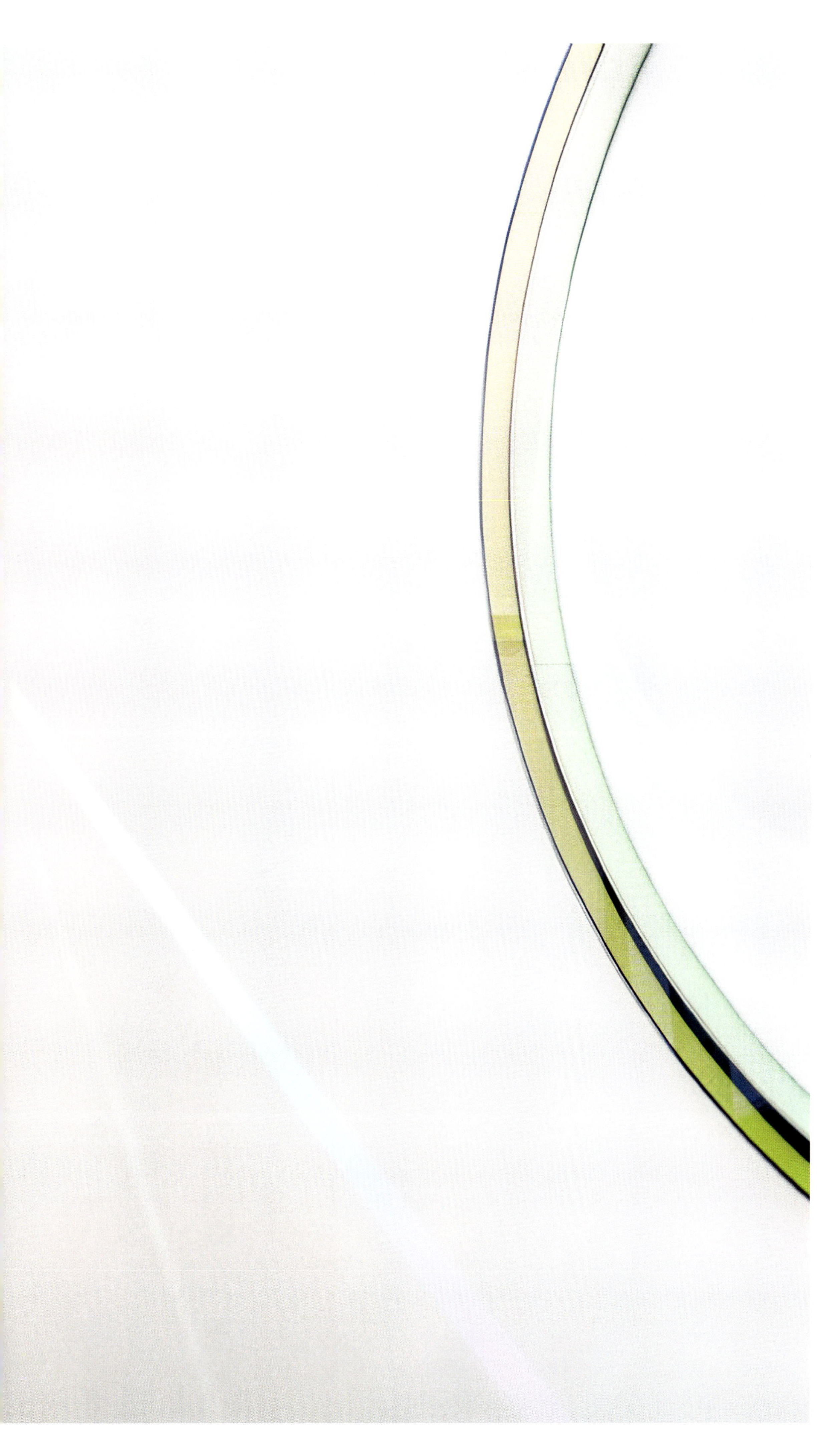

400–700 / 2, 2015
Coated glass with gradient,
Optiweiss glass,
multiplex board
108 × 4.2 × 4 cm

František Vízner

born 1936 in Prague, Czechoslovakia;
died 2011 in Žďár nad Sázavou,
Czech Republic

František Vízner is considered one of the leading glass artists of the twentieth century. His works are characterized by a mastery of glassmaking processes and a profound aesthetic sensibility. Vízner began his artistic career at the glass schools in Nový Bor and Železný Brod before continuing his education at the Academy of Applied Arts in Prague. While still a student, he perfected a technique and a sense of form that would accompany him throughout his fifty-year career as a designer for the glass industry and later as a freelance artist. He has become *the* specialist in cut studio glass.

Vízner's work is characterized by a minimalist aesthetic, featuring clean lines, geometric shapes and a subtle use of color. He is known for the unique way he uses glass's transparency and play of light. After acquiring a raw block of solid colored glass, he would work on it with grinding stones, diamond tools, and drills, employing a series of fine grinding wheels, glass templates, carborundum powder, and hydrofluoric acid to optimize the shapes and clean the surfaces. From this he produced vessels, vases, bowls, and plates exclusively.[1]

An outstanding example of Vízner's work is his deep green *Bowl*. This piece, created in 2000, embodies many of his style's characteristic features. The glass's color gives the object a mysterious yet calming aura, and the bowl has a simple yet perfectly proportioned form that emphasizes the purity and beauty of the glass. The matte surface reflects and refracts light in a beguiling way. Vízner has always been concerned with the relationship between material, form, and light, and the masterful workmanship of *Bowl* demonstrates his technical skill and attention to detail. Indeed, it almost looks like a still pool of water in which light gently moves and plays, imbuing the work with a meditative calm and lasting elegance.

Vízner's *Bowl* is not only an aesthetic object, but also an example of the deep connection between art and craftsmanship. Vízner understands how to apply a modern, minimalist language of design to traditional glass processing techniques. This synthesis of tradition and innovation makes his works timeless and universally understandable.

In art history, František Vízner is recognized as an artist who took the medium of glass to a new level. His works, including the *Bowl,* testify to his ability to unite beauty and functionality in perfect harmony. Vízner's extraordinary objects continue to impress collectors all over the world and are included in leading museum collections. BK

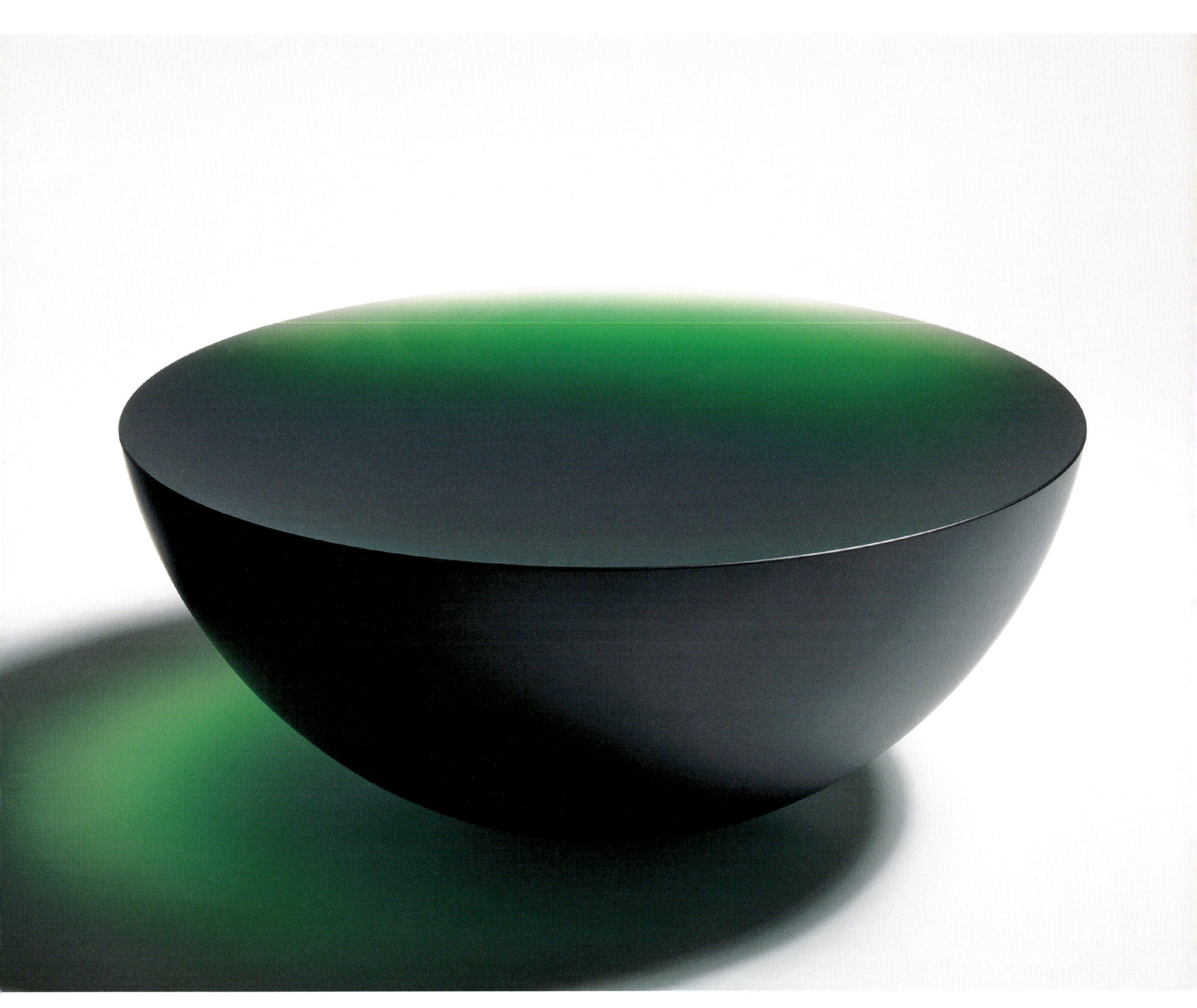

Bowl, 2000
Polished glass
approx. 18 × 32 × 32 cm

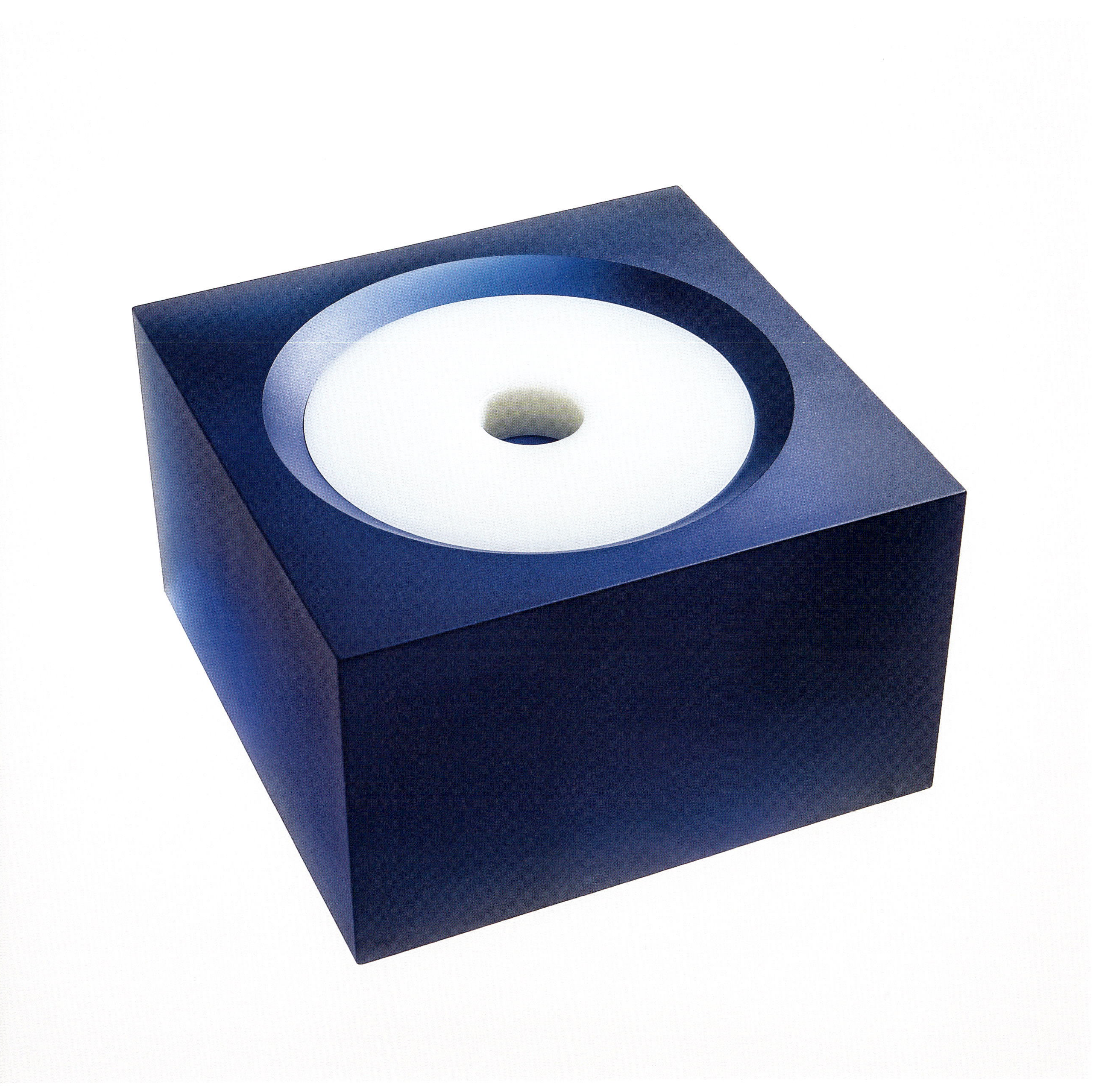

Eckige Vase, 2000
Polished glass
approx. 18 × 20 × 20 cm

Ursula von Rydingsvard

born 1942 in Deensen, Germany;
lives and works in New York City, USA

In a career spanning more than five decades, Ursula von Rydingsvard has become one of the most influential sculptors of our time. Her large-scale, often monumental, sculptures form landmarks, whether in urban spaces or the countryside—as brilliantly shown, for example, at the 56th Venice Biennale (2015). She assembles her sculptures from pieces of cedar, painstakingly cutting and composing them into a structured, faceted surface that she then rubs with graphite patina; more recently, she has also made spectacular sculptures in bronze and copper. The works have abstract forms that seem to draw from everyday items, such as vessels, bowls, or tools, in which the human signature merges with forms of nature to create something larger, archaic, and almost spiritual.

The large wall piece *Luminosa* (2013) appears like a metaphor of flowing light. Here, von Rydingsvard has exchanged her accustomed material, cedar, for glass—an exception in her work. As with her wooden sculptures, it appears organic, as if shaped by wind and weather. Composed of individual glass forms in the same way that she works with wood, this gold-colored work, created in Venice, has visual associations with a coat or collar for providing warmth and protection; like her other sculptures, it has a "tremendous dignity" and is imbued "with a profound sense of humanity and gravity."[1] Von Rydingsvard's sculptural practice relates, in her own words, to her family's history as Polish farmers and refugees of the Second World War. The manual process, the handling of the material, connects her and the piece to the real world and becomes a vehicle of memory and introspection.

Von Rydingsvard received her MFA from Columbia University, New York, in 1975. Her works are in major collections around the world, including the Whitney Museum of American Art, the Metropolitan Museum of Art, the Museum of Modern Art, and the Brooklyn Museum, all in New York. PGH

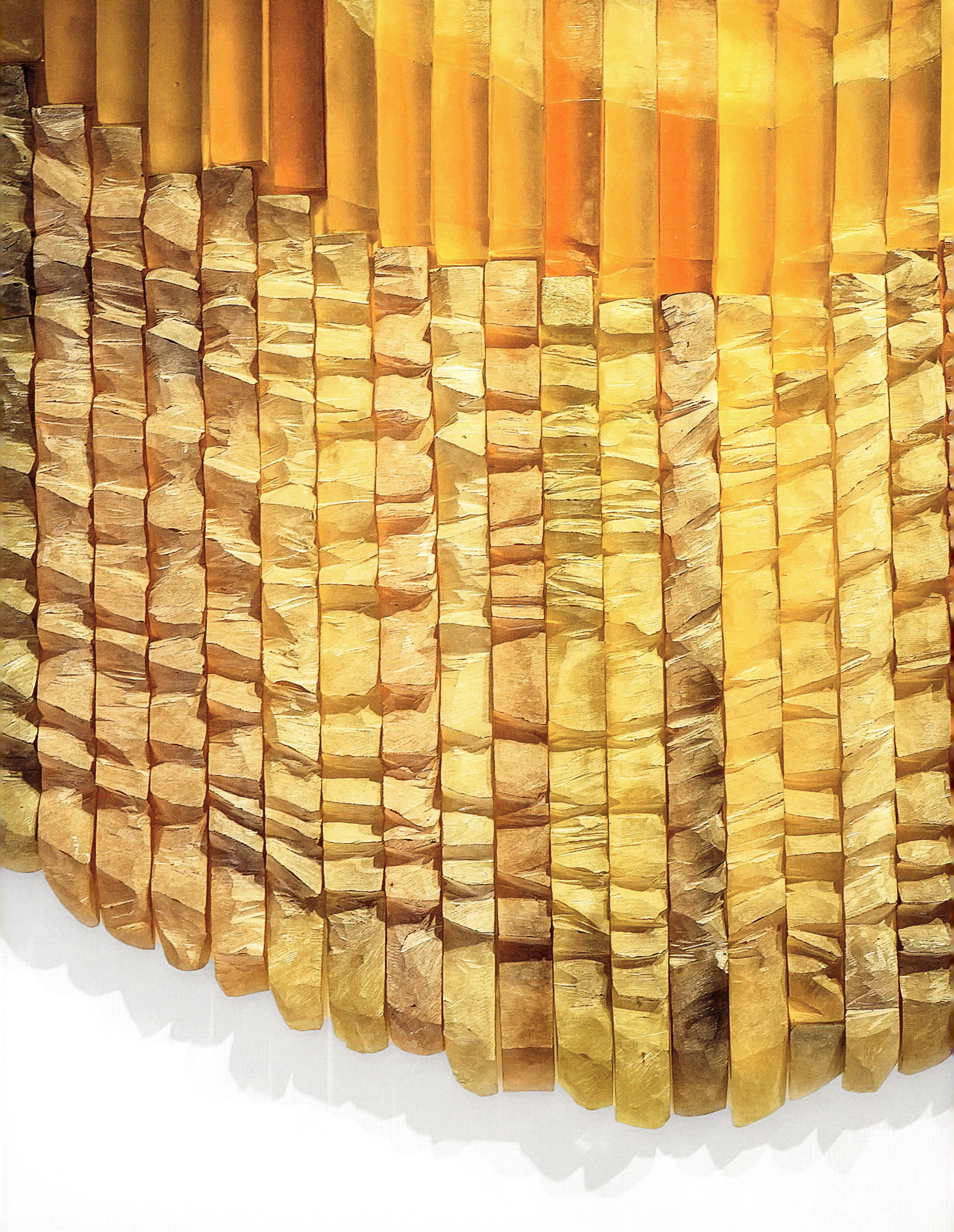

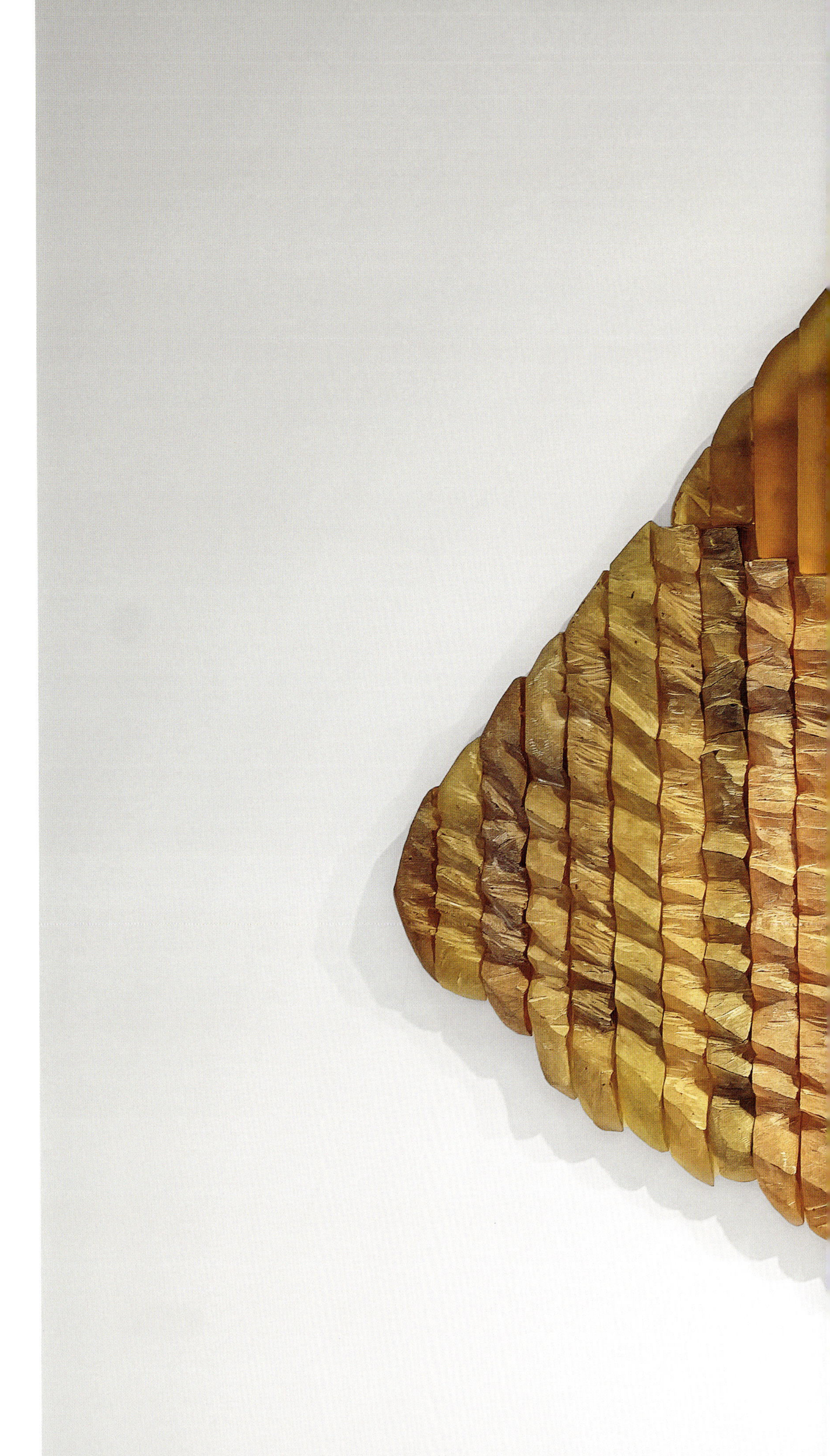

Luminosa, 2013
Glass
185.4 × 228.6 × 25.4 cm

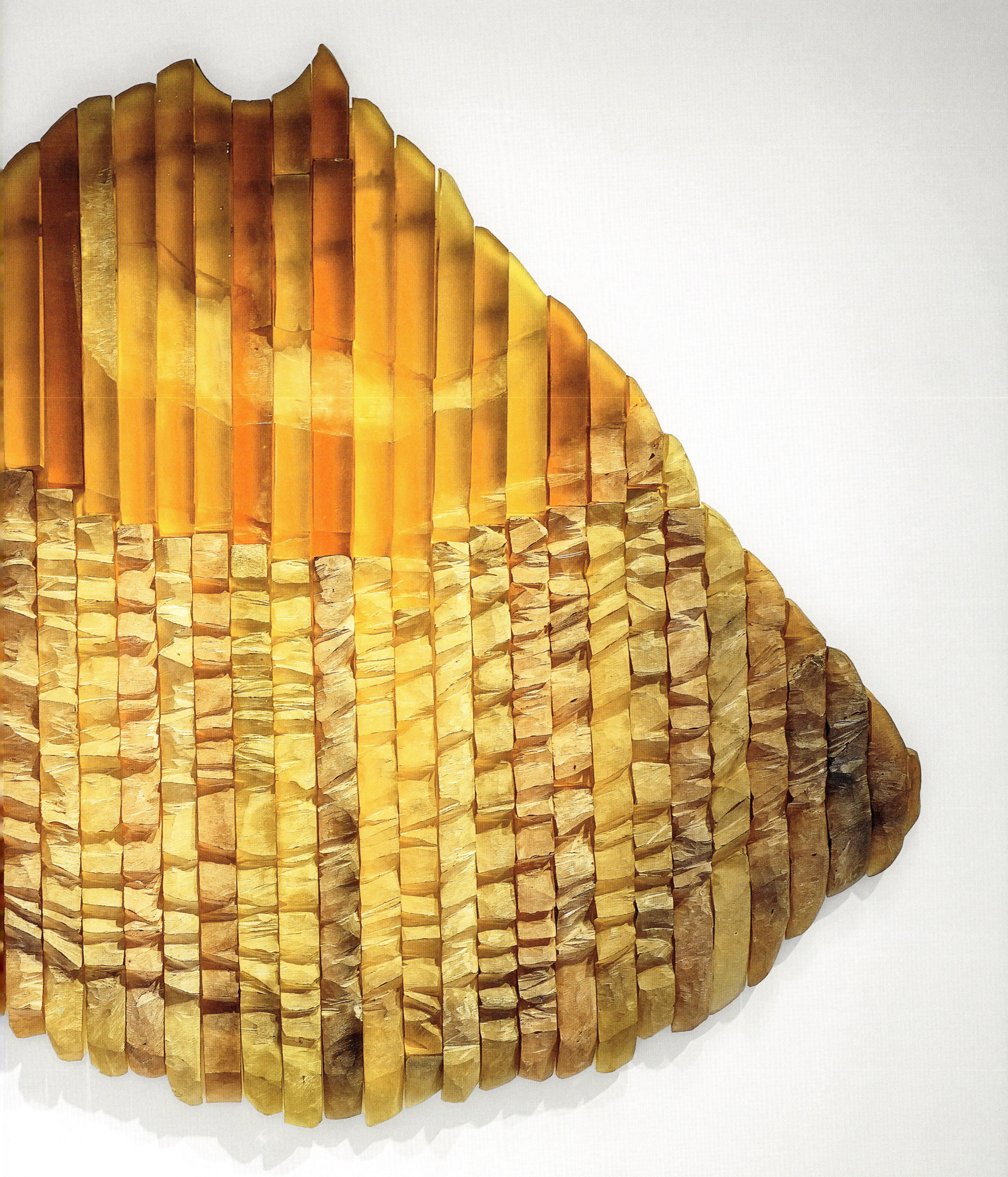

Janusz Walentynowicz

born 1956 in Dygowo, Poland;
lives and works in Skagen, Denmark

Janusz Walentynowicz is a glass artist renowned for his figurative studio glass work.

Encased in a thick slab of murky glass, a young naked woman stands upright. Her immobile pose and closed eyes exude a strong sense of stillness and detachment. Like Walentynowicz's numerous other figures engulfed in solidified glass, Standing may be a tacit allusion to a personal tragedy: the artist's father was a commercial fisherman who drowned during a haul when Walentynowicz was still a boy. The artist, however, wants his work to transcend biographical references. "My sculptures are points of balance," Walentynowicz says: "moments of the future." He urges the viewer, in the best tradition of contemporary art, "to put his or her own experiences in it."

Black Box, 2013
Cast glass
49 × 36 × 36 cm

Walentynowicz masterfully rendered his submerged inert nude *Standing* in a decisive moment of imminent awakening reminiscent of Lessing. *Standing* in a further reading seems reminiscent of the spray-drenched birth of Venus, whom Jean-Auguste-Dominique Ingres portrayed in 1808 as rising from the sea with her arm elevated iconically above her head. The closed eyes and graceful aloofness hint at the semiconscious daze of a mythological goddess being born. In another association, the dreamy haze of the glass encasement may remind the viewer of the crystal coffin in the fairy tale of the Brothers Grimm, in which a sleeping beauty awaits her resurrection. Science-fiction movies of the late twentieth century could also spring to mind, as many featured incubator-like glass tanks in which the protagonist floated in translucent liquid—to heal, to mature, or to be preserved for future action. The sense of awakening, of renewal and immanent activity in Walentynowicz's work is heightened by the body's proportion: the youthful anatomy and elongated legs speak of a teenager experiencing a growth spurt.

Despite the full-bodied presence, Walentynowicz's *Standing* is not a solid figure submerged in glass. It is a body-shaped cavity, a negative bas-relief the artist then painted on the reverse in order to give the illusion of a woman. The artist has been using this extraordinary technique since 1988.

Walentynowicz's *Black Box* (2013) piques the viewer's curiosity like a big wrapped present. Stuffed inside a black garbage bag, the bulging shape gives no clue as to its content. The outer edges hint at a rectangular box, while from all faces protrusions swell. *Black Box* is an extraordinary fusion of cube and square, a powerful conflation that only four sturdy leather straps with cam buckles can hold together and secure. To the initial feeling of playful curiosity Walentynowicz adds an undercurrent sense of danger: bursting at the seams, *Black Box* turns perilous and uncanny. The all-too-familiar announcement "If you see unattended baggage, report it to staff immediately" rings in one's ears. Technically, Walentynowicz has created a black box in the truest sense of the word. His package is solid cast glass. It cannot be opened. Its contents will remain a mystery forever. JG

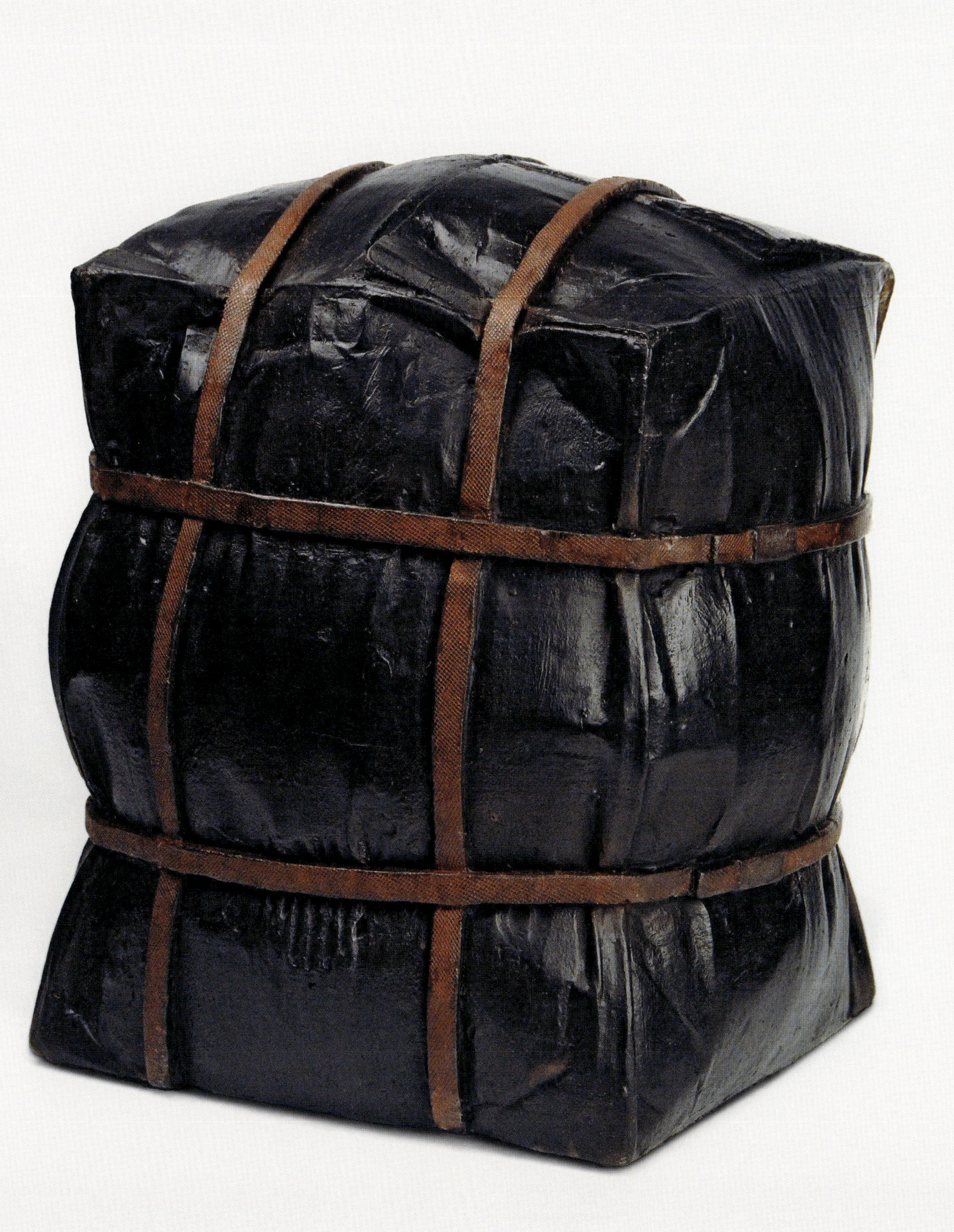

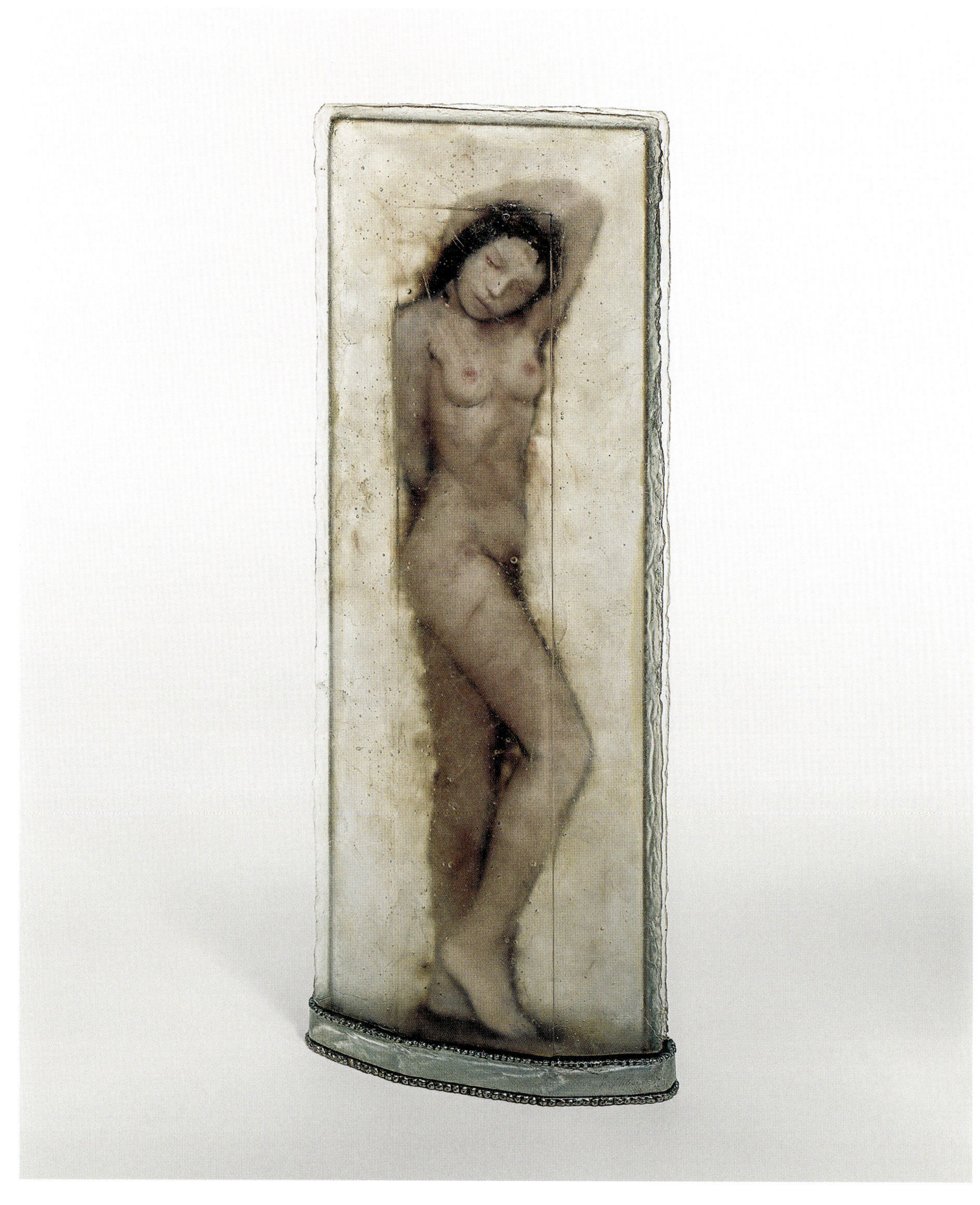

Standing, 2000
Cast glass
93 × 63 × 11 cm

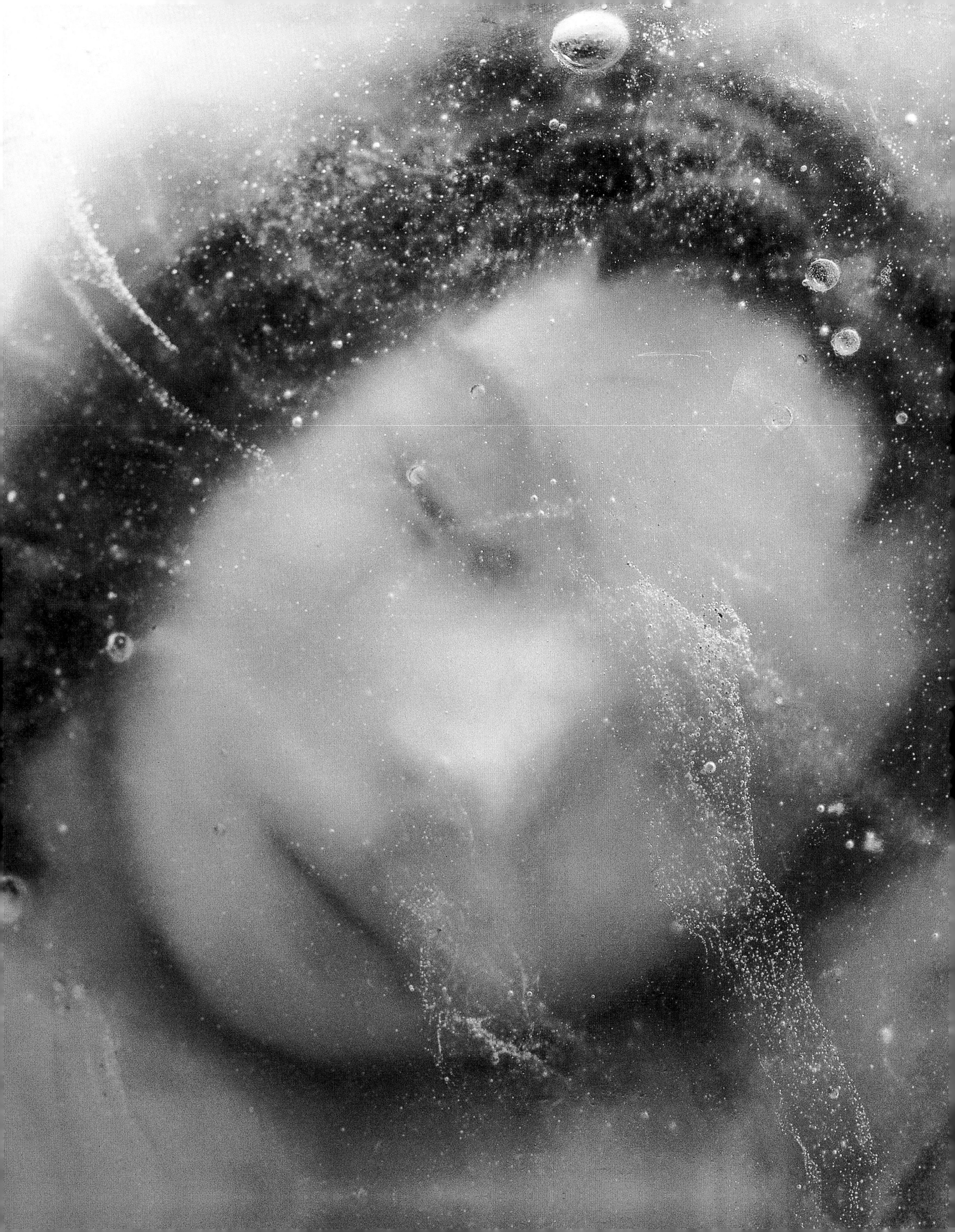

Qin Wang

born 1978 in Jingdezhen, China
lives and works in Shanghai, China

Qin Wang is considered one of the leading glass artists in China, and his works are represented in exhibitions and collections around the world. He graduated from the Jingdezhen ceramics institute in 2000, and in 2008 he received his degree in fine art from Shanghai University, where he now teaches.

At the beginning of his career, Qin Wang worked with ceramics, and his familiarity with this material can also be seen in his glass art.[2] It is important to note that the studio glass movement in China is still relatively young and at the start was pursued mainly by ceramics artists. Since then, glass has been understood by the art academies in China as an area of specialization in its own right and is now established with well-equipped studios.[3]

As the title suggests, Faraway Mountain (2007), made of molded glass, looks like a pale blue landscape with the outline of a distant mountain rising up in the background. The organic-looking forms below are reminiscent of a topography, while at the same time the work evokes lightness and transparency through its materiality. It is a semi-transparent object that the viewer can see through.

Qin Wang's works are the results of his explorations and experiments with glass. As the artist says about his work, melting glass in the kiln is a kind of Zen moment for him. This often leads to unexpected results, which can lead to new concepts and insights.[4] His works are characterized by philosophical and cultural themes as well as challenges in the modern world. JH

Ascend, 2007
Cast glass
55 × 21 × 11 cm

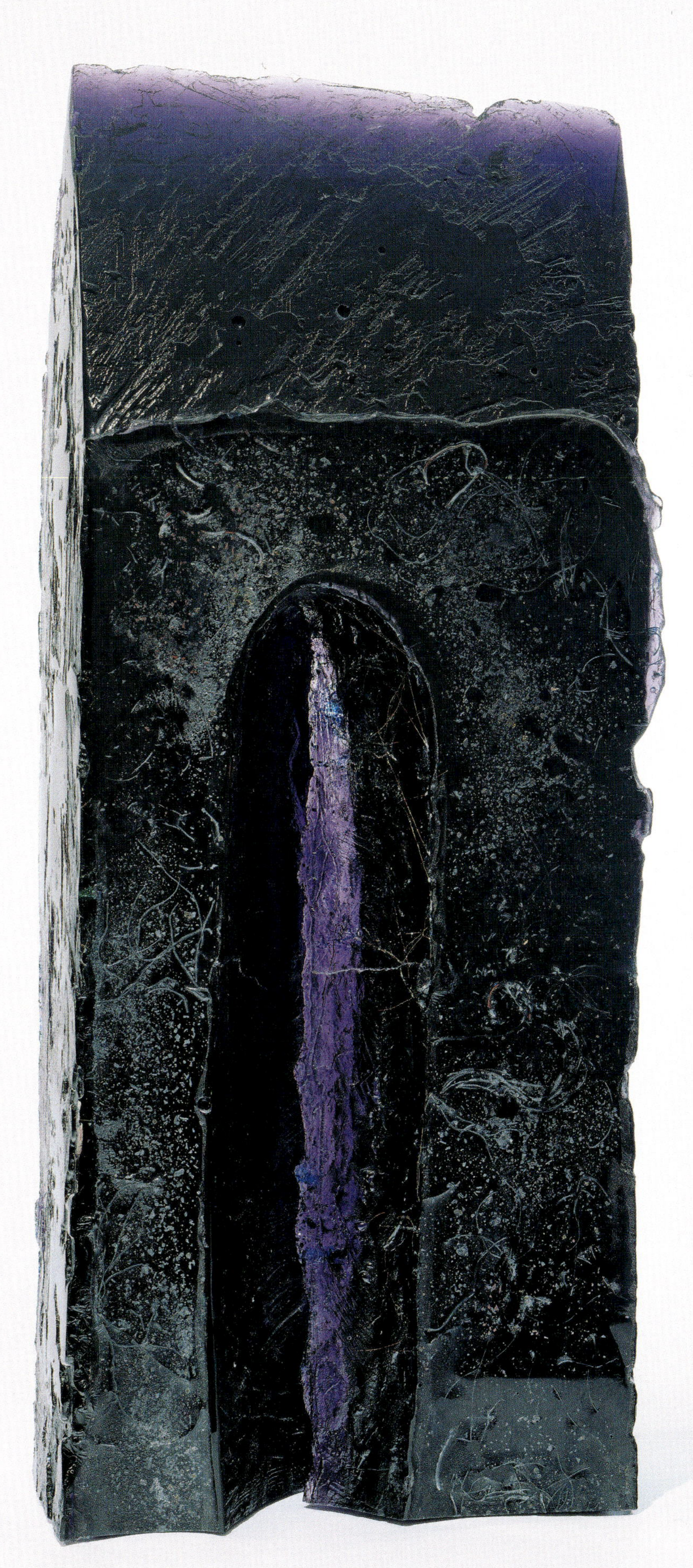

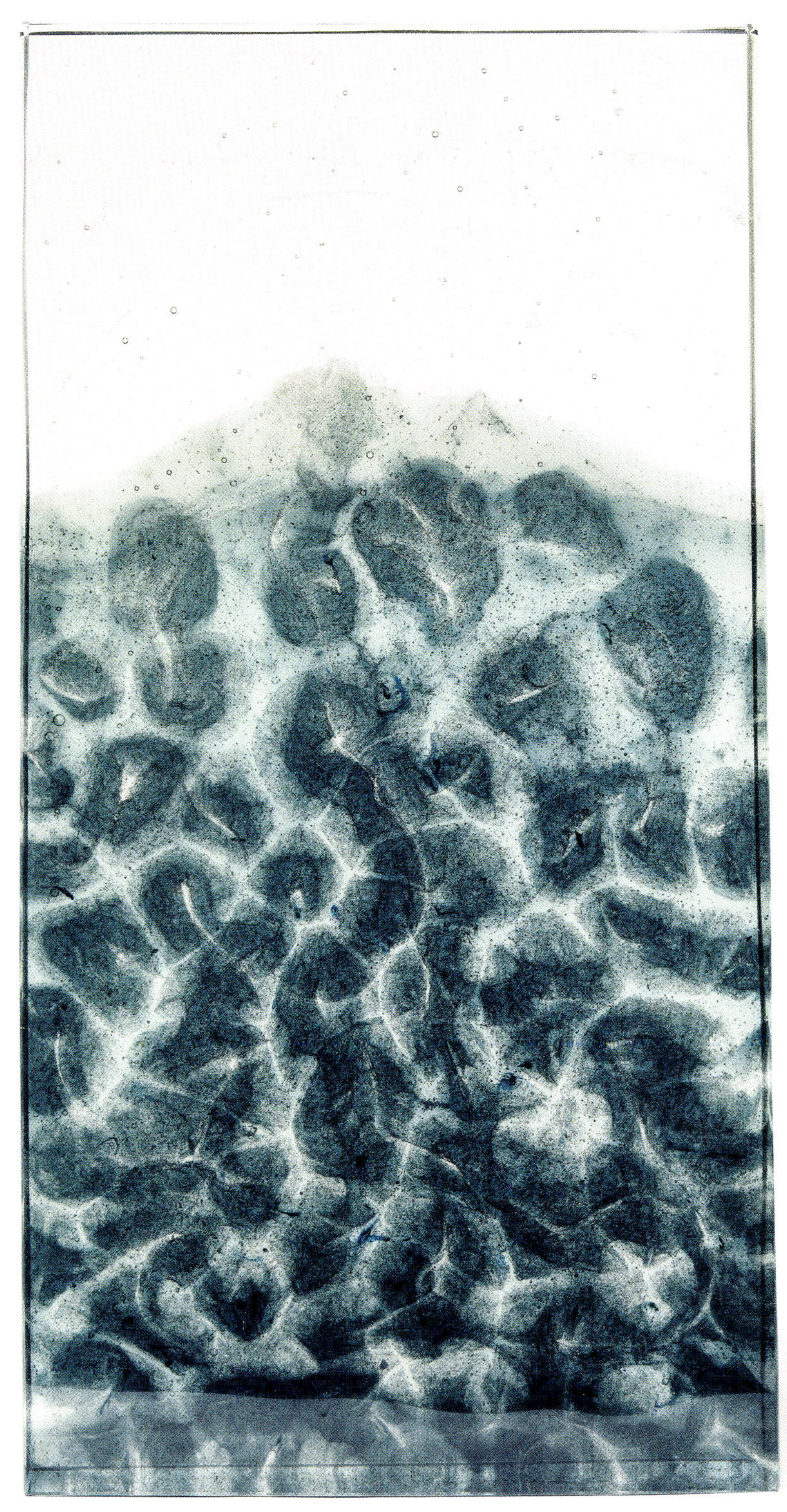

Faraway Mountain, 2007
Cast glass
63 × 32 × 8 cm

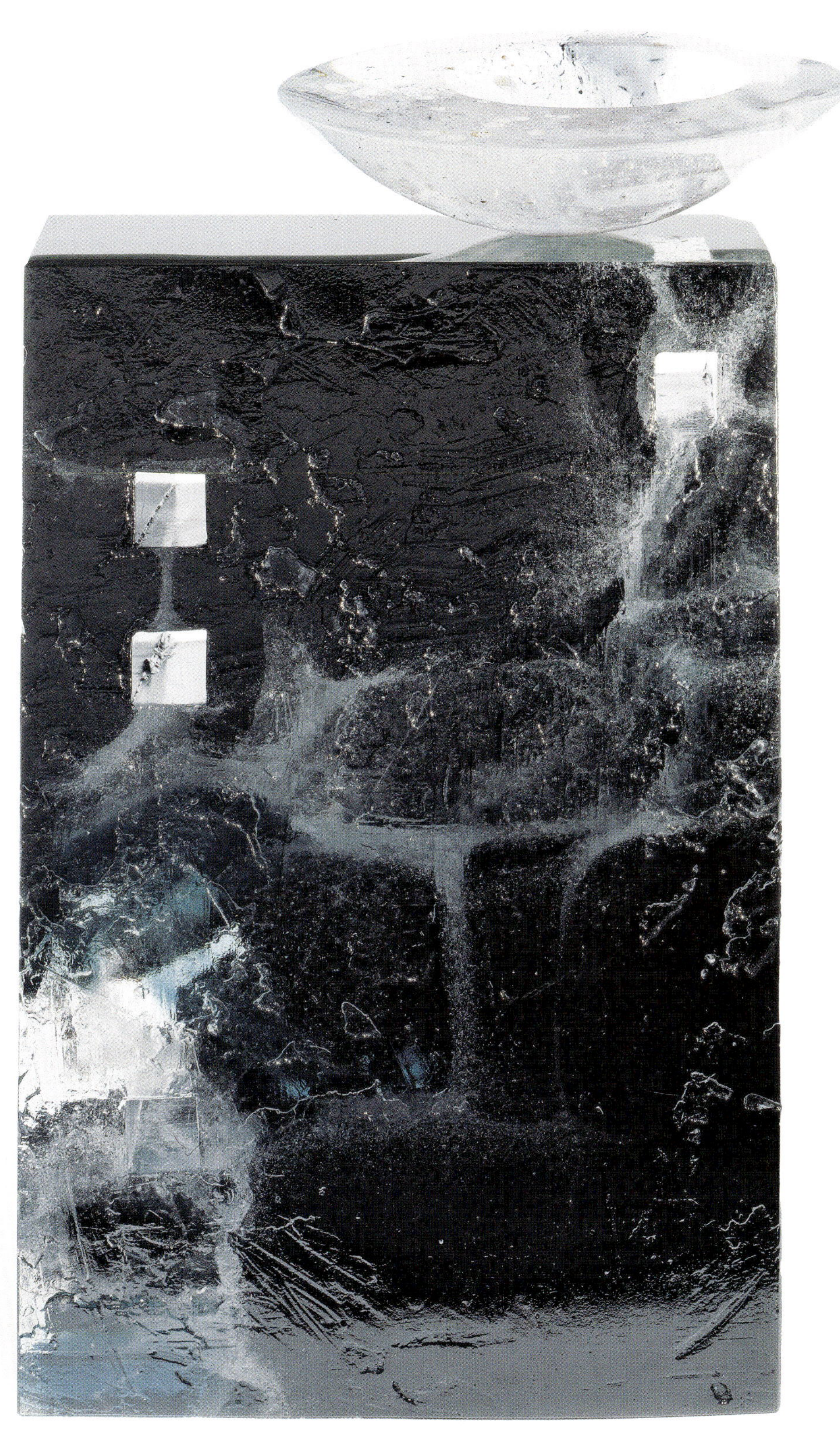

Summer Sitting II, 2006
Cast glass
45 × 26 × 9 cm

Sunny Wang

born 1972 in Yunlin, Taiwan;
lives and works in Hong Kong, China

Sunny Wang describes her artworks as originating from a synthesis of personal meditation and the inspiration she draws from her abundant impressions of life.[1] This broad spectrum finds multidimensional expression in her work, which extends well beyond purely visual and aesthetic pleasure.

The two hot-formed objects *Almost Self* and *More Than Self* come from her *Self* series. Related in terms of content, they also resemble each other in their design: solidly formed, organic, and harmoniously balanced. Yet behind this impression is concealed a meaning that is scarcely perceptible at first: the sculptures are an abstraction of the Chinese character for "self" (自), referring to its structure in their design. The bubbles trapped in the glass represent the space between the lines of the character, and the number of bubbles, therefore, is by no means random. For example, three bubbles in the base—imitating the calligraphic structure of the character—correspond to the "Self," while two bubbles symbolize the "Almost Self" and four bubbles the "More Than Self."[2] It is an almost mathematical materialization of the profoundly human struggle to realize one's identity—a struggle that often, as here, occurs on the inside.

Almost Self, 2006
Furnace glass hot formed
40 × 25 × 8 cm

At the same time, the bubbles can be understood as the artist's preserved breath trapped in the glass. Whether the "self" is written, formed from glass, or expressed through the breath—according to Chinese philosophy, all of this requires qi (氣),[3] the energy that underlies all life and that plays a central role in Wang's conceptual approach. Qi, neither material nor immaterial, eludes fixed categories, much like glass, which exists in a perpetual, barely perceptible state of flux.

As one of the leading glass artists in East Asia, Wang has been awarded numerous major awards from across the world. Since 2007, she has been an associate professor at Hong Kong Baptist University, where she researches and teaches the material possibilities and potential significance of glass in contemporary art. AB

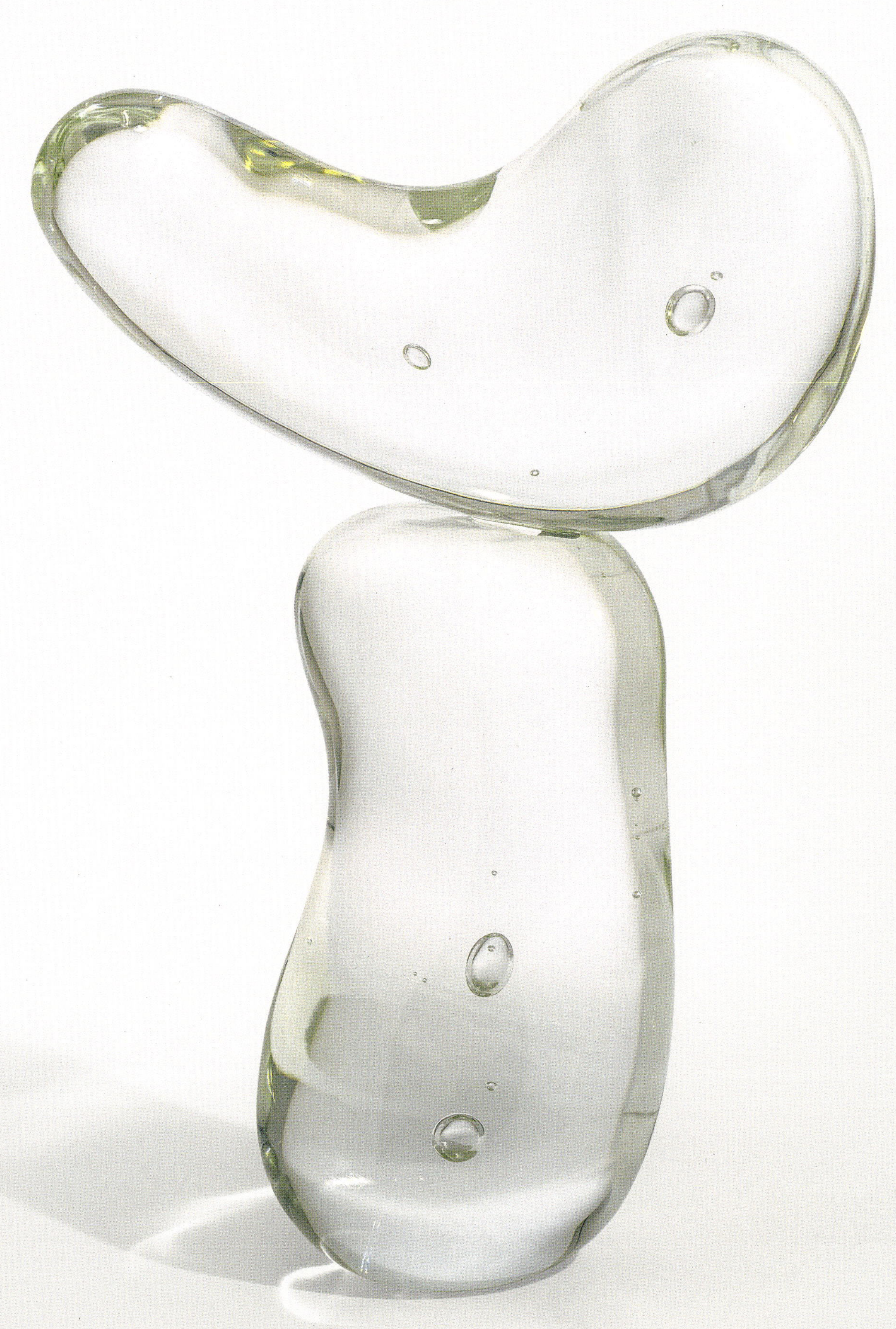

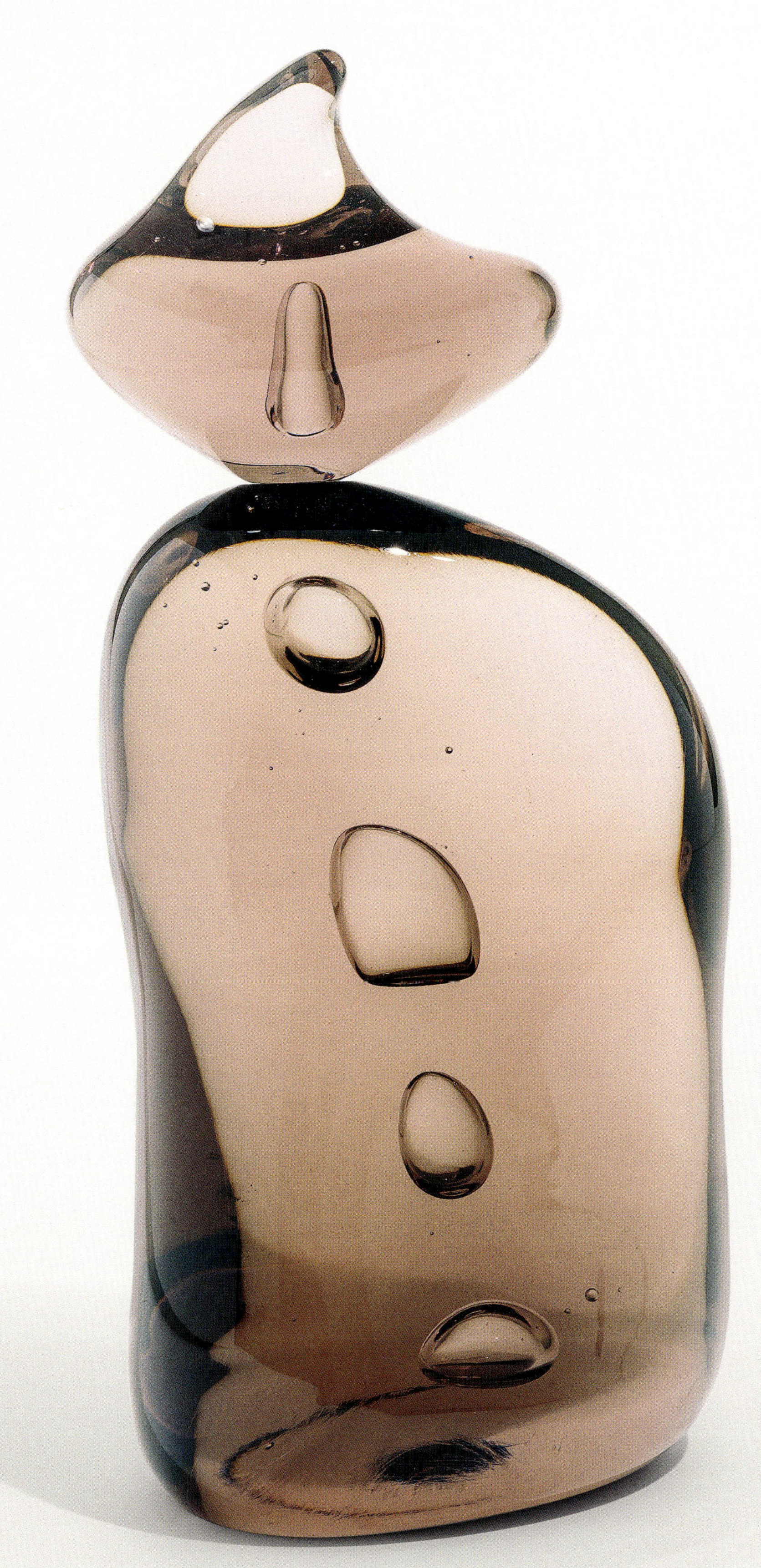

More Than Self, 2006
Furnace glass hot formed
38 × 18 × 8 cm

Pae White

born 1963 in Pasadena, California, USA;
lives and works in Los Angeles, USA

Pae White is a multimedia artist. She focuses on the “normal,” on the objects of everyday life, as well as on the ephemeral and neglected. White makes artwork that emerges from experimenting with materials, an approach that often combines high tech and artisanal crafts to produce ephemeral objects and quotidian motifs. She is interested in the “exploration of the neglected, the forgotten, the spaces between things,” as she herself puts it. With an interest in materials as varied as ceramics, neon, wallpaper, spray paint, and aluminum foil, and her dedication to the craft process, she transcends the boundaries between art, applied art, design, and architecture. White is known for her monumental site-specific installations with threads extended through the space or shimmering mobiles. The medium of glass plays a major role in her work. For the 2017 Venice Biennale, she built a 75-meter-long curved wall using 3,000 hand-cast clear and colored glass bricks. The monumental piece, entitled *Qwalala,* was presented on the island of San Giorgio Maggiore, and in 2023 as a permanent installation on the campus of Claremont McKenna College in southern California, where it reveals its light and colors spectacularly when illuminated at night.

Overserved (2017) is also made from glass bricks. “I’ve always been fascinated by the simple module of a brick, the basic brick,” says White. “So to have this kind of module of energy as something you make architecture with, is something I was really interested in.”[1] Overserved is a conceptual, minimalist, and at the same time very poetic work. Made of blown, reflective glass bricks in deep blue, a wall of irregular height stretches across the corner of the floor. By using what is actually a banal building block, White hones our vision to discern the beauty and visual complexity of everyday life: “My goal is to cause viewers to stop and consider the bits and pieces of our lives that are most often overlooked, perhaps suggesting a more comprehensive reconsideration of the world around us, even to ask ourselves: What is important to us? What are we seeing? What are we not seeing?”[2] PGH

Overserved, 2017
52 blown mirrored glass bricks
24.1 × 10.1 × 6.9 cm each
24 × 533 × 184 cm

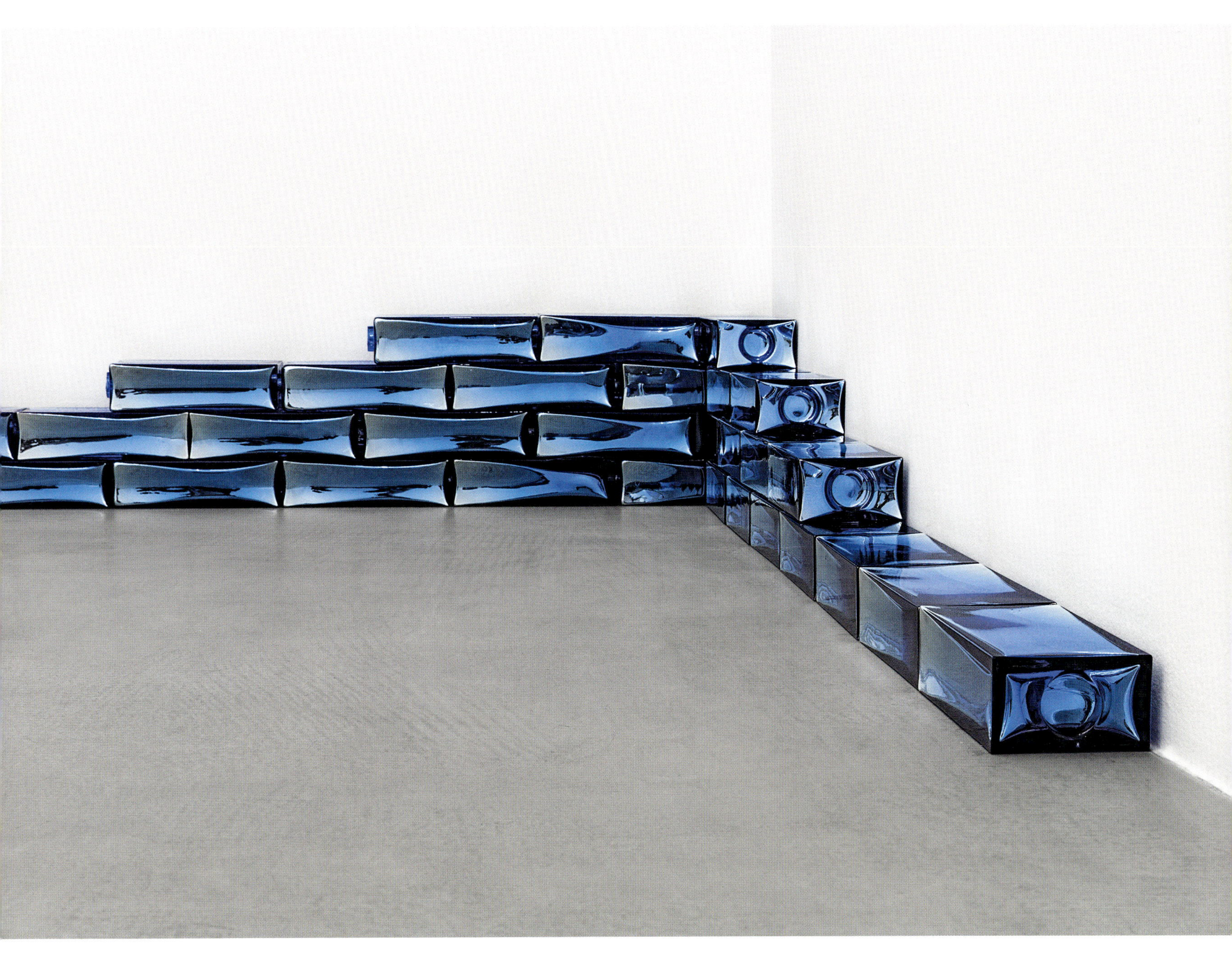

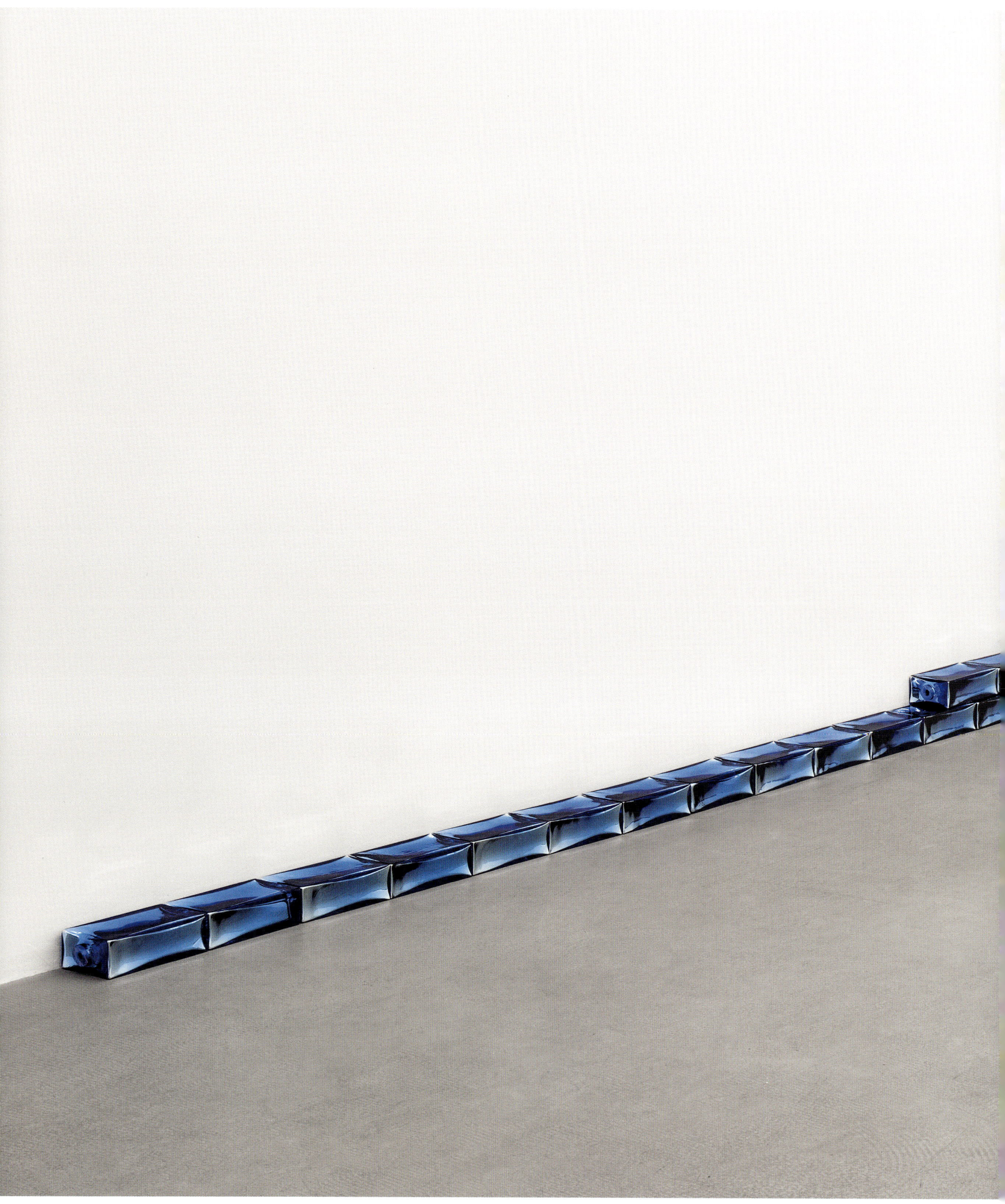

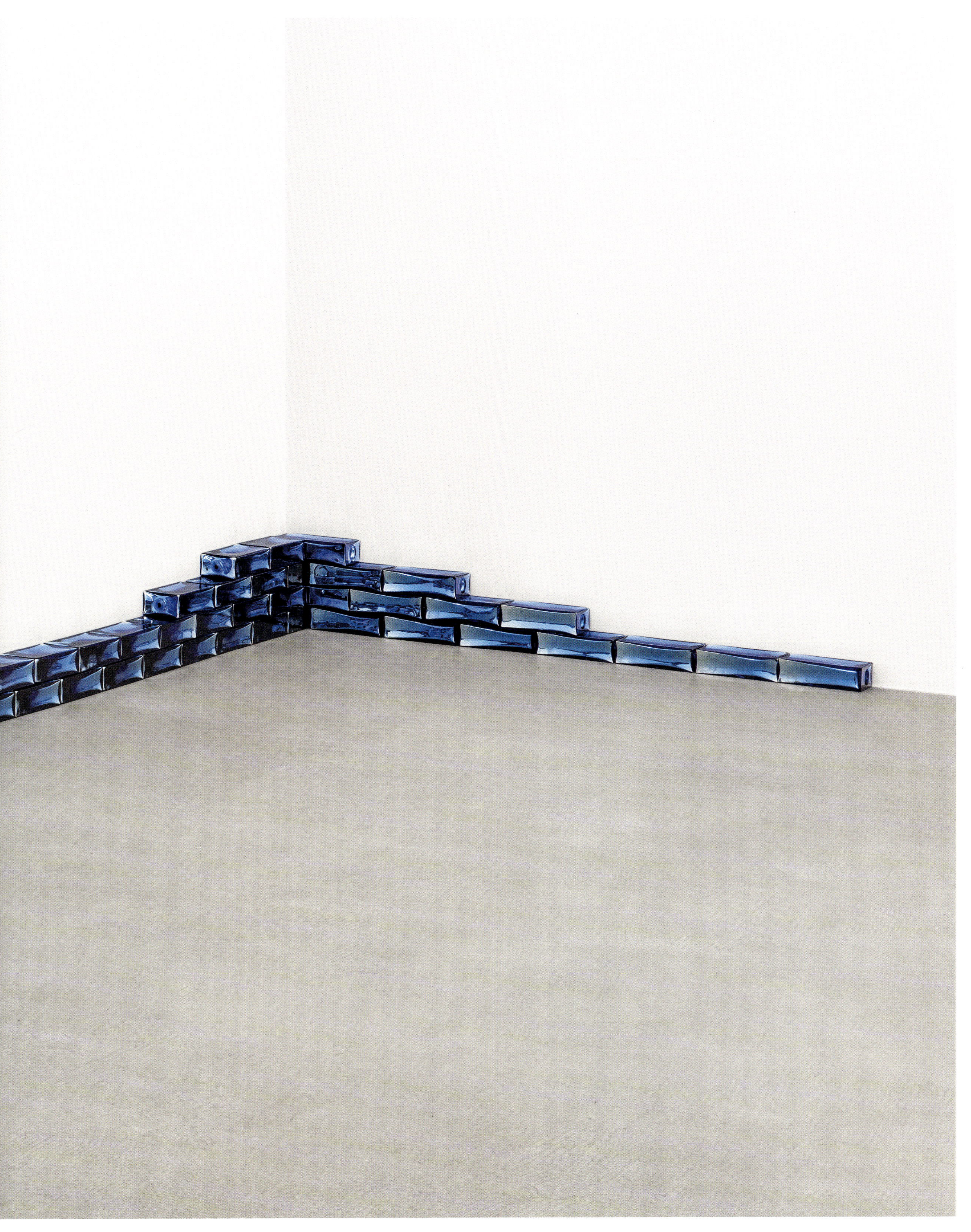

Terry Winters

born 1949 in Brooklyn, New York City, USA;
lives and works in New York City and
Columbia County, New York, USA

The American artist Terry Winters has been a prominent member of the New York art scene since the 1970s, with solo exhibitions at the Whitney Museum, New York; the Metropolitan Museum of Art, New York; the Whitechapel Gallery, London; and the Pinakothek der Moderne, Munich. Known for his paintings, drawings, and prints, he has enriched the language of abstraction by using a wealth of expressive colors, forms, and figures. In Winters' art, one discovers a pictorial language reminiscent of structures and constellations in nature, of micro- and macrocosms in the sciences, of complex networks and architectural patterns.

It is a stroke of luck that Winters also experiments with glass and has entrusted four of his glass sculptures from the *Marseille Templates* series (2004–06) to the Alexander Tutsek-Stiftung. What fascinates him about painting applies even more to glass: the ability to explore intuitively, tapping into a desire to unleash his own imagination and allow things to emerge on their own—only then does something happen that was not originally intended. Winters works with glass as simply another instrument, and his concerns are the same as when painting or drawing: the underlying aim is to bring about a kind of transformation. The *Marseille Templates* may appear to be derived from lab beakers, and yet they are not functional: they cannot stand on their own and are held up, provisionally it seems, by pieces of wood. Varying in shape and size, they all originate from the same matrix: abstract forms, transparent bodies that stretch into space in rhythmic curves, moving as though in the act of drawing.

Glass is a mixture of raw minerals, and blowing hot glass into a hollow shape is, along with modeling clay, the original process for creating a form. Through fire and "inspiration" (literally "breathing into"), the air develops bubbles and spheres as places to inhabit, as a space for thoughts. Vessels are created, each one unique, through a difficult process that involves calculation, skill, and pure chance. PGH

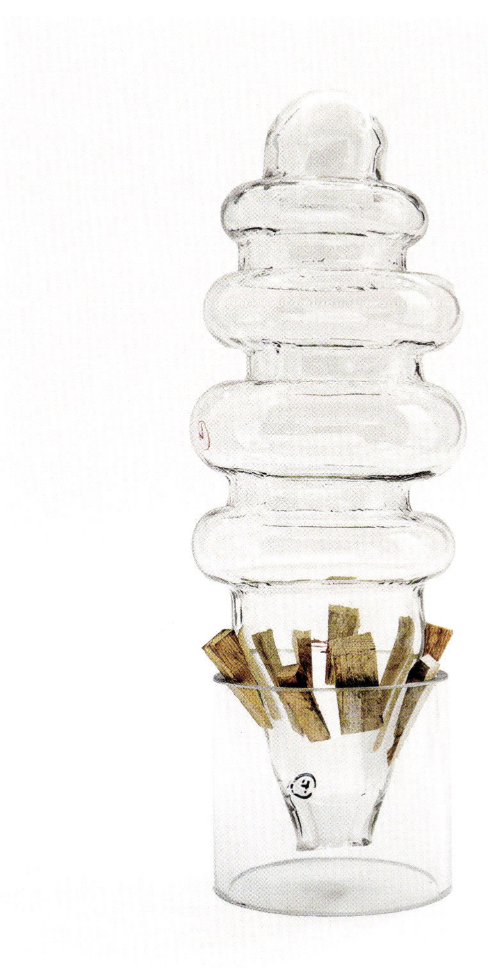

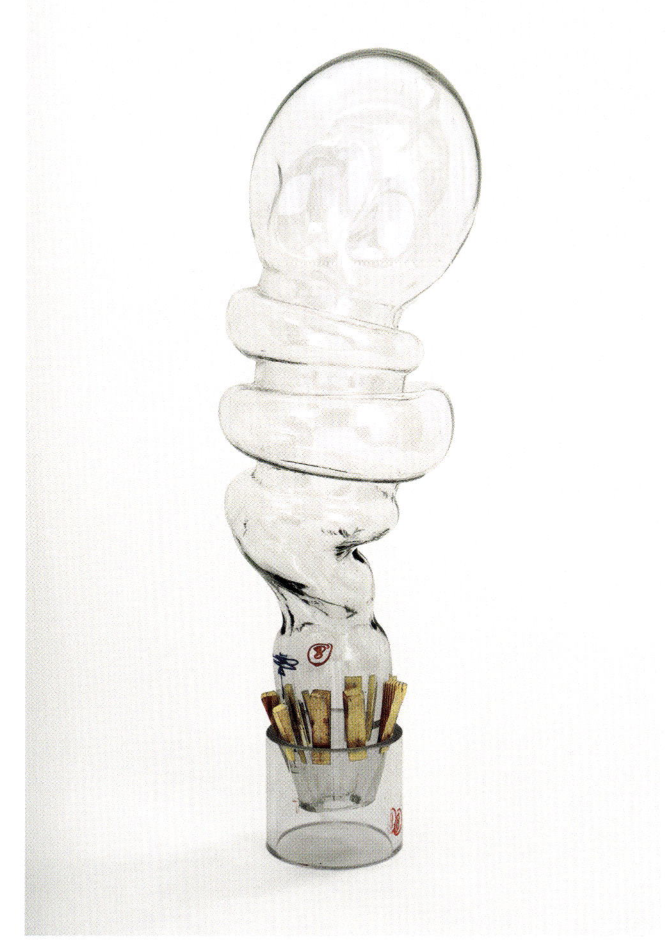

Marseille Template/4, 2004–06
Glass and wood
height 68 cm, diameter 25 cm

Marseille Template/8, 2004–06
Glass and wood
height 84 cm, diameter 25 cm

Marseille Template/16, 2004–06
Glass and wood
height 75 cm, diameter 34 cm

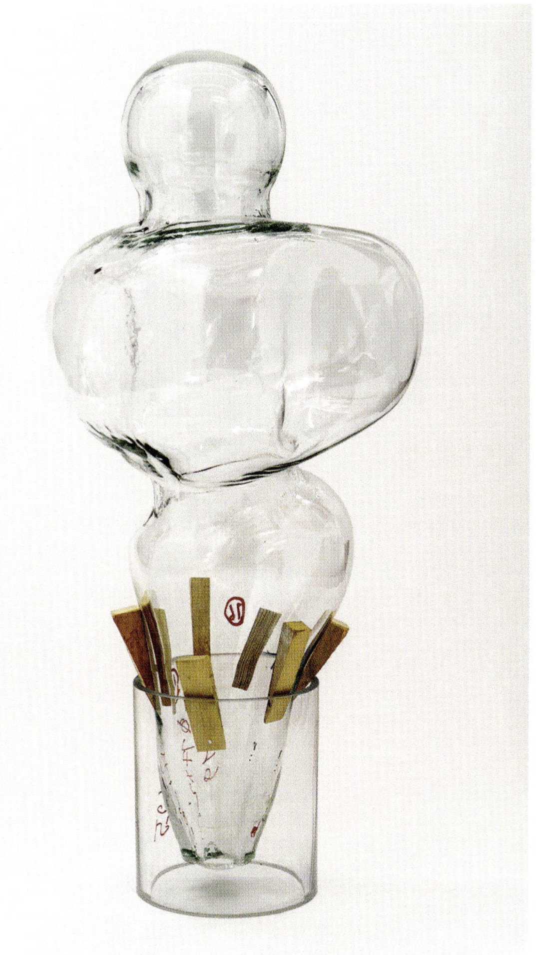

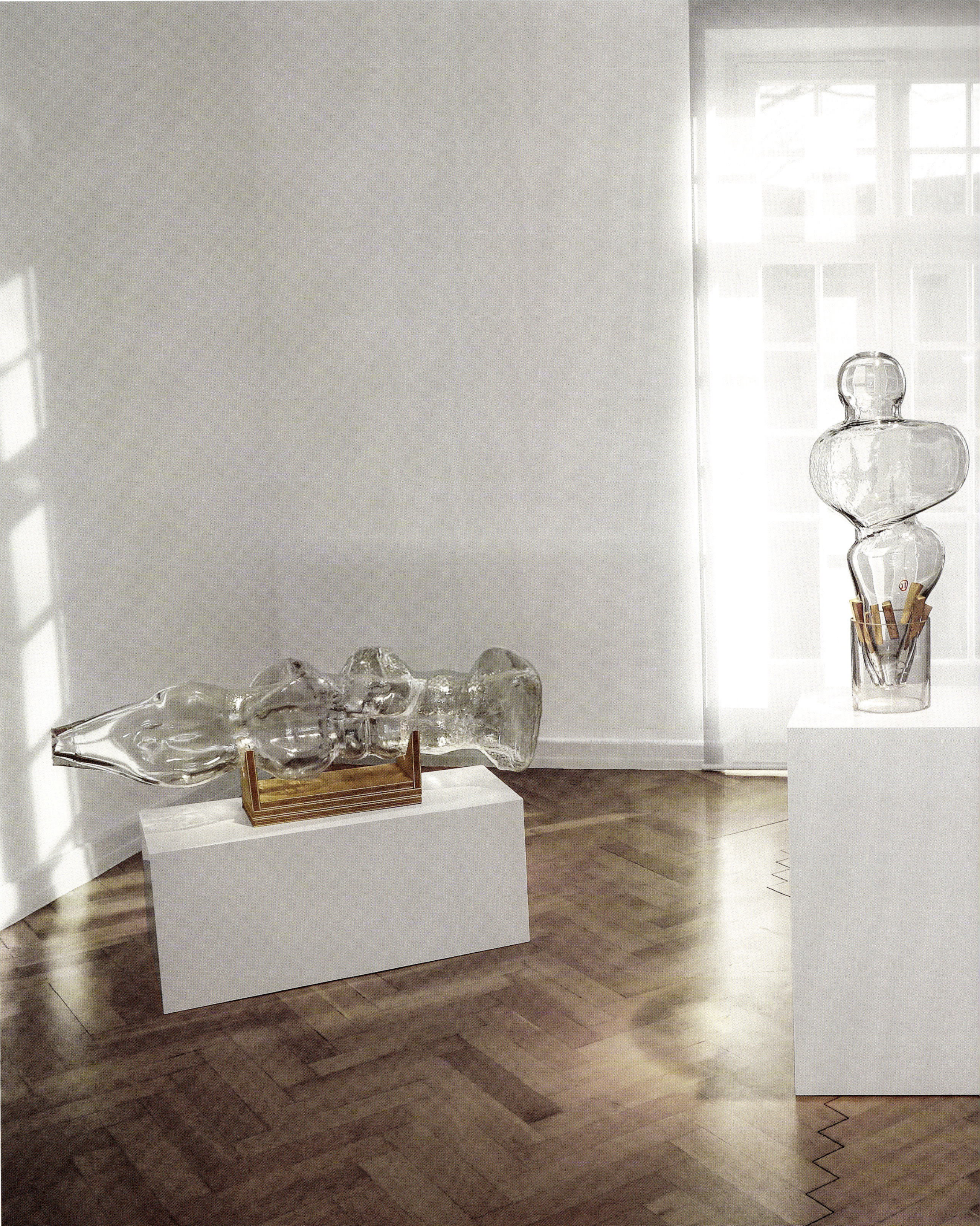

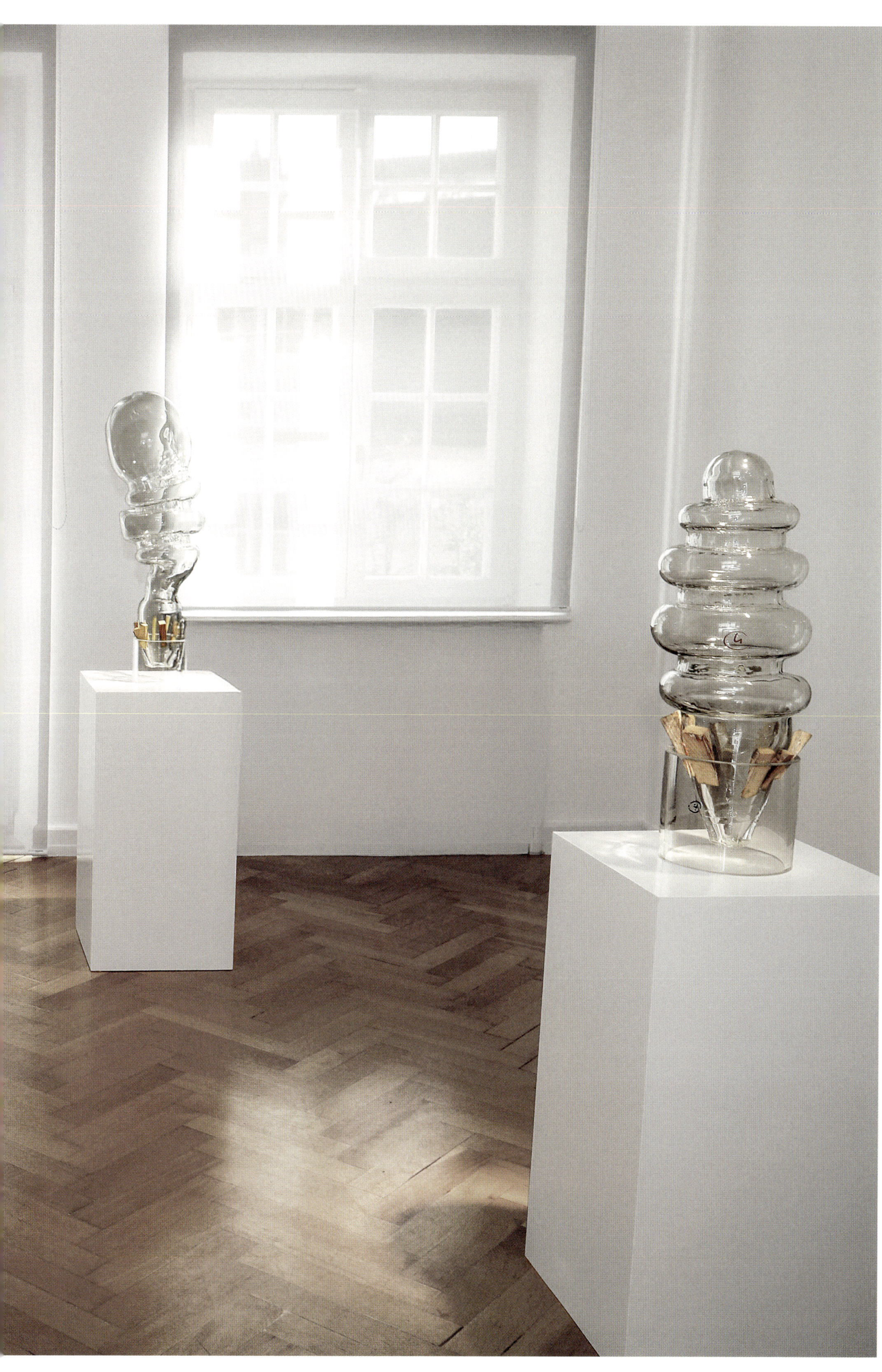

Installation view
Alexander Tutsek-Stiftung
from left to right:
Marseille Template/20,
2004–06
Marseille Template/16,
2004–06
Marseille Template/8,
2004–06
Marseille Template/4,
2004–06

Ann Wolff

born 1937 in Lübeck, Germany;
lives and works in Gotland, Sweden

Ann Wolff's comprehensive oeuvre comprises sculptural works made from glass, concrete, wood, aluminum, and stone as well as drawings and photography. For her works, she seeks the medium and the material that will allow her to express that which interests her.

A recurring theme in her work is the self. This is the point of departure for Wolff's interest in the world and the mainspring for her artistic work.[1] The human figure—the face in particular—serves as a narrator. It allows her to explore existential questions of being human, to reflect on questions of identity, and to study inner human states. In her work since 2000, the human figure, whether single or double or in a group, made of kiln-molded glass, stands in the foreground.[2] Wolff plays with the resulting forms, the negative and the positive, the hollow space and the body, the interior and the exterior. In the massive, 50-centimeter-high work *Andante* (2006), Wolff reveals herself to be a student of the interchanging relationship of body, space, and time. *Andante*—the striding woman, the moving woman—is a doubled female figure that runs from the right side as a negative form into the glass, only to emerge from the glass on the left as a positive form. Time, and also history, has passed in the meantime. Where is the figure going? What has she experienced?

Andante, 2005
Cast glass
50 × 18 × 50 cm

Starting with a clay model, Ann Wolff produces elaborate plaster molds into which, in a further process, the glass is melted. The fissured surface of the clay is clearly visible in the glass. In *Head and Head* (2012), a glass head has a doppelganger made of concrete. In *Domus I* (2006), the head is given a protective covering in the form of a house. Her large work *River* (2011), inspired by an altar, is a fusion of two halves that fit into each other, one positive and one negative, opened like a book.

After training at the School of Design in Ulm, Germany, Ann Wolff moved to Sweden in 1959 and had a successful career as a designer for Kosta Boda and others. In the 1970s, she became part of the international studio glass movement and regularly taught at the Pilchuck Glass School. In 1977, Ann Wolff was the first recipient of the now well-known Coburg Glass Prize and began her career as a freelance artist. Since then, Ann Wolff has had a decisive influence on artists working with glass. From 1993 to 1998, she was a professor at the University of Fine Arts Hamburg. In 2011, she was awarded the European Culture Prize for her artistic achievements.[3] AC

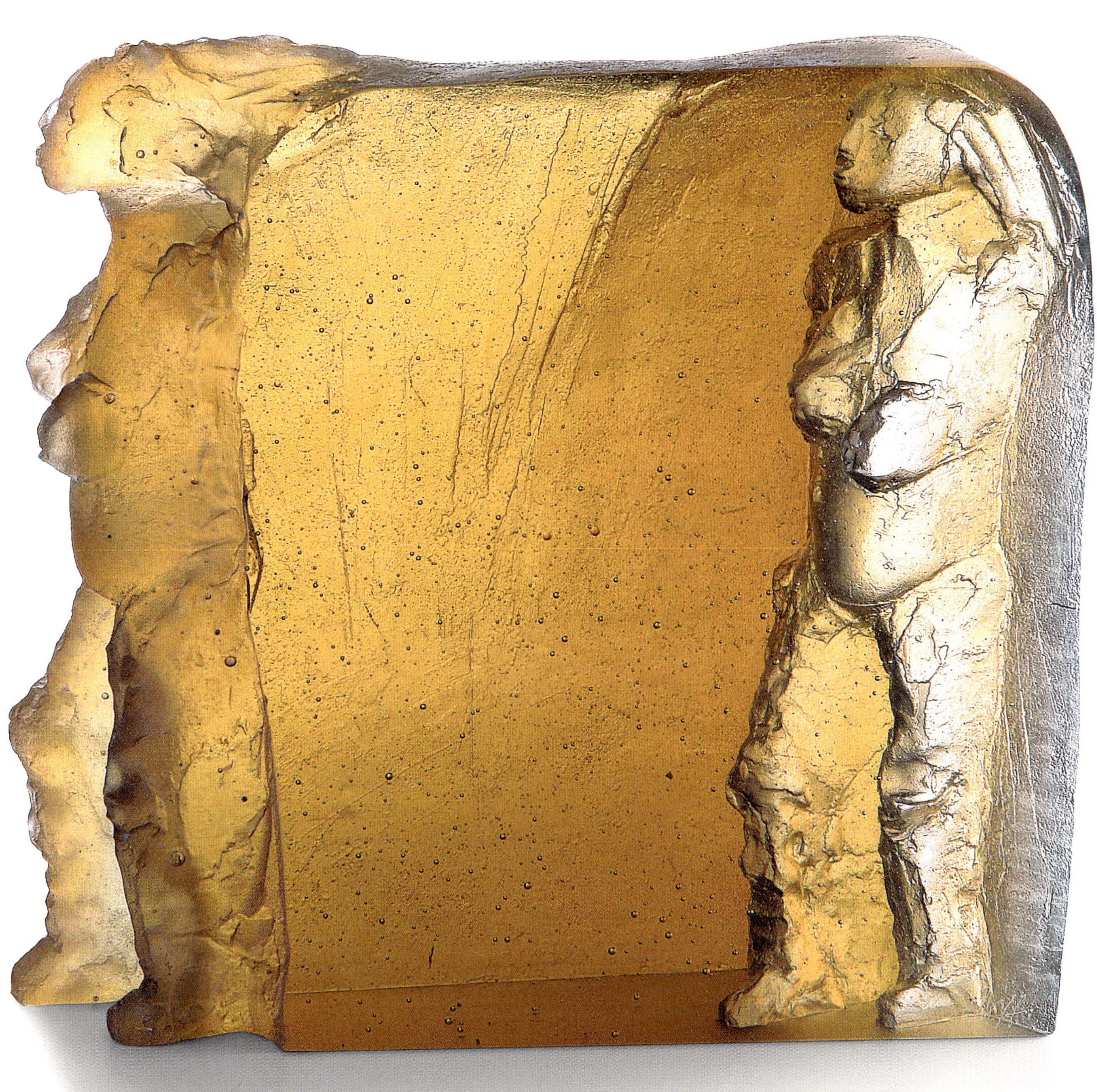

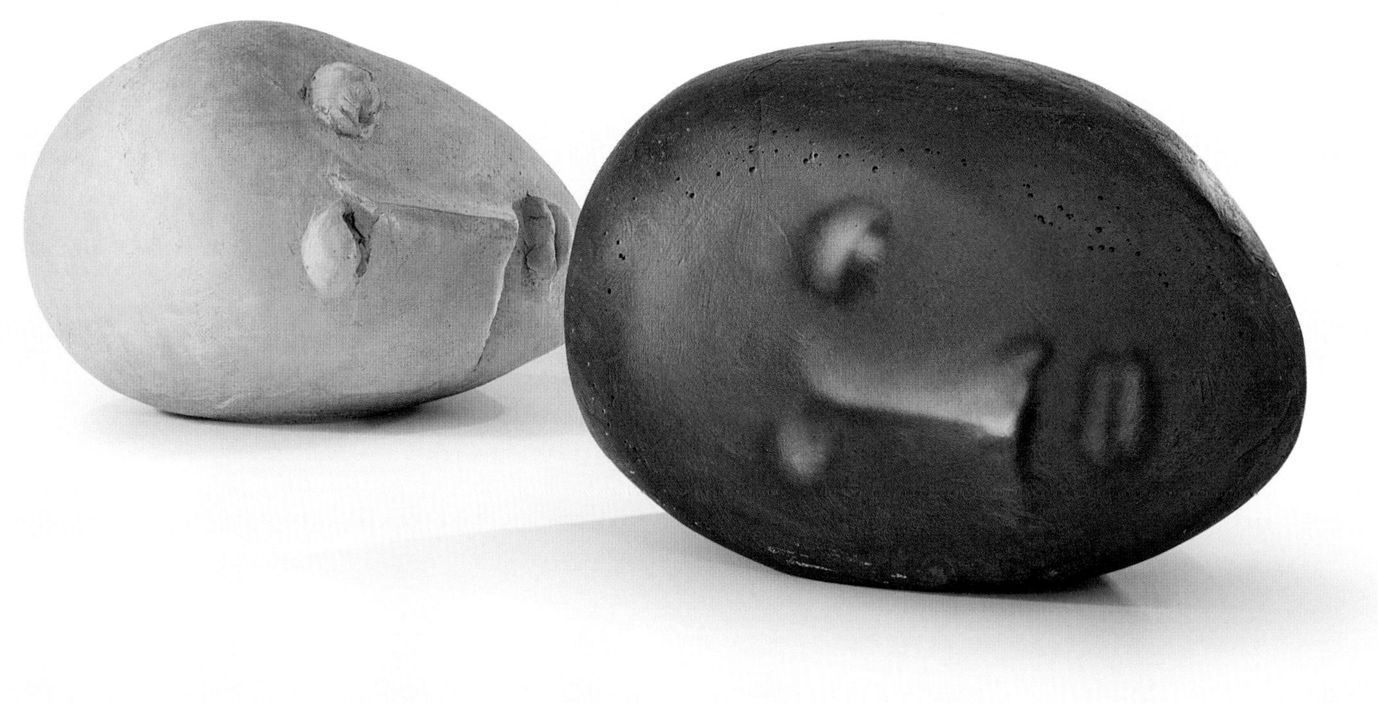

Head and Head, 2012
Cast glass
Glass head: 47 × 70 × 38 cm
Concrete head: 45 × 63 × 47 cm

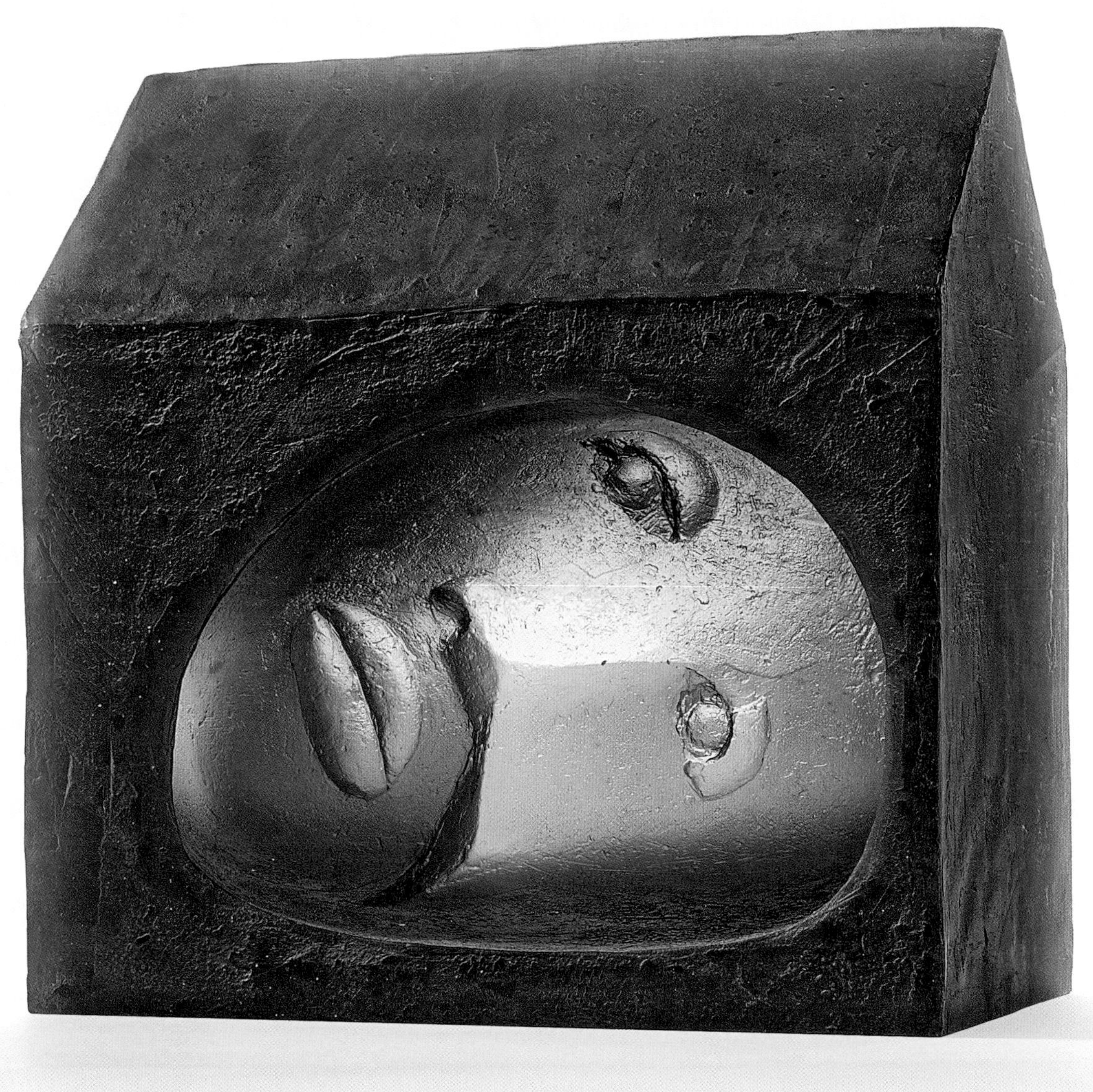

Domus I, 2006
Cast glass
37 × 35 × 23 cm

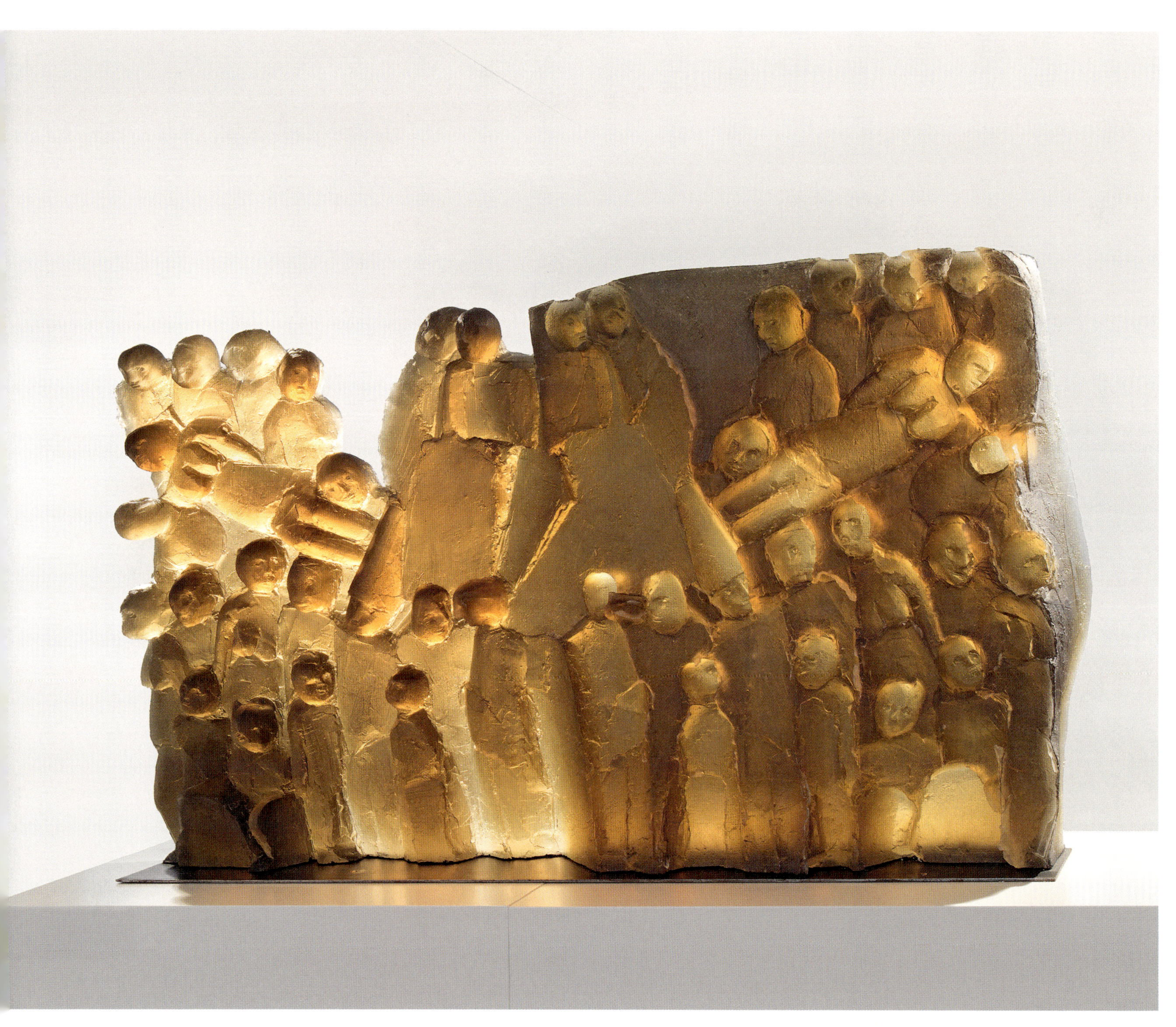

River, 2011
Cast glass
75 × 130 × 14 cm

References

The texts on the artists are based on generally available information (monographs, exhibition catalogues, the artists' websites, museums, galleries, platforms) which is not listed in detail here. The sources of the quotations follow in alphabetical order by artist.

NIKO ABRAMIDIS &NE

1 Max Goelitz, https://www.maxgoelitz.com/en/content/feature/396/artworks-358-niko-abramidis-ne-agenda-table-muc-manila-2020/.

PHILIP BALDWIN AND MONICA GUGGISBERG

1 Cf. *Baldwin / Guggisberg: Au-delà du verre / Beyond Glass*, exh. cat. Musée Ariana, Geneva, October 13, 2011–March 25, 2012 (Milan, 2011), 45–53.

2 Cf. *Amphore. Métaphore. Baldwin Guggisberg. Guggisberg Baldwin,* exh. cat. Musée du Verre François Décrochemont, June 25–November 27, 2022 (Conches-en-Ouche, 2022), 12–14.

MONICA BONVICINI

1 Performance in the Hercules Hall of the Munich Residence, 2017.

MARK BRADFORD

1 *Borsa* is indeed the third bag that Mark Bradford has made in Venice. In 2017 he and Rio Terà collaborated with Isotta Dardilli on a special-edition bag. In 2018, Bradford and Rio Terà teamed up with the architect Francesco Tencalla and interior designer Giada Mabrin for a second bag, marking the first anniversary of *Process Colletivo*. See Nicole R. Fleetwood, ed., Mark Bradford – Process Collettivo (Zurich: Hauser & Wirth, 2024), 68.

KRISTI CAVATARO

1 Claire Voon, "Kristi Cavataro Is a Fast-Rising Sculptor Breathing New Life into an Ancient Medium: Stained Glass," *Artnet*, September 23, 2022, https://news.artnet.com/art-world/sculptor-kristi-cavataro-breathes-new-life-into-stained-glass-2179677.

2 Rachel Wetzler, "Kristi Cavataro Pushes Stained Glass into Striking New Sculptural Directions," *Art in America*, May 5, 2022, 52–53, https://www.artnews.com/art-in-america/features/kristi-cavataro-new-talent-stained-glass-1234627684/.

3 Christopher Alessandrini, "The Evocative Sculptures of Kristi Cavataro Can't Be Pinned Down," *Interview*, April 21, 2021, https://www.interviewmagazine.com/art/the-evocative-sculptures-of-kristi-cavataro-cant-be-pinned-down.

DALE CHIHULY

1 Dale Chihuly in *Chihuly Jerusalem 2000* (Seattle: Portland Press, 2000), 30.

2 Chihuly in a fax to his son Jackson, dated June 13, 1999; reprinted in *Chihuly Jerusalem Cylinders* (Seattle: Portland Press, 1999), 140.

TONY CRAGG

1 Tony Cragg, quoted by the Leila Heller Gallery (2017), https://www.leilahellergallery.com/exhibitions/tony-cragg-at-difc-gate.

JIMMIE DURHAM

1 Jimmie Durham, Berlin, November 8, 2016, published by Michel Rein, Paris, 2017, https://michelrein.com/expositions/presentation/177/glass-with-jimmie-durham.

ERWIN EISCH

1 Cf. Charles Hajdamach, "Die Glasköpfe – 'eine allgemeine Menschlichkeit,'" in *Erwin Eisch. Wolken waren schon immer mein letzter Halt. Glas und Bilder,* ed. Katharina Eisch-Angus (Munich: Hirmer, 2012), 181–205.

2 Cf. Ines Kohl, "Ihr sollt Euch nicht vom Zweck, der Funktion der Dinge erniedrigen lassen," in *Erwin Eisch. Der Himmel fängt am Boden an,* ed. Uta Spies (Passau: Dietmar Klinger Verlag, 2007), 19–23.

CARLOS GARAICOA

1 Victor Sattler, "Achtung, zerbrechlich," *Monopol: Magazin für Kunst und Leben* (July 28, 2022), https://www.monopol-magazin.de/achtung-zerbrechlich-alexander-tutsek-stiftung.

2 Mario Merz, *Tavola spirale* (Spiral Table), 1982, aluminum, glass, fruit, vegetables, branches, steel, tar paper, beeswax. See Dimitris Lempesis, *Traces: Mario Merz,* http://www.dreamideamachine.com/?p=22126.

3 Carlos Garaicoa, quoted by Galleria Continua.

DONGHAI GUAN

1 Guan Donghai and Anthony Brewerton, in *Glass Art: Ausstellungskatalog von Objekten 2003 bis 2007* (2007).

MONA HATOUM

1 Mona Hatoum, "It's About Shattering the Familiar," interview by Emma Robertson, *The Talks,* http://the-talks.com/interview/mona-hatoum/.

2 Ibid.

SHIRAZEH HOUSHIARY

1 Shirazeh Houshiary, quoted in Farah Nayeri, "As Tensions Rise with Iran, So Does Interest in Art It Inspired," *The New York Times,* March 8, 2020, https://www.nytimes.com/2020/03/08/arts/iran-artists.html.

2 Shirazeh Houshiary in 2013, quoted in "Shirazeh Houshiary Becomes a Royal Academician," Lisson Gallery, July 13, 2022, https://www.lissongallery.com/news/shirazeh-houshiary-becomes-a-royal-acdaemician.

ANN VERONICA JANSSENS

1 Ann Veronica Janssens, "Making the Invisible Visible," interview by Margot Heller, in *Ann Veronica Janssens: Hot Pink Turquoise,* exh. cat. Louisiana Museum of Modern Art, Humlebæk, Denmark (2022), 83.

2 Ibid., 86.

3 Ibid., 86.

4 Ann Veronica Janssens, *Grand Bal,* ed. Roberta Tenconi, exh. cat. Pirelli HangarBicocca, Milan (2023), 122.

KI-RA KIM

1 Ki-Ra Kim, artist statement, https://kirakimglass.com/about/.

NAMDOO KIM

1 Namdoo Kim, artist statement, https://www.namdookim.com/art-works.html.

2 Namdoo Kim, statement on the work *Present,* https://www.namdookim.com/present-2012ndash.html.

YOSHIAKI KOJIRO

1 Cf. statement by Kojiro Yoshiaki, https://taimodern.com/artist/kojiro-yoshiaki/?section=statement (accessed January 19, 2025).

2 Cf. https://www.mouvementsmodernes.com/en/artist/yoshiaki-kojiro/biography (accessed January 19, 2025).

3 E-mail correspondence with Kojiro Yoshiaki on February 5, 2017.

SILVIA LEVENSON

1 Silvia Levenson, quoted in "Silvia Levenson: Personal and Political Revelations in Glass," *Talking Out Your Glass* (n.d.), https://talkingoutyourglass.com/silvia-levenson/.

2 Silvia Levenson, artist statement, Murano Glass Museum (2016), https://museovetro.visitmuve.it/en/mostre-en/archivio-mostre-en/silvia-levenson-exhib/2016/03/16612/identidad-desaparecida-levenson/.

STANISLAV LIBENSKÝ
JAROSLAVA BRYCHTOVÁ

1 Cf. Eva-Maria Fahrner-Tutsek, *Glas der Gegenwart. Katalog eins. Contemporary Glass* (Munich: Edition EMF / Alexander Tutsek-Stiftung, 2004), 6.

2 Cf. ibid., 13.

3 Cf. ibid., 32.

4 Cf. the website of the Victoria & Albert Museum, London, https://collections.vam.ac.uk/item/O5059/arcus-1-sculpture-libensky-stanislav/ (accessed January 17, 2025).

HAROON MIRZA

1 Max Goelitz, https://www.maxgoelitz.com/artists/35-haroon-mirza/works/1312-haroon-mirza-aurora-b-solar-powered-led-circuit-composition-43-2021/.

MASAYO ODAHASHI

1 Website of Art Alliance for Contemporary Glass, https://contempglass.org/artists/entry/masayo-odahashi (accessed January 4, 2025).

SIBYLLE PERETTI

1 Sibylle Peretti, https://sibylleperetti.com/page/2-Artist%27s%20Statement.html (accessed January 19, 2025).

2 E-mail correspondence with Sibylle Peretti on January 15, 2025.

LAURE PROUVOST

1 Laure Prouvost, "Laure Prouvost on Seduction, Language, and Bodily Provocations," interview by Natasha Hoare, *Extra Extra* no. 9, https://extraextramagazine.com/talk/laure-prouvost-seduction-language-bodily-provocations/.

COLIN REID

1 Colin Reid, Adrian Sassoon Gallery, London, https://www.adriansassoon.com/artists/70-colin-reid.

2 Colin Reid, Adrian Sassoon Gallery, London, https://www.adriansassoon.com/artists/70-colin-reid.

GIZELA ŠABÓKOVÁ

1 Website of Gizela Šabóková, https://gizelasabokova.com/ (accessed January 3, 2025).

ANRI SALA

1 Efi Michalarou, "Architecture into Art: A Dialogue," *Dream Idea Machine*, http://www.dreamideamachine.com/?p=63339.

2 Anri Sala, "What Interests Me the Most Is Not the Gesture, but the Becoming of the Gesture," interview, in *Bourse de Commerce: Pinault Collection* (October 10, 2022), https://www.pinaultcollection.com/en/boursedecommerce/what-interests-me-most-not-gesture-becoming-gesture-anri-sala.

MASAHIRO SASAKI

1 *Glashaus: Internationales Magazin für Studioglas* (April 2010): 10–11.

2 Ibid.

3 Website of the Corning Museum of Glass: https://people.cmog.org/bio/masahiro-sasaki (accessed December 29, 2024).

ERIC SIDNER

1 Eric Bell, "Eric Sidner: Capillary Refill," review of exhibition at Deborah Schamoni, Munich, 2022, *Art Viewer*, https://artviewer.org/eric-sidner-at-deborah-schamoni-2/.

JANA STERBAK

1 Jana Sterbak, "CICA Presents Jana Sterbak," notes written in collaboration with Huguette Epinat, *Conversations in Contemporary Art*, Concordia University (January 21, 2013), https://conversationsincontemporaryart.tumblr.com/post/41123525500/cica-presents-jana-sterbak.

JENNA SUTELA

1 Text by Max Goelitz Contemporary.

2 See exh. cat. Serpentine Gallery.

NERINGA VASILIAUSKAITĖ

1 Cf. *Neringa Vasiliauskaitė. repeat and remain again and again*, exh. cat. Städtische Galerie Villingen-Schwenningen, August 5 – October 7, 2018 (Villigen-Schwenningen, 2018), 7–8.

FRANTIŠEK VÍZNER

1 William Warmus, "Vizner's Vision," in Glass 82 (Spring 2001): 42–47.

2 František Vízner, Sklo/Glass (Rijen, 1994).

URSULA VON RYDINGSVARD

1 Helaine Posner, "Introduction," in *Ursula von Rydingsvard: Sculpture, 1991–2009*, exh. cat. Sculpture Center, New York (Munich: Prestel, 2011), 17.

QIN WANG

1 See *Glass Serendipity: Wang Qin Works 2005–2010*.

2 See ibid., 4.

3 See Xue Lu, "Akademisches Glas in China," in *Glass.China*, ed. Eva-Maria Fahrner-Tutsek (Munich: Edition EMF / Alexander Tutsek-Stiftung, 2009), 36.

4 See *Glass Serendipity*, 40.

SUNNY WANG

1 *Sunny Wang Glass*, exh. cat. KORU Touch of New Zealand (Split, Croatia, 2004).

2 Website of the HKBU library, https://heritage.lib.hkbu.edu.hk/routes/view/scripts/en/starts/0/owners/Faculty/sorts/title/languages/en (accessed January 9, 2025).

PAE WHITE

1 Amelia Bertsch, "'An Evening with Pae White': The Artist behind CMC's *Qwalala*," *The Student Life*, Claremont Colleges, November 8, 2024, https://tsl.news/an-evening-with-pae-white/.

2 Pae White, artist statement, California Community Foundation, https://www.calfund.org/fva/2009-gallery/pae-white/.

ANN WOLFF

1 Cf. Karin Sidén, "Preface," in *Ann Wolff*, exh. cat. Prins Eugens Waldemarsudde (Stockholm, 2022), 161.

2 Cf. Uli Seitz, ed., *Ann Wolff: Live* (Bielefeld: Kerber Christof Verlag, 2010), 9.

3 Dagmar Brendstrup, "Powerful, but Fragile Too: The Artist Ann Wolff – Strong and Sensual," in *Ann Wolff: Andante*, exh. cat. Toyama Glass Art Museum (Toyama, 2017), 19–23.

List of Works

Picture Credits

Niko Abramidis &NE / p. 29

Agenda Table (Muc-Manila), 2020
Steel, screen, glass, steel plate, smartphone dummy, drawing on Post-It and Google Earth video loop (27'13")
125 × 80 × 72 cm
© Niko Abramidis &NE, courtesy max goelitz, Photo: Dirk Tacke

Philip Baldwin and Monica Guggisberg / p. 31

First Memories, 2010
Blown-glass vessel with cold-worked surface
139.7 × 34.9 × 40 cm
© Philip Baldwin Monica Guggisberg, Photo: Gaëtane Fiona Girard

Monica Bonvicini / pp. 33–39

Small Pendant (2), 2021
Glass, cable, cast aluminum
Cast aluminum: 9.5 × 39 × 4 cm
Overall: 26 × 39 × 6 cm
© Monica Bonvicini / VG Bild-Kunst, Bonn 2025, courtesy Galerie Peter Kilchmann, Zurich, Photo: Jens Ziehe

In My Hand, 2019
Glass, metal
35 × 20 × 20 cm
© Monica Bonvicini / VG Bild-Kunst, Bonn 2025, courtesy Galerie Peter Kilchmann, Zurich, Photo: Sebastian Schaub

Fleurs du Mal (pink), 2019
Steel, hand-blown glass
Approx. 170 × 150 × 150 cm
© Monica Bonvicini / VG Bild-Kunst, Bonn 2025, courtesy Galleria Raffaella Cortese, Milan, Photo: Andrea Rossetti

Bonded, 2017
Glass, metal, mirror, table
Sculpture: 84 × 47 × 47 cm
Table: 70 × 100 × 60 cm
© Monica Bonvicini / VG Bild-Kunst, Bonn 2025, courtesy Galerie Peter Kilchmann, Zurich, Photo: Sebastian Schaub

Mark Bradford / p. 41

Borsa, 2024
Murano glass
66 × 17.8 × 33.3 cm
Edition 25/30 + 5 AP
© Mark Bradford, courtesy Hauser & Wirth, Photo: Keith Lubow

Kristi Cavataro / pp. 43–45

Untitled, 2019
Stained glass
86.4 × 53.3 × 22.9 cm
© Kristi Cavataro, courtesy RAMIKEN

Untitled, 2022
Stained glass
59.7 × 94 × 94 cm
© Kristi Cavataro, Photo: Mark Waldhauser, courtesy Lisson Gallery

Dale Chihuly / p. 47

Jerusalem Cylinder, 2000
Mold-blown glass, chunks of crystals applied hot
59 × 17 × 17 cm
© Dale Chihuly / VG Bild-Kunst, Bonn 2025, Photo: Hans-Joachim Becker, courtesy Alexander Tutsek-Stiftung

Tony Cragg / pp. 49–51

Untitled, 2015
Glass
47 × 26 × 27 cm
© Tony Cragg / VG Bild-Kunst, Bonn 2025, Photo: Michael Richter

Listeners, 2015
Glass
37 × 35 × 21 cm / 36 × 40 × 18 cm
© Tony Cragg / VG Bild-Kunst, Bonn 2025

Jimmie Durham / p. 53

Verre en plein air 1, 2017
Steel structure with glass
165.5 × 87 × 89.5 cm
© Jimmie Durham, Permission to publish by estate of Jimmie Durham and Michel Rein, Paris/Brussels, Photo: Marion Vogel, courtesy Alexander Tutsek-Stiftung

Erwin Eisch / pp. 55–59

Der Bruch ist die Sünde, 1997
Mold-blown glass, painted
58 × 26 × 30 cm
© Erwin Eisch, Photo: Hans-Joachim Becker, courtesy Alexander Tutsek-Stiftung

Bodisatwa, die Erleuchtete, 1985
Mold-blown glass, painted, engraved
54 × 24 × 24 cm
© Erwin Eisch, Photo: Hans-Joachim Becker, courtesy Alexander Tutsek-Stiftung

Buddha, 1982
Mold-blown glass, mirrored, painted
50 × 24 × 22 cm
© Erwin Eisch, Photo: Hans-Joachim Becker, courtesy Alexander Tutsek-Stiftung

Buddha Heads
Installation view: Alexander Tutsek-Stiftung
© Erwin Eisch, Photo: Hans-Joachim Becker, courtesy Alexander Tutsek-Stiftung

Die Einsicht, 1989
Mold-blown glass, engraving, gold leaf
47 × 30 × 24 cm
© Erwin Eisch, courtesy Galerie B, Photo: Michael Bode

Jes Fan / pp. 60–61

Networks (for Expansion), 2021
Borosilicate glass, silicone, *Phycomyces* zygospore liquid culture
116.8 × 61 × 127 cm
© Jes Fan, courtesy Empty Gallery, Photo: Pierre Le Hors

Carlos Garaicoa / pp. 63–65

Jardín Frágil (Versión I) / Fragile Garden (Version I), 2019 (Detail)
Installation
Murano crystal, metal, glass
25 + 5 blowpipes, each 200–220 cm
Overall: approx. 90 × 230 × 620 cm
© Carlos Garaicoa / VG Bild-Kunst, Bonn 2025, courtesy Galleria Continua, San Gimignano / Beijing / Les Moulins / Habana

Jardín Frágil (Versión I) / Fragile Garden (Version I), 2019
Installation view: Alexander Tutsek-Stiftung
© Carlos Garaicoa / VG Bild-Kunst, Bonn 2025, Photo: Marion Vogel, courtesy Alexander Tutsek-Stiftung
In the background:
Laure Prouvost
Cooling System 3 (For Global Warming), 2018
© Laure Prouvost / VG Bild-Kunst, Bonn 2025
Anri Sala
No Window No Cry (Luigi Cosenza, La Fabbrica Olivetti, Pozzuoli), 2015
© Anri Sala / VG Bild-Kunst, Bonn 2025

Donghai Guan / pp. 67–69

Regime, 2006
Cast glass
25 × 11 × 49 cm
© Guan Donghai, Photo: Hans-Joachim Becker, courtesy Alexander Tutsek-Stiftung

City Gate #7, 2006
Cast glass with bronze detail
47 × 32 × 13 cm
© Guan Donghai, Photo: Hans-Joachim Becker, courtesy Alexander Tutsek-Stiftung

White City Gate, 2008
Cast glass
60 × 38 × 10 cm
© Guan Donghai, Photo: Hans-Joachim Becker, courtesy Alexander Tutsek-Stiftung

Jens Gussek / pp. 71–73

The Blue Flower, 2007
Blown glass, wood
Object: 62 × 48 × 32 cm
Wood: 68 × 36 × 11 cm
© Jens Gussek, Photo: Hans-Joachim Becker, courtesy Alexander Tutsek-Stiftung

Dreams Behind Me, 2007
Blown glass
180 × 130 × 35 cm
© Jens Gussek, Photo: Hans-Joachim Becker, courtesy Alexander Tutsek-Stiftung

Mona Hatoum / pp. 75–79

Korb V, 2014
Hand-blown glass and steel
33 × 49.5 × 45 cm
© Mona Hatoum, courtesy Alexander and Bonin, New York, Photo: Joerg Lohse

Turbulence (black), 2014
Black glass marbles
3 × 250 × 250 cm
© Mona Hatoum, courtesy Galerie Chantal Crousel, Paris, Photo: Sebastiano Pellion

Drowning Sorrows (cachaça), 2014
Cut glass bottles
15 × 200 × 200 cm
© Mona Hatoum, Photo: Hans-Joachim Becker, courtesy Alexander Tutsek-Stiftung

Shirazeh Houshiary / pp. 80–81

Alar, 2016–17
Glass and mirror-polished stainless steel
145 × 118 × 118 cm
© Shirazeh Houshiary / VG Bild-Kunst, Bonn 2025, courtesy Lisson Gallery

Ann Veronica Janssens / p. 83

Magic Mirror CL9E166, 2021–22
Dichroic composite glass consisting of crash glass, float glass, and gelatin filters
120 × 120 × 1.8 cm
Edition 1 + 1 AP
© Ann Veronica Janssens / VG Bild-Kunst, Bonn 2025, courtesy Esther Schipper, Berlin/Paris/Seoul, Photo: Jörg von Bruchhausen

Hassan Khan / p. 85

The Knot, 2012
Glass sculpture and stainless-steel stand
10 × 72 × 6 cm / 120 × 92 × 40 cm
Edition 3/3 + 1 AP
© Hassan Khan, courtesy Galerie Chantal Crousel, Photo: Anders Sune Berg (Installation view: documenta 2012)

Ki-Ra Kim / p. 87

Glass Feather-65 III, 2015
Kiln-formed glass, steel frame
diameter 65 cm
© Ki-Ra Kim, Photo: Nikolaus Steglich, courtesy Alexander Tutsek-Stiftung

Namdoo Kim / p. 89

Present III, 2022
Ceramic, glass, copper, and mixed media
67 × 40 × 40 cm
© Namdoo Kim, courtesy Gallery Sklo, Photo: Myoung-June OH

Yoshiaki Kojiro / pp. 91–93

Be, 2005
Cast glass with calcium carbonate, kiln-fired
54 × 48 × 16 cm
© Yoshiaki Kojiro, Photo: Hans-Joachim Becker, courtesy Alexander Tutsek-Stiftung

Hatate II, 2012
Cast glass with calcium carbonate, kiln-fired
56 × 77 × 63 cm
© Yoshiaki Kojiro

Raimund Kummer / pp. 95–97

Gespräch unter drei Augen (Aus dem Albinokomplex), 1990
Eyes: 3 pieces, Bohemian glass, each 23 cm in diameter
Stools: 3 pieces, Karacabey Black Marble, each 44 × 48 × 40 cm
© Raimund Kummer / VG Bild-Kunst, Bonn 2025, Installation view: Neue Nationalgalerie, Berlin

Sternengewölbe, 1990
Eye: Bohemian glass, height approx. 18.5 cm, diameter approx. 35 cm
Stars: cast steel, 23 pieces, height 1.5–2.5 cm, diameter approx. 2–5 cm
Case: steel, vulcanized rubber and Plexiglas, overall: 96 × 62 × 53.5 cm
© Raimund Kummer / VG Bild-Kunst, Bonn 2025

Alicja Kwade / p. 99

Hemmungsloser Widerstand, 2019
Mirror, found stones, safety glass
86.5 × 71 × 122 cm
© Alicja Kwade

Glenda León / p. 101

Listening to the Rain, 2023
Blown glass, sound
270 × 43 × 43 cm
© Glenda León, courtesy Max Estrella Gallery

Antoine Leperlier / pp. 103–105

Flux et Fixe XIV, 2012
Pâte de verre
30 × 9.5 × 31 cm
© Antoine Leperlier / VG-Bild Kunst, Bonn 2025

La Chute (Vanité au Lapin VI), 2001
Crystal pâte de verre, hot-sculpted
47 × 26 × 13 cm
© Antoine Leperlier / VG-Bild Kunst, Bonn 2025, Photo: Hans-Joachim Becker, courtesy Alexander Tutsek-Stiftung

Silvia Levenson / pp. 107–109

She flew away II, 2014
Kiln-cast glass
Shoes: 6 × 7 × 17 cm each
Swing: 3 × 40 × 20 cm
© Silvia Levenson, Photo: Marion Vogel, courtesy Alexander Tutsek-Stiftung

Recovered Identity, 2014–present (Detail)
Kiln-cast glass, 133 pieces
© Silvia Levenson, Photo: Marion Vogel, courtesy Alexander Tutsek-Stiftung

I see you are a bit nervous II, 2006
Mixed media, kiln-formed glass, wood
approx. 120 × 120 × 200 cm
© Silvia Levenson, Photo: Hans-Joachim Becker, courtesy Alexander Tutsek-Stiftung

Stanislav Libenský and Jaroslava Brychtová / pp. 111–113

Empty Throne, 1989–2004
Cast glass
90 × 70 × 26 cm
© Stanislav Libenský / Jaroslava Brychtová, Photo: Hans-Joachim Becker, courtesy Alexander Tutsek-Stiftung

Arcus I, 1990–99
Cast glass
75 × 102 × 21 cm
© Stanislav Libenský / Jaroslava Brychtová, Photo: Hans-Joachim Becker, courtesy Alexander Tutsek-Stiftung

Jessica Loughlin / pp. 115–117

Open Space 19, 2005
Kiln-formed and wheel-cut glass
67.3 × 74 × 3.8 cm
© Jessica Loughlin, Photo: Grant Hancock

Between Spaces 5, 1999
Glass, fused, engraved, wheel-cut, slumped
81.9 × 15.9 × 4.1 cm
© Jessica Loughlin, Photo: Hans-Joachim Becker, courtesy Alexander Tutsek-Stiftung

Haroon Mirza / pp. 119–121

Illuminated Amanita Harvest (Solar Cell Circuit Composition 22), 2023
Solar cells, polyurethane resin, copper tape, electrical wire, magnetic wire, LED tape, miniature painting by Brishna Amin Khan, cables on glass, and anodized aluminum
146.8 × 146.8 × 7.6 cm
© Haroon Mirza, courtesy max goelitz, Photo: Dirk Tacke

Aurora B (Solar Powered LED Circuit Composition 43), 2021
Addressable LEDs, electrical wire, copper tape, magnetic wire, LED matrix, polyurethane resin, metal pigments, acetate, oil on canvas, and QT Py on photovoltaic panel
164 × 100 × 8 cm
© Haroon Mirza, courtesy max goelitz, Photo: Milena Wojhan

Masayo Odahashi / pp. 123–125

Calm of Water V, 2004
Cast and enameled glass
50 × 17 × 18 cm
© Masayo Odahashi, Photo: Hans-Joachim Becker, courtesy Alexander Tutsek-Stiftung

Two Directions, 2009
Cast and enameled glass
26 × 45 × 18 cm
© Masayo Odahashi, Photo: Hans-Joachim Becker, courtesy Alexander Tutsek-Stiftung

Sibylle Peretti / p. 127

Twins, 2002
Pâte de verre, glass droplets
27 × 23 × 13 cm
© Sibylle Peretti, Photo: Hans-Joachim Becker, courtesy Alexander Tutsek-Stiftung

Laure Prouvost / p. 129

Cooling System 3 (For Global Warming), 2018
Glass, wooden stick, framed drawing
Fountain: 224 × 127 × 126 cm
© Laure Prouvost / VG Bild-Kunst, Bonn 2025, courtesy Lisson Gallery, Photo: George Darrell

Colin Reid / p. 131

Ring of Fire R1739, 2013
Kiln-cast glass, ground, polished
91 × 92 × 10 cm
© Colin Reid

Gizela Šabóková / p. 133

The Slim One, 1998
Cast glass
70 × 12 × 12 cm
© Gizela Šabóková / VG Bild-Kunst, Bonn 2025, Photo: Hans-Joachim Becker, courtesy Alexander Tutsek-Stiftung

Anri Sala / p. 135

No Window No Cry (Luigi Cosenza, La Fabbrica Olivetti, Pozzuoli), 2015
Music box, glass, metal, window frame
202.5 × 60 × 3.5 cm
Edition 1 + 1 AP
© Anri Sala / VG Bild-Kunst, Bonn 2025, courtesy Galleria Alfonso Artiaco, Napoli, Photo: Luciano Romano

Masahiro Sasaki / pp. 137–139

Tensei 0911, 2009
Blown glass, sandblast
30 × 31 × 73 cm
© Masahiro Sasaki

Tensei 1108, 2011
Blown glass, sandblast
71 × 19 × 19 cm
© Masahiro Sasaki

Alejandra Seeber / pp. 140–141

Speech Bubble (iride), 2014
Murano glass and steel cable
39 × 48 × 20 cm
© Alejandra Seeber, courtesy Häusler Contemporary München | Zürich

Speech Bubble (verde iride), 2014
Murano glass and steel cable
46 × 33 × 18 cm
© Alejandra Seeber, courtesy Häusler Contemporary München | Zürich

Speech Bubble (opalina), 2014
Murano glass and steel cable
45 × 62 × 20 cm
© Alejandra Seeber, courtesy Häusler Contemporary München | Zürich

Speech Bubbles, 2014
Installation view: Alexander Tutsek-Stiftung
© Alejandra Seeber, courtesy Häusler Contemporary München | Zürich, Photo: Nikolaus Steglich, courtesy Alexander Tutsek-Stiftung

Eric Sidner / p. 143

Drops, 2022
Glass, bronze, brass
145 × 85 × 32 cm
© Eric Sidner, courtesy Deborah Schamoni, Photo: Ulrich Gebert

Kiki Smith / pp. 145–149

Sainte Geneviève and the Deer, 1999
Fired paint on glass panels
2 panels ranging from 137.8 × 122.9 cm to 226.1 × 118.7 cm
© Kiki Smith, courtesy Pace Gallery, Photo: Kerry Ryan McFate

Ashen, 2010
Wood and lamp glass
Overall installation dimensions variable
Coffin open: 83.8 × 156.2 × 56.5 cm
Coffin closed: 30.5 × 158.1 × 56.5 cm,
Drop-leaf table: 75.56 × 101.6 × 48.26 cm,
15 dandelion puffs: 21.9 × 2.5 × 2.5 cm to 26 × 7.9 × 7.9 cm
© Kiki Smith, courtesy Pace Gallery, Photo: Thomas Dashuber, courtesy Diözesanmuseum Freising

Untitled (Oil Color Flowers), 2008
Oil paint on mouth-blown clear antique glass with white and yellow gold leaf
3 framed glass panels, each 60.3 × 50.2 × 4.4 cm
© Kiki Smith, courtesy Pace Gallery

Mine, 1999 (Detail)
Glass
9.5 × 11.4 × 12.1 cm to 17.8 × 18.4 × 9.5 cm, 38 units, each installation dimensions variable
© Kiki Smith, courtesy Pace Gallery, Photo: Thomas Dashuber, courtesy Diözesanmuseum Freising

Jana Sterbak / p. 151

Hard Entry, 2003
Glass, hand-blown, hand-shaped, 8 pieces
height 28.5 cm, diameter 32 cm
© Jana Sterbak, courtesy Barbara Gross Galerie

Jenna Sutela / p. 153

Indigo, Orange and Plum Matter (I Magma cycle), 2021
3 pieces, blown glass, goo, heating and lighting equipment, custom plinths with motors and LED lights with projectile lenses
Each head approx. 35 × 23 × 18 cm
© Jenna Sutela, Photo: Rob Battersby

Hui Tao / p. 155

Money Grab Hand, 2024 (Detail)
Cast glass
380 pieces, each approx. 14 × 4 × 4 cm
© Tao Hui, commissioned by Tai Kwun Contemporary, courtesy Tai Kwun and Esther Schipper, Berlin/Paris/Seoul, Photo: South Ho

Neringa Vasiliauskaitė / p. 157–159

400–700 / 1, 2015
Curved coated glass, Optiweiss glass, multiplex board
diameter 117 × 3.8 × 4 cm
© Neringa Vasiliauskaitė

400–700 / 2, 2015
Coated glass with gradient, Optiweiss glass, multiplex board
108 × 4.2 × 4 cm
© Neringa Vasiliauskaitė

František Vízner / pp. 161–163

Bowl, 2000
Polished glass
approx. 18 × 32 × 32 cm
© František Vízner / VG Bild-Kunst, Bonn 2025, Photo: Hans-Joachim Becker, courtesy Alexander Tutsek-Stiftung

Eckige Vase, 2000
Polished glass
approx. 18 × 20 × 20 cm
© František Vízner / VG Bild-Kunst, Bonn 2025, Photo: Hans-Joachim Becker, courtesy Alexander Tutsek-Stiftung

Ursula von Rydingsvard / pp. 165–167

Luminosa, 2013
Glass
185.4 × 228.6 × 25.4 cm
© Ursula von Rydingsvard / VG Bild-Kunst, Bonn 2025, Photo: Marion Vogel, courtesy Alexander Tutsek-Stiftung

Janusz Walentynowicz / pp. 169–171

Black Box, 2013
Cast glass
49 × 36 × 36 cm
© Janusz Walentynowicz

Standing, 2000
Cast glass
93 × 63 × 11 cm
© Janusz Walentynowicz, Photo: Hans-Joachim Becker, courtesy Alexander Tutsek-Stiftung

Qin Wang / pp. 173–175

Ascend, 2007
Cast glass
55 × 21 × 11 cm
© Wang Qin, Photo: Hans-Joachim Becker, courtesy Alexander Tutsek-Stiftung

Faraway Mountain, 2007
Cast glass
63 × 32 × 8 cm
© Wang Qin, Photo: Hans-Joachim Becker, courtesy Alexander Tutsek-Stiftung

Summer Sitting II, 2006
Cast glass
45 × 26 × 9 cm
© Wang Qin, Photo: Hans-Joachim Becker, courtesy Alexander Tutsek-Stiftung

Sunny Wang / pp. 177–178

Almost Self, 2006
Furnace glass hot formed
40 × 25 × 8 cm
© Sunny Wang, Photo: Hans-Joachim Becker, courtesy Alexander Tutsek-Stiftung

More Than Self, 2006
Furnace glass hot formed
38 × 18 × 8 cm
© Sunny Wang, Photo: Hans-Joachim Becker, courtesy Alexander Tutsek-Stiftung

Pae White / pp. 181–183

Overserved, 2017
52 blown mirrored glass bricks
24.1 × 10.1 × 6.9 cm each
24 × 533 × 184 cm
© Pae White, courtesy kaufmann repetto, Milano / New York, Photo: Andrea Rossetti

Terry Winters / pp. 185–187

Marseille Template/4, 2004–06
Glass and wood
height 68 cm, diameter 25 cm
© Terry Winters, courtesy Matthew Marks Gallery

Marseille Template/8, 2004–06
Glass and wood
height 84 cm, diameter 25 cm
© Terry Winters, Courtesy Matthew Marks Gallery

Marseille Template/16, 2004–06
Glass and wood
height 75 cm, diameter 34 cm
© Terry Winters, courtesy Matthew Marks Gallery

Marseille Templates, 2004–06
Installation view: Alexander Tutsek-Stiftung

Ann Wolff / pp. 189–192

Andante, 2005
Cast glass
50 × 18 × 50 cm

Head and Head, 2012
Cast glass
Glass head: 47 × 70 × 38 cm
Concrete head: 45 × 63 × 47 cm

Domus I, 2006
Cast glass
37 × 35 × 23 cm

River, 2011
Cast glass
75 × 130 × 14 cm

Contributors and Editor

Dr. Eva-Maria Fahrner-Tutsek studied sociology, political science, and psychology. After earning a master's degree in psychology and a PhD in natural sciences, she became a research psychologist at the Max Planck Institute of Psychiatry and the Technische Universität München as well as a group manager at a nonprofit research institute. She has published numerous scientific essays and books. Eva-Maria Fahrner-Tutsek has been Chairwoman of the Executive Board of the Alexander Tutsek-Stiftung since the nonprofit foundation was established in 2000, and is responsible for its conception and development. Located in Munich, Germany, the foundation supports art and science. A major focus of its activities lies in organizing exhibitions and assembling a high-quality collection of photography and contemporary sculpture, emphasizing glass as a material. On her many travels around the world, Eva-Maria Fahrner-Tutsek has used her eye for photography and glass sculpture to discover extraordinary artworks and acquire them for the foundation's collection. As Art Director, she curates art exhibitions and is the author of publications on international contemporary glass art and photography.

Dr. Petra Giloy-Hirtz a former associate professor of medieval literature at the Heinrich-Heine-Universität Düsseldorf and a lecturer at the Ludwig-Maximilians-Universität Munich, has been an independent curator of contemporary art since the 1990s. Since 2017 she has been the Artistic Advisor of the Alexander Tutsek-Stiftung. She has produced numerous exhibitions and publications, including *Kiki Smith: Empathy*, Diözesanmuseum Freising (2024); *Berlinde De Bruyckere: City of Refuge II*, Diözesanmuseum Freising (2023); *Kiki Smith: I Am a Wanderer*, Modern Art Oxford, Oxford (2019); *Kiki Smith: Procession*, Haus der Kunst, Munich (2018), Sara Hildén Museum, Tampere, Finland (2019), Belvedere, Vienna (2019); *Dennis Hopper: The Lost Album*, Royal Academy of Arts, London (2014), Martin-Gropius-Bau, Berlin (2012); *David Lynch: The Factory Photographs*, The Photographers' Gallery, London, MAST, Bologna (2014); *Julian Schnabel: Polaroids*, Hague Museum of Photography, The Hague, Netherlands (2010); and such monographs as *Acosta Danza: Fusion* (2022) and *Anselm Kiefer: The Women* (2025).

Tina Oldknow is an independent curator and art historian specializing in contemporary art, craft, and design in glass. In 2015, she retired from her post as senior curator of modern and contemporary glass at the Corning Museum of Glass in Corning, New York, a position she'd held for 16 years. Oldknow has curated more than 30 exhibitions during her career and has written more than 100 books, articles, and essays on glass. Books authored by Oldknow include *Pilchuck: A Glass School* (1996); *Chihuly: Persians* (1996); *Richard Marquis: Objects* (1997); *Dante Marioni: Blown Glass* (2000); *William Morris: Animal Artifact* (with James Yood, 2000); *25 Years of New Glass Review* (2005); *Dan Dailey* (with William Warmus, 2007); *Contemporary Glass Sculptures and Panels: Selections from the Corning Museum of Glass* (2008); *Voices of Contemporary Glass: The Heineman Collection* (2009); *Collecting Contemporary Glass: Art and Design after 1990 from the Corning Museum of Glass* (2014); *Contemporary Glass Vessels: Selections from the Corning Museum of Glass* (2015); and *Venice and American Studio Glass* (with William Warmus, 2020).

The team of
the Alexander Tutsek-Stiftung

The texts on selected artists
were written by
Alexandra Baringer (AB)
Ayşegül Cihangir (AC)
Dr. Jörg Garbrecht (JG)
Julia Hürner (JH)
Barbara Kunze (BK)
Dr. Sally Oey (SO)
Katharina Wenkler (KW)

Alexander Tutsek-Stiftung

The foundation in Munich supports contemporary art and science. This nonprofit foundation was established in 2000 by the entrepreneur Alexander Tutsek and Dr. Eva-Maria Fahrner-Tutsek, who together envisioned a vibrant world of art and science driving social progress and human coexistence. The Alexander Tutsek-Foundation focuses on areas in art and science that are often neglected or overlooked and aims to strengthen them sustainably.

In its internationally oriented temporary exhibitions on current issues and in its collecting pursuits, the Alexander Tutsek-Stiftung focuses on contemporary photography as well as contemporary glass sculptures and installations. The aim is to open up new perspectives on important questions of our time and to expose these two artistic media to a broader public. The acquisitions of recent years include works by such young and internationally renowned artists as Tony Cragg, Mona Hatoum, Kiki Smith, Robin Rhode, Nan Goldin, Rinko Kawauchi, and Robert Rauschenberg. As the collection's focus on photography in Asia expanded, important works by Chinese artists, including Ren Hang, RongRong, and Cao Fei, entered the collection.

Art: promoting young talent and artists

A key objective of funding in the arts is the promotion of young talent. The Alexander Tutsek-Stiftung aims to improve the training opportunities for artists working in contemporary photography and in the medium of glass. Areas of financial support range from experimentation with materials to student exhibition projects to the creation of elaborate works of art. In tandem with universities, glass schools, and academies, the Alexander Tutsek-Stiftung strives to broaden and advance the development of training programs and the acquisition of suitable technical equipment. Equally important to the foundation is offering support to individual artists who work with glass or in the field of photography. The foundation has committed itself to the further education of these artists by offering assistance through scholarships and grants, and with course fees and travel expenses to institutions both in Europe and overseas.

Art: institutional support

The Alexander Tutsek-Stiftung supports ambitious exhibition projects at renowned art institutions, long-term funding programs, and the financing of significant acquisitions. Since 2016, the foundation has been the primary supporter of a carefully selected few museums of international standing. Its support of innovative photography exhibitions throughout Germany is a further ongoing commitment.

The Alexander Tutsek-Stiftung is proud to support one of the most prestigious German young talent awards in photography and the leading national glass prize for senior artists.

Science: advancing research and supporting young talent

In the academic realm, the Alexander Tutsek-Stiftung primarily supports research and teaching in the engineering sciences. These apply the knowledge gained in the natural sciences to our daily lives and make an important—often overlooked—contribution to the technical progress of society. The funding focuses on basic and applied research into glass, ceramics, stones, and earths. These subjects yield important insights that are relevant to other subfields of engineering but that are increasingly being neglected in general funding. To ensure that these subjects remain the center of attention at technical universities, the foundation teams up with institutions to maintain their attractiveness to students and support innovative research projects. The Alexander Tutsek-Stiftung has been awarding doctoral scholarships and has been one of the biggest partners of Deutschlandstipendien in Munich for half a decade. In selected cases it also funds the acquisition of high-quality equipment for laboratories and equipment necessary for teaching at technical colleges and universities of applied sciences.

Imprint

Published by
Hirmer Verlag GmbH
Bayerstrasse 57–59
80335 Munich
Germany

Edited by
Alexander Tutsek-Stiftung
Munich
www.atstiftung.de

Editorial Coordination
Eva-Maria Fahrner-Tutsek
Petra Giloy-Hirtz

Photo Management
Ayşegül Cihangir

English Translation
James Copeland

Copy Editing and Proofreading
Michael Pilewski

Design, Layout, Typesetting
Christian Hölzl, Nina Hardwig,
h.und.b, Munich

Hirmer Project Management
Rainer Arnold

Pre-press and Repro
Reproline Mediateam, Unterföhring

Printing and Binding
Printer Trento s.r.l.

Paper
120 g/m², Arena White Smooth
135 g/m², Symbol Tatami White
by Fedrigoni

Printed in Italy

The Deutsche Nationalbibliothek lists this publication in the Deutsche Nationalbibliografie; detailed bibliographic data is available on the Internet at http://www.dnb.de.

www.hirmerpublishers.com

Front cover
Shirazeh Houshiary
Alar, 2016–17
145 × 118 × 118 cm
© Shirazeh Houshiary /
VG Bild-Kunst, Bonn 2025,
courtesy Lisson Gallery

ISBN 978-3-7774-4582-3

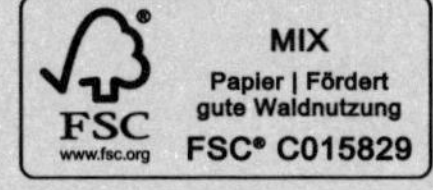